# THE FENIANS IN ENGLAND
## 1865 — 1872

**Other books in the Historical Perspective series:**

THE GENERAL STRIKE OF 1926: The Economic, Political and Social Causes.    *R.A. Florey*

HISTORICAL PERSPECTIVES

# THE FENIANS IN ENGLAND 1865 — 1872

## A Sense of Insecurity

Patrick Quinlivan and Paul Rose

JOHN CALDER·LONDON
RIVERRUN PRESS · NEW YORK

First published in Great Britain 1982 by
John Calder (Publishers) Ltd.,
18, Brewer Street,
London W1R 4AS

First published in the U.S.A. 1982 by
Riverrun Press Inc.,
175 Fifth Avenue,
New York, N.Y. 10010

BRITISH LIBRARY CATALOGUING IN PUBLICATION DATA

---

Quinlivan, Patrick
  The Fenians in England, 1865-1872. — (Historical
  perspectives; vol. 1).
  1. Fenian Brotherhood — History
  I. Title     II. Rose, Paul     III. Series
  322.4'2'0942     DA954     80-40575

  ISBN 0-7145-3775-6

SUBSIDISED BY THE
**Arts Council**
OF GREAT BRITAIN

Typeset in 10/12 Janson by Alan Sutton Publishing Ltd. Gloucester

Printed and bound in Great Britain by
the Hillman Press, Frome, Somerset

# CONTENTS

Chapter 1   *Who were the Fenians?*   1

Chapter 2   *Ricard O'Sullivan Burke and the Fenians in England*   9

Chapter 3   *The Chester Castle Raid*   16

Chapter 4   *The Murphy Riots*   33

Chapter 5   *The Manchester Rescue*   43

Chapter 6   *The Clerkenwell Explosion*   76

Chapter 7   *Reactions and Relief*   95

Chapter 8   *The Clerkenwell Trials*   105

Chapter 9   *The Last Public Execution*   133

Chapter 10   *Aftermath*   139

Chapter 11   *The Amnesty Movement*   144

Chapter 12   *The Fenians — An Assessment*   161

BIBLIOGRAPHY   173

INDEX   187

# List of Illustrations

*Facing page*

| | |
|---|---|
| Ricard O'Sullivan Burke | 10 |
| Jenny and Laura Marx | 11 |
| Chester Castle sketch | 26 |
| Fenian stamp | 27 |
| The Irish Frankenstein | 36 |
| The English Frankenstein | 37 |
| Charles Bradlaugh | 68 |
| Bradlaugh Statue | 69 |
| Not Belfast 1981, but London 1867 | 86 |
| Clerkenwell Explosion scene | 87 |
| Thomas Billis Beach | 98 |
| Clerkenwell verse | 99 |
| Five IRB members | 134 |
| Robert Anderson | 135 |
| St. James Church plaque | 142 |
| Cork National Monument | 143 |
| Friedrich Engels | 168 |
| The Order of the Day | 169 |

# Chapter 1

## Who were the Fenians?

*Fenianism — the noblest and most terrible manifestation of this unconquered nation.*
Padraig Pearse[1]

Led by Finn Macumhall, the legendary Fenians of the pre-Christian era were a band of warriors similar to the Knights of King Arthur. Their high ideals of chivalry went with the national spirit. The magical undertones were matched by heroic conduct calculated to inspire heroism and so protect the country. In one story Finn says the Fenians would not give up Ireland in exchange for the whole world and the country of ever-lasting youth with it.[2]

The early Fenians had to pass tests of physical prowess that were as astonishingly difficult as they were dangerous. 'The number of *fianna* of Ireland at that time was seven score and ten chief men. every one of them having nine fighting men under him, and each of them was bound to three things — to take no cattle by oppression, not to refuse any man, as to cattle or riches, no one of them to fall back before nine fighting men ... and there was no man taken into the *fianna* till he knew twelve books of poetry.'[3]

The legends of the Fenians bear the same connection with elemental feeling for nature as the Psalms of David. The same nostalgia over the mighty fallen is revealed in Creda's lament for Cael, as in the lament for Saul and Jonathan:

> *Sad is the sound of the wave against*
> *the beach to the North,*
> *Breaking over a white rock,*
> *Weeping for Cael that he is gone.*[4]

Or in Oisin's sorrow after the death of Finn in the Battle of the White Strand against the King of the World:

> *It is bad the way I am after Finn*
> *of the fianna: since he is gone*
> *away, every good is behind me*
> *Without great people, without mannerly ways*
> *It is sorrowful I am after our King that is gone.*[5]

But there is a ring of defiance and anti-clericism in the saga which may have been injected at a later era. Nature is contrasted with the man-made trappings of religion, for in one later saga when St. Patrick pronounces doom of hell upon the Fenians, he receives the response:

> *Better to be in Hell with Finn, than in Heaven*
> *with pale and flimsy angels.*[6]

In another story Caolite told St. Patrick that the Fenians were maintained by 'the truth that was in our hearts and the strength in our arms and the fulfilment in our tongues'.[7]

Again the ballad of the blackbird of Derrycarn recalls:

> *When Finn and the Fenians lived*
> *They held dearer the mountains than the church*
> *Sweet to them were the blackbirds' notes*
> *The ringing of bells was not sweet.*[8]

But Lady Gregory's translation is less explicit:

> *The time Finn lived and the fianna*
> *It was sweet to them to be listening*
> *to the whistle of the blackbird*
> *The voice of the bells would not have been sweet to them.*[9]

The combination of self-reliance, attachment to the earth, and specifically the Irish earth, and independence from clericalism together with the organization under centres and sub-centres by the 'Fenian chief' James Stephens, was the inspiration bequeathed by Finn MacCumhall and Oisin and their warriors of antiquity. The name 'Fenian' was selected by John O'Mahony for the new embodiment of Irish national feeling in the mid-nineteenth century.

John O'Mahony (1819-1877) was described by John O'Leary as 'the manliest and handsomest man' he had ever seen, 'the soul of truth and honour'.[10] Apart from his revolutionary activities, he had a keen interest in languages and history. He translated Keating's *History of Ireland* from the Irish.[11] To him the word Fenian represented the yearning for nationhood embodied in an ancient ideal. All nations have their myths, and legend and history combine to create their sense of identity. The sense of identity bequeathed by the Fenians was an unbroken thread leading to another Battle of the White Strand fought from a Dublin Post Office in 1916. Creda's lament for Cael was to be echoed by a nation lamenting for Padraig Pearse, James Connolly and his latter day Fenians with a yearning for social justice merged with the Fenian tradition exemplified by Pearse's address 'To the Boys of Ireland', delivered in February 1914.

Finally, we believe with Thomas Davis that 'righteous man must make our land a nation once again.' Hence, we endeavour to train our boys to be pure, truthful, honest, sober, kindly, clean in heart as well as body; generous in their service to their parents and companions now as we would have them generous in their service to their country hereafter. We bear a very noble name and inherit very noble traditions, for we are called after the Fianna of Finn, that heroic companionship which, according to legend, flourished in Ireland in the second and third centuries of the Christian era.

> *We, the Fianna never told a lie*
> *Falsehood was never imputed to us.*

said Oisin to St. Patrick; and again when St. Patrick asked Caolite MacRonain how it came that the Fianna won all their battles, Caolite replied:

> *Strength that was in our hands, truth that was on our lips*
> *and purity that was in our hearts.*

If his translation differs from that of Myles Dillon, the message is nevertheless identical. Fused with the agrarian socialism of Davitt and the Marxism of James Connolly, the Fenian ideal was written in blood and still inspires a wide variety of Irish political groups today.

But Fenianism as an ideal is not to be confused with the Irish Republican Brotherhood which rose against Britain in 1867, and whose exploits in England itself are described in this book.

From the warrior hosts of the ancient Fianna there sprang through the poetic and historical mind of John O'Mahony a link with the past, a word both military and lyrical, 'Fenian'. His choice of name caught public imagination. It was not a new word, for the term had been used in English language publications as early as 1816[12] to describe Irish soldiers, but by 1864 the term was in world wide use to denote Irish rebels against British rule. The name was used to describe members of the Irish Republican Brotherhood in the nineteenth century, as well as of the Fenian Brotherhood in America. These two organizations were so closely linked they were often thought of and referred to as one. The Irish Republican Brotherhood was a political organization for the overthrow of British rule in Ireland and for the establishment of a republic. It was founded in Dublin on St. Patrick's Day, 1858, and soon afterwards the Fenian Brotherhood was formed in the United States. The object of the Fenian Brotherhood was to assist the Irish Republican Brotherhood in every way to secure the freedom of Ireland.

The Fenian Brotherhood received strong support from the Irish who had suffered in the great famine of 1845-48 and from the harsh treatment of English landlords; the forced emigrations gave Irish-Americans a detestation of English rule that has lasted to the present day. In 1864 and 1865 Fenian rallies in America attracted scores of thousands. Funds were raised by collections, subscriptions, and the sale of bonds redeemable when the Irish Republic was established. There was even an issue of postage stamps, perhaps the first example of philatelic propaganda, and the stamps today are valued at over £1,000 each.[13]

Armed Fenian units paraded in American towns; Fenian periodicals and song books proliferated, and there was a popular brand of Fenian tobacco.[14] Despite this support from first and second generation Irish-Americans, the Fenian Brotherhood was often weak and divided. In the latter part of the eighteen-sixties it was split into three distinct sections, each in theory supporting the Republican Brotherhood in Ireland but in practice sharply divided by personalities and policies.

The political roots of Fenianism are to be found, not in the legends of Finn and Oisin, but in the rising of the United Irishmen in 1798 and in the words of the leader, Theobald Wolfe Tone, who gave to Irish nationalism the highest expression of its objects:

> To break the connection with England, the never-failing source of all our political evils; and to assert the independence of my country — these are my objects. To unite the whole people of Ireland, to abolish the memory of past dissensions, and to substitute the common name of Irishman in place of the denominations of Protestant, Catholic and Dissenter — these were my means.[15]

The Irish Republican Brotherhood always emphasized republicanism in the manner of Theobald Wolfe Tone and the United Irishmen. One version of the Fenian constitution stated:

> The object of the IRB is to establish and maintain a free and independent Republican government in Ireland ... the Supreme Council of the IRB is hereby declared in fact, as well as by right, the sole Government of the Irish Republic. Its enactments shall be the laws of the Irish Republic until Ireland secures absolute national independence, and a permanent Republican Government is established.

The Young Ireland revolt of 1848 gave further inspiration to the Brotherhood. One of the original founders of the movement, James Stephens, who had been wounded in the 1848 revolt, spent part of his exile in Paris and gained experience from continental revolutionary secret societies.[16] He and John O'Mahony took part in the Paris rising of 1851. The Fenian movement provided the link between the risings of 1848 and 1916 when the first signatory of the Declaration of Independence was that of the Fenian Thomas Clarke (1857-1916), while the whole period was spanned by John Devoy's life-time (1842-1928) of Fenian agitation.[17] By 1947 a former member of the Brotherhood, Sean T. O'Kelly (1882-1966) was elected President of the Republic of Ireland.

The mainspring of Fenian activities was always in the United

States but groups worked continuously in Ireland, Great Britain, France, Australia, Canada and South America. In 1865 British rule in Ireland was threatened for the first time by a world-wide organization with a secure base. The primary object of the Irish Republican Brotherhood was to organize a revolt in Ireland. Arms were smuggled in and men trained for combat. Experienced soldiers from the American Civil War were sent to Ireland to act as instructors and leaders. Fenians in Ireland joined various armies, particularly the French Foreign Legion, to gain battle experience. The published correspondence of the leading Fenian organizer, John Devoy, shows the wide range of Fenian activities. They varied from rescuing political prisoners in Ireland, England and Australia, to organizing three raids on Canada, and to financing experiments that led to the building of the first practical submarine, over $60,000 being given to John Holland (1840-1914) for research work on a weapon to use against British naval power.[18] Meetings were held with French, Russian and Spanish Government representatives to discuss possible action in time of war. One such discussion took place with the Spanish Premier, Canovas del Castillo, and concerned the proposed capture of Gibraltar by Irish-American Fenians.[19] Aid to countries fighting Britain was always readily available. One Fenian group planned to supply rifles to the Zulus,[20] while a more successful group organized a Brigade to assist the Boer Army.[21]

Everything from constitutional Parliamentary opposition to agrarian demonstrations was used by the Irish as a weapon. The Land League, the Home Rule League, the Irish Volunteers and Sinn Fein have often appeared to supercede the Irish Republican Brotherhood as political forces, but Fenians were active in all these organizations and showed their strength at a critical moment in 1916. The Brotherhood is by no means dead and its lineal descendants have been the organizing power behind the Irish Republican activities in diverse and sometimes conflicting forms in recent years. There was no Gandhi to lead Ireland to independence through a creed of non-violence. The Ulster Unionists showed their determination to use violence to over-rule the ballot box, and the saddest lesson of the period is that it took the method of violence to bring about an independent Irish Republic.

The Irish Republican Brotherhood of the nineteenth century differed from previous Irish nationalist organizations in that the main base was outside Ireland. The *Pall Mall Gazette* in 1867 noted that the Brotherhood was the first case of such an organization, with political objects in view, being established in England and added 'it will probably annoy us for years and at intervals produce catastrophies'[22] The Republican Brotherhood did not secure the support of the Catholic Church; indeed two Encyclicals condemned Fenian activities. Many of the clergy were hostile and Paul Cullen, Archbishop of Dublin, was a bitter critic. In 1867 Cardinal Manning in London devoted a whole pastoral letter to an attack on the Fenians.[23]

The Fenians had personal links with many radical organizations. Most members belonged to the working class and had marked socialist tendencies. Many had a strong anti-clerical bias. James Stephens joined the First International[24] and Fenian leaders in England enjoyed the confidence and friendship of Friedrich Engels and Karl Marx. The First International had several Irish branches in England[25] and the members of these were mostly Fenians.

The rise of the Fenians came just too late to take advantage of the problems caused to the British Government by the Crimean War (1854-56) and the Indian uprising of 1857. The most favourable year for Fenian activities was 1865, when thousands of troops in the British Army were ready to mutiny and support an Irish uprising.[26] Many of the demobilized veterans of the American Civil War had not settled down to civilian pursuits and would have welcomed the opportunity of winning fame and freeing Ireland. Irish participation in the ranks of the Union Army was a spawning ground for Fenian ideas and a training ground for their military methods. French and Russian feeling was strongly hostile to Britain and there were numerous points of friction between the British and American governments; the dearest hope of the Irish-Americans was for an Anglo-American war. The American Secretary of State, William Seward, felt that war with England would help to bind the States together and give a sense of national unity. President Andrew Johnson was willing to give the Fenians every chance of succeeding in Canada and elsewhere. Many British leaders were pessimistic about the future of Anglo-American relations. Queen Victoria noted in her diary on 12 February 1865, 'Talked of America and the danger, which seems approaching, of our having a war with her as soon as she makes peace; of the impossibility of our being able to hold Canada ...'[27] while about the same time Charles Dickens wrote: 'If the Americans don't embroil us in a war before long it will not be their fault ... what with their claims for indemnification, what with Ireland and Fenianism, and what with Canada, I have strong apprehensions.'[28] A struggle in Ireland could have started a chain reaction leading to American intervention on behalf of Ireland.

In 1865 the Fenians had a chance of success, but delay by James Stephens brought arrests and defeat. Stephens hesitated from month to month until the British Government became aware of the dangerous situation and acted swiftly. The Fenian leaders in Ireland were arrested, scores of court martials dealt with Fenians in the

British Army and Irish regiments were hastily drafted to distant parts of the Empire.

James Stephens was among those arrested in Ireland. The Fenians led by Colonel Thomas J. Kelly (1833-1908), rescued him from Richmond Gaol in November, 1865, and he went to the United States and talked of fighting in 1866. Stephens failed to put his war talk into action and finally at a conference in New York in December, 1866, he was deposed and went into retirement in France. Control of the Irish Republican Brotherhood was taken over by a Supreme Council under the leadership of Colonel Kelly.

The new leader gave the order for a rising in Ireland on 11 February 1867 and for simultaneous action in England. The Fenians in Ireland would be led by experienced military officers; supplies of arms and volunteers would be sent from America to the first Irish port held by the rebels. The Fenians in England were expected to create diversions and several imaginative schemes were put forward; some Irish-American officers were sent to England to help organize the attacks. Colonel Kelly sent his deputy, Ricard O'Sullivan Burke, to be in charge of operations in England.

**NOTES**

1. Padraig Pearse's address to the Boys of Ireland *Selected Political meetings of Padraig Pearse*, p.39.
.2. For reference to the Fenian Cycle and Sagas see Augusta Gregory *Gods and Fighting Men*; Myles Dillon, *Early Irish Literature*; Proinsias MacCana, *Celtic Mythology*, 1970, pp. 106-115.
3. *Ibid.*
4. *Ibid.*
5. *Ibid.*
6. *Ibid.*
7. *Ibid.*
8. *Ibid.*
9. *Ibid.*
10. J. O'Leary, *Recollections of Fenians and Fenianism* Vol. 1., 1896, p. 102.
11. G. Keating, *History of Ireland* (Ed. J. O'Mahony), (1857).
12. W. Scott, *The Antiquary* (1816)
13. *Stamps of Ireland*, (D. MacDermott, Ed.) (1979, p. 9).
14. W.D. D'Arcy, *The Fenian Movement in the USA*, 1947, p. 294.
15. C. Dickson, *Revolt in the North*, 1960, p.183.
16. *Irishman* 3 March 1866.
17. Conor Cruise O'Brien (Ed.) *The Shaping of Modern Ireland*, 1960, Chapter 1.
18. *Devoy's Post Bag*, Vol. 1, 1948, p. 470.
19. *Ibid.*, p.293.
20. *Ibid.*, p.408.
21. *Ibid.*, Vol. 2, 1953. p. 347.

22. Quoted in *Dublin University Magazine*, January 1868.
23. H.E. Manning, Pastoral letter 17 March 1867.
24. Letter from Karl Marx, 30 November 1868, quoted in N. Mansergh, *Ireland in the Age of Reform and Revolution*, 1940, p.71.
25. *Irish Workers Voice*, October 1953.
26. J. Devoy, *Recollections of an Irish Rebel*, 1929, p.63.
27. S.F. Bemis, *A Diplomatic History of the United States*, 1942, p. 381.
28. T.A. Bailey, *A Diplomatic History of the American People*, 1950, p.406.

# Chapter 2

## *Ricard O'Sullivan Burke and The Fenians In England*

Ricard O'Sullivan Burke was well suited for his difficult and dangerous job. Although only twenty-eight years old he had shown ample proof of ability and daring. He was born in Kinneigh, near Dunmanway, County Cork, on 24 January 1838[1] the youngest son of Denis Burke, a tenant-farmer. The Burke family was relatively prosperous but when Denis Burke voted against a conservative candidate their landlord, the Earl of Bandon, immediately evicted them thus forcing several members of the family to emigrate. Ricard was educated in Dunmanway and became a student-teacher in Kinneigh. Teaching was not attractive to him so he enlisted in the South Cork Militia. On St. Patrick's Day, 1855, at the age of seventeen, he was made a lance-corporal.[2] Soon after this he had a disagreement with an officer and took French leave. He went to sea and became a supercargo. During the next five years he visited many Mediterranean ports, Japan, South America and the United States. He stayed some time in Chile, learning Spanish and serving in the Chilean cavalry.[3] He also spent nearly a year in Paris and studied art; he was a linguist and a writer.

At the outbreak of the American Civil War Ricard O'Sullivan Burke was in New York for the second time. He joined the Federal Army and soon afterwards became a member of the Fenian Brotherhood. Burke served in the 15th New York Light Infantry at the Battle of the Bull Run. When his regiment was sent back to New York to train as an engineering unit he made quick progress in the engineering school.[4] In 1862 he took part in the siege of Yorktown and later saw action at the Battle of Gloucester. He served in the Army of the Potomac in the other struggles of the Civil War until Appomattox. On his discharge at the end of the War he was Captain of Engineers with a colonel's brevet.[5] He fought throughout the War without being wounded but was hit in the hand by a stray bullet during a victory celebration after a mustering-out parade.[6]

Soon after leaving the American Army Burke was sent to England by the Republican Brotherhood where he became senior agent for the purchase of arms and ammunition, showing considerable skill in his work. Posing as a representative of the Chilean Government, he obtained over 2,000 rifles and sent them to Ireland.[7] He had returned to America for a short time in 1866 and had been in Ireland to take charge of the Waterford area in the rising of March, 1867. When the rising collapsed he had to go to Sligo Bay to meet the ship *Erin's Hope* and warn the crew that their cargo of arms from America could not be used or even landed. The ship had sailed from New York with 5,000 rifles and other arms to be handed over to the Fenians at any port held by them.[8]

It must have been a galling moment for Burke when he boarded the ship and had to report the complete failure of all plans for a national uprising. A lesser man might have given up then. Burke had seen the failures of 1865, 1866 and 1867 but he went on to prepare for a rising in 1868. He returned to England and went to Birmingham, where he had set up an office as a cover for his work in obtaining arms for the Fenians.

Burke was noted for his lively humour and intelligence. He was tall, good looking and powerfully built. A contemporary wrote 'there never was a more agreeable companion ... suave, good natured, always bouyant, with a gay bonhomie.'[9] A hostile source refers to him as 'the cleverest of the Fenians', while the *Gaelic American* of 27 May 1922 calls him 'by long odds the most remarkable man the Fenian movement produced, and also one of the ablest.'[10] A jaundiced official of the United States Embassy in London described Burke as 'boastful, silly and pompous'[11], but most contemporaries refer to his good humour and jokes. Margaret O'Donovan Rossa in her autobiography recounts several humorous stories of Burke: she knew him over a period of fifty years and refers to him as a 'happy comedian'.[12]

At the time of Burke's return to England the outlook for the Fenians there was still promising. The long tradition of Irish emigration, together with the flood of refugees at the time of the Famine, meant that most towns in Britain had Fenian sympathizers. In 1867 some 600,000 Irish-born were living in England.[13] In London they formed more than three per cent of the population and in Liverpool more than 20 per cent.[14]

The Irish colonies in England were usually disliked by the native English, a dislike in which racial antipathy, religious bigotry and economic rivalry played their parts. A *Times* editorial advised Irish people in England to keep as quiet as possible as their habits and

Ricard O'Sullivan Burke in American Civil War Uniform. Head of Irish Republican Brotherhood in England 1867. (Courtesy of Mrs. T. Lynch of Coachford)

Jenny and Laura Marx. Daughters of Karl Marx and ardent supporters of the Fenians in England. (Courtesy of Marx Memorial Library)

manner of life had made them unpopular.[15] A less restrained publication summed up the Irish in Britain as being 'unclaimed by civilization, uneducated as the brutes that perish, knowing nothing of religion save in an idolatrous form, and professing rebellion as a principle'[16] Many of the enforced emigrants certainly looked forward to the day when an Irish Republic would be proclaimed; they echoed the prayer of rebel John Mitchell 'Send war in our time, O Lord'[17], and hoped that the great new republic of the West would repay with interest the help given by Irish soldiers in the American War of Independence.

Added to the 600,000 Irish-born were many born in England of Irish parents; in the census returns they were classed as English but they often proved more nationalistic in feeling and activities than their parents. The ranks of the Republican Brotherhood teemed with English-born Fenians, attached by strong sentiment to the idea of a free Ireland, the country of their dreams and often a country they had never seen. Representative of this group are Thomas Clarke and Edward Pilsworth. Thomas Clarke was born in the Isle of Wight and spent years in British goals for his Fenian activities.[18] During the 1916 Easter Week Rising in Dublin, Clarke, by then an old man, was the only signatory of the Declaration of Independence to vote for a fight to the finish. Pilsworth was born in Birmingham and became the leading Fenian organizer in the British Army.[19]

Most of the Irish emigrants in England belonged to the working class and joined the struggle for reform and the improvement of working conditions. They were the natural allies of the radical movements that led to the formation of the Labour Party. The Fenians were favourably regarded by some of the English working class movements. English Radical support for Irish freedom movements had a long history. The mutiny at the Nore in 1797 showed links between Irish rebels and English radicals.[20] The ephemeral United Englishmen movement was linked with the United Irishmen and the rising of 1798.[21] The names of John Docherty, Feargus O'Connor and Bronterre O'Brien stand out among the Chartist leaders, and in 1848 the Chartists of Clerkenwell demonstrated in favour of the Young Ireland movement.[22]

As most of the Irish emigrants were Catholic by religion they were prevented from complete acceptance of communist theories, but the Fenians had close personal links with communist leaders. Friedrich Engels' home in Manchester was a centre of Fenian activity and was even decorated in the Fenian colours of green and black.[23] Engels doubted if the English workers were strong enough to overcome their 'historic sentiments of nationality'[24] though he was encouraged by the sympathy for the Fenians shown by some of the

London workers. He was critical of many Fenian activities as being
'Bakunistic, braggart, aimless propaganda through action.'[25]

Karl Marx was prominent in activities in support of Irish political
freedom. In 1870 he wrote:

> The decisive blow against the English ruling classes cannot be delivered
> in England but only in Ireland ... England possesses a working class
> divided into two hostile camps, English proletarians and Irish prolet-
> arians. The ordinary English worker hates the Irish worker as a com-
> petitor who lowers his standard of living ... the Irishman regards the
> English worker as both sharing the guilt of English domination in Ireland
> and at the same time acting as its stupid tool, The antagonism is arti-
> ficially kept alive by the press, the pulpit, the comic papers, in short by
> all the means at the disposal of the ruling classes. This is the secret of the
> impotence of the English working classes ... to hasten social revolution in
> England is the most important object we have ... the sole means of
> hastening it is to make Ireland independent.[26]

In the first volume of *Capital* Marx analyzed and condemned
British rule in Ireland; he drew up the resolutions in favour of Irish
self-government passed at the International Working Men's Association from 1864 onwards and he drafted a programme of reform for
Ireland to be carried out through the assistance of the English
working class. The three main points of the programme were self-
government for Ireland, an agrarian revolution, and protective
tariffs against England. This was hardly a programme to arouse
enthusiasm in the English working classes, but in 1867 Marx still
believed that the English rule in Ireland could be overthrown by the
efforts of the English working class.[27]

Among the working class members were many from the tailoring
trade; a leading Fenian was editor of *The Tailor* for several years.[28]
Doctors and journalists played prominent parts in the movement.
One member, Dr. Mark Ryan (1844-1940), served the Brotherhood
for sixty years in England. His life story covers the history of
Fenianism in England. He became a member in Bacup, Lancashire,
soon after 1860. Like many other Fenians he received his training with
the Lancashire Rifle Volunteers and he left with his rifle to join the
rising of 1867.[29] After the collapse of the rising he returned to
England where he worked as a doctor in Clerkenwell and other parts
of London until his retirement. He always escaped arrest and lived
to take the salute of Irish Army units in Dublin. A Presbyterian
minister, David Bell, was the London representative of the Fenian
paper *Irish People*.[30] Another member, the writer, Edmund O'Donovan, while war correspondent in Egypt was caught in the Hicks
Pasha debacle and achieved a memorial plaque in St. Paul's
Cathedral.[31]

The Irish Republican Brotherhood in England existed to support the revolutionary movement in Ireland. Members were expected to make their way to Ireland for the Rising but a number of diversionary attacks in England were planned, the most notable being the capture of Chester Castle with the arms and ammunition stored there. Military instruction, arms and ammunition were sought by the Fenians; their usual source of supplies being the county militias. This was the time of the Napoleon III scare in England and volunteers were welcomed into the militia units. Arms for Ireland were bought or stolen and there were social activities to raise funds for the purchase of arms. The organization and activities of the Brotherhood in England varied considerably according to place and circumstances. Sometimes constitutional organizations were supported but the basic aim of freedom for Ireland remained the same.

Following the plan of James Stephens the Fenians in England were organized in 'circles' led by an officer known as the 'centre'.[32] In theory at least each circle consisted of 820 men, each section of nine men had a sergeant, nine sergeants were under the control of a captain, nine captains in turn came under the orders of the centre of the circle. By 1867 Fenian circles had been established in all the large cities of England. The erratic financial support from America meant that the organization depended on small groups, strong in some districts of Northern England, but with little central direction or cohesion. General policy was decided by the Supreme Council of the Irish Republican Brotherhood. The Council usually consisted of eleven members of whom two represented the Fenians in England. Meetings were held in Ireland, England or France. Contact with the Fenian Brotherhood in America was maintained by 'visitors' who were elected delegates.

The organization of the Fenian movement by James Stephens was simple and effective in the early days. When the time came for military action in 1865 he hesitated and control of the movement passed to other hands; he found it impossible to arrange a partnership between the political and military leaders at the time of crisis. Perhaps the key to his indecision was his mistrust of General Millen, the senior army man sent by the American Brotherhood to aid the rising. His mistrust was justified, for in 1865 Millen had called on the British Consul in New York and by early March, 1866, had offered to supply valuable information on the military arrangements of the Fenians in the United Kingdom, their numbers and distribution, and secret places of deposit of arms.[33] He also reported that Ellen O'Leary and Mrs O'Donovan Rossa made frequent visits to Paris and brought back funds for the payment of men and arms. The Dublin Police were in favour of arresting and detaining the women, but Lord Wodehouse, Lord Lieutenant of Ireland, demurred. He felt they should be arrested, searched by 'polite policemen' and released because it was 'ticklish work to meddle with women.'[34]

The period of uncertain leadership within the Fenian movement in Ireland coincided with a split in the American organization. Unease and uncertainty spread among the Fenians in England. They heard of the toll taken by British police and secret agents while the Fenian leaders tried to work out a policy. Committees and councils debated and delayed action as each group tried to find out what the other groups thought or were doing. Messages and messengers crossed and recrossed the Atlantic, the Irish Sea and the English Channel. The date of the Rising in Ireland was postponed, putting a new strain on communications between the Fenian groups. One result, perhaps typical of the postponement, was the collapse of the plan to seize Chester Castle in England.

## NOTES

1. *Gaelic American* 27 May 1922.
2. *South Cork Militia Order Book*, 1855.
3. *Irishman*, 4 January 1868.
4. *Devoy's Post Bag*, Vol. 1, p.35.
5. J. Devoy, *Recollections of an Irish Rebel*, 1929, p.358.
6. *Gaelic American*, 27 May 1922.
7. M. Ryan, *Fenian Memories*, 1946, p.126.
8. D. Ryan, *The Phoenix Flame*, 1937, p.180.
9. *Irishman*, 4 January 1868.
10. *Gaelic American*, 27 May 1922.
11. *Diary of Benjamin Moran*, 6 December 1865.
12. M. O'Donovan Rossa, *My Mother and Father were Irish*, 1939, p.14.
13. J.A. Jackson, *The Irish in Britain*, 1963, p. 11.
14. Census Reports 1861 and 1871 H.C.(1863) and H.C.(1873).
15. T. de V. White, *The Road of Excess*, 1946, p.164.
16. *Blackwoods Magazine* September 1848.
17. N. Mansergh, *Ireland in the Age of Reform and Revolution*, 1940, p.57.
18. J. Devoy, *Op. Cit.*, p.232.
19. *Devoy's Post Bag*, Vol. 1, p.14.
20. G.D.H. Cole, *The Common People*, 1961, p.166.
21. E.H. Stuart Jones, *The Last Invaders of Britain*, 1950, p.247.
22. T.A. Jackson, *Clerkenwell Green*.
23. G. Mayer, *Friedrich Engels*, 1936, p. 191 (letter from Engels to Karl Marx 29 November 1867).
24. N. Mansergh, *Ireland in the Age of Reform and Revolution*, 1940, p.82.
25. *Ibid.*
26. R. Dixon (Ed.), *Marx and Engels on Ireland*, 1971, p. 294 (letter from Karl Marx to Siegfried Mayer and August Vogt 9 April 1870).

27. N. Mansergh, *Op. Cit.*, p.71.
28. M. Ryan, *Op. Cit.*, p.61.
29. *Ibid.*
30. Clogher Record, 1967, p.270.
31. Letter from Registrar of St. Paul's Cathedral 24 March 1966.
32. J. Devoy, *Op. Cit.*, 1929, p.27.
33. L. O'Broin, *Fenian Fever*, 1971, p.48.
34. *Ibid.* p.51.

# Chapter 3

## *The Chester Castle Raid*

The Chester raid was in a sense a non-event in that it ended in anti-climax and undramatic failure. But it demonstrated the ability of Irishmen in England to organize in significant numbers. If the Fenians could call at will upon such a measure of support in the North of England, it was not surprising that they were able to succeed in the later Manchester episode. The plan to capture Chester Castle in February 1867 was in every sense one of the most astonishing exploits of the Fenians, frustrated only by treachery from within their own ranks.

The first sign that something extraordinary was afoot was described in the inimitable patronizing style of the London *Times*, the voice of the establishment:

> In the course of the morning a large body of ruffians made their appearance in Chester. The city police were at once armed, the regulars and volunteers were ordered to assemble in the Castle, an attack being apprehended.[1]

The epithet 'ruffians' excluded reference to nationality but reading between the lines it indicated the nature of the apprehended attack and of those assembling at Chester. The telegraph from Chester had caused *The Times* to report that a rumour prevailed in London that 'an attack by a considerable body of men supposed to be Fenians, and chiefly from Liverpool was premeditated if it had not actually been made, upon Chester Castle.'[2] It asserted that there was some ground for the rumour.

Chester had meanwhile telegraphed to report that several hundred young men of between 18 and 25 had poured into the city since noon. They were described as being 'apparently of the labouring and operative class' but again nothing overtly indicated their nationality. They poured into the city, going to various parts of the town and the telegraph gave an estimate of their numbers as between five to eight hundred.

*The Times* could give no definite information at that stage as to the plan afoot but it commented that 'it is certain that their spontaneous arrival from Liverpool, Preston, Manchester, Halifax and other surrounding towns showed that a premeditated action of some kind must be in view.' Indeed it was, and the object was described succinctly by Crilly nearly forty years later.

> It was resolved that the Circles of Lancashire should co-operate with the Dublin movement by a proceeding which for daring and audacity could hardly be excelled. They had information that Chester Castle contained 20,000 stand of arms, besides accoutrements and ammunition to a large extent, and that the place had only a nominal garrison. A Fenian military Council in Liverpool decided to attack Chester Castle, seize the arms, cut the telegraph wires, 'impress' the railway rolling stock, load trans with men and arms, and make for Holyhead. Here, they were to seize all the steamers in port, and speed for Dublin, in the expectation of landing in that city before intelligence of their astounding feat could possibly have reached Ireland.[3]

It is idle to speculate on their own intelligence concerning train and ship movements or the warnings that may have preceeded them. The sheer audacity of the scheme might have carried them through. Curiously, the Castle built as a fortification against another branch of Celts was to be the springboard for an Irish rising. The Castle of Chester was built in 1084 by William the Conqueror at the gateway to Wales and, since the advent of the railway, to Ireland via the Holyhead ferry. It was originally a considerable fortress but a great part of it was dismantled about 1870 for the purpose of erecting the County hall. On the Western side was the spacious armoury. Assizes, County Courts, Petty Sessions and meetings of the County Council were held in the area but, more significantly, the Castle also served as barracks as well as an arsenal.

If the arsenal was the target, arms would be needed to make the assault. It would seem that what the '2,000 unarmed irregulars'[4] planned was to obtain 300 rifles from a building known as the cockpit (but no longer used for the sport.) It estimated that 30,000 stands of arms, ammunition, cannon, shells and balls would be the next to fall into the hands of the newly-armed men. Prior to 1830 an entire regiment had been established at Chester, but Chester was apparently considered less important from a strategic point of view now that Wales was absorbed into the United Kingdom without the dissent felt in Ireland. For the Romans or the Normans Chester was a key bastion. No one would have anticipated an attack of this kind from the rear, using Chester as the road to Dublin. Consequently only one company of the 54th Regiment under Captain Edwards was stationed inside the Castle, a maximum of sixty-six men to repel an attack.

Another suggestion made was a plan to fire the town, while all correspondents regarded jewellers' shops as apparent targets. There was, however, no evidence to substantiate this; no looting took place. But the first conjecture stems from a curious incident reported on 14 February following a statement that 'we have been informed that one point in the Liverpool resolution was that Chester was to be fired in several plates'.[4] It then went on to describe how on Monday a stranger speaking with an American accent, applied at the works of the Chester Waterworks Company for permission to inspect the machinery. The man in charge said he had no power to grant the request. The stranger said he had no time to wait to see the manager, but that if the man would take him through he would make it worth his while to do so. This was against the rules and the stranger left.

Not long after, another stranger called with a similar request which was also refused. This excited the 'Cestrian's' curiosity and he watched the second man join the first and walk with him to the banks of the canal where they dropped a goodly sized parcel into the water. The supposition was that this was something intended to sabotage the machinery so that if the city were fired there would be no water available for fire fighting.[5] This may have been due to private enterprise, for there seems to have been little serious attempt to carry it through if it was an essential part of the plan. Nor is there any authoritative Fenian source to indicate this intention.

Whatever the details decided upon, the proposed attack was the result of a special mission organized in New York of the fifty men whose special purpose was to sail to England and Ireland to revive the flagging Fenian movement in Ireland after it had lost its chance to rise at the most appropriate time, 1865, when its leader, James Stephens, was not prepared to act. Irish-Americans like Thomas Kelly, William Halpin and John McCafferty were impetuous and eager for the fray although the opportune moment to strike had long past. Fifteen of them were stationed in London and eight of them were ex-officers of the American army. There were similar groups or directories in Glasgow, Leeds, Liverpool and Manchester.[6]

'For some time past', the *Annual Chronicle* stated, 'those Directories had been making arrangements to concentrate their forces upon some place which was to have been afterwards designated. This was not done, but a meeting was called for Sunday the 10th at Liverpool, and it was resolved to attack Chester Castle the following day, seize the arms deposited there, cut the telegraph wires, tear up the rails, and make good their escape by rail to Holyhead and trust to fortune to get across to Ireland.'[7]

The *Annual Chronicle* was remarkably accurate in its information. Similarly, it was significant that while the events had scarcely got underway, the *Manchester Guardian* was able to state authoritatively that 'we are informed that the Chief Constable of Chester has in his possession a list of ex-Federal officers with the rank they held in the Federal army who are now in Chester and who are believed to be in command of the present movement.' Such remarkably accurate information about the activities of a secret society must have had a source high in the ranks of the Fenian movement. It was this which was to prove crucial in the events which followed.

Years later, John Denvir[8] gave his highly personal account of what was planned at Chester:

> The idea was to bring sufficient men from various parts of England, armed with revolvers, to overpower the garrison, which at the time was a very weak one, and to seize the large store of arms then in the Castle. In connection with this, arrangements had been made for the cutting of wires, the taking up of rails, and the seizure of sufficient engines and waggons to convey the captured arms to Holyhead, whence, a steamer having been seized there for the purpose, the arms were to be taken to Ireland and the standard of insurrection raised. Of John Ryan, one of the leaders of this raid, I have already spoken. Another of them, Captain John McCafferty, was one of the Irish-American officers who had crossed the Atlantic to take part in the projected rising in Ireland . . .
>
> Most of the American officers I came in contact with during these years had served in the Federal Army, but McCafferty fought on the side of the South in the American Civil War. He was a thorough type of a guerilla leader. With his well-proportioned and strongly-knit frame, and handsome resolute-looking bronzed face, you could imagine him just the man for any dashing and daring enterprise.
>
> I frequently met John Flood, too, whose name, with that of McCafferty, is associated with the Chester raid. He was then about thirty years of age, a fine handsome man, tall and strong, wearing a full and flowing tawny-coloured beard. He had a genial-looking face, and, in your intercourse with him, you found him just as genial as he looked. He was a man of distinguished bearing, who you could imagine would fill with grace and dignity the post of Irish Ambassador to some friendly power. He was a Wexford man, full of the glorious traditions of '98. He took an active part in aiding the escape of James Stephens from Ireland. With Colonel Kelly he was aboard the hooker in which the C.O.I.R. escaped, and to his skill and courage and rare presence of mind was largely due the fact that Stephens did not again fall into the hands of his enemies.
>
> Father McCormick, of Wigan, a patriotic Irish priest, used to tell me, too, of the men coming to confession to him on their way to Chester, and afterwards to Ireland, for the rising on Shrove Tuesday . . .
>
> When John Ryan informed me of the plans that were being matured for the seizure of the arms and ammunition in Chester Castle, I volunteered for any duty that might be allotted to me. It was settled that I should hold myself in readiness to carry out, when called upon, certain mechanical arrangements in connection with the raid with a view to prevent reinforcements from reaching Chester.
>
> These arrangements were to consist of the taking up of the rails on certain railway lines and the cutting of the telegraphic wires leading into

Chester. I, therefore, surveyed the ground, and besides the required personal assistance, had in readiness crowbars, sledge hammers, and among other implements, the wrenches for unscrewing the nuts of the bolts fastening the fishplates which bound together the rails, end to end. I now held myself prepared for the moment when the call to action would meet me.

The plan was to concentrate quickly several hundred men on Chester on 11 February. The men were to be divided into companies of about fifty; each company had an allotted duty to perform. One company led by McCafferty himself was to surprise and overpower the small company of soldiers guarding the Castle.[9]

Once the Castle was in McCafferty's possession, the telegraph wires were to be cut in and around the city. This would isolate the city and so cut it off from help outside. (Here the order of operations seems curiously reversed from what one would expect.)

A second company of men was allotted the task of transporting the war material from the Castle to the station in drays. Once the arms and ammunition were aboard the train the driver was to drive at the point of a revolver, full speed for Holyhead. As soon as the train had pulled out of Chester station a task party was to tear up the rails of all the lines leading out of Chester.

The captured material was to be put aboard the mail boat at Holyhead. If the mail boat was not there any other steamer would be used. Once the captured arms and ammunition were aboard the steamer, the Captain was to be compelled at the point of a revolver to sail for Wicklow where the cargo was to be unloaded. The destination of Wicklow seems more sensible from a military point of view than Dublin, but one marvels at the lack of precision as much as at the audacity of the plan. But audacity may succeed where careful planning may fail, as McCafferty had no doubt learned during other daring exploits in the American Civil War. The event was timed to take place on the night of Monday, 11 February, The *Manchester Guardian* stated the timing to be for 7 p.m.

Denvir was told a few days later by John Ryan that the word had been sent round to a certain number of Fenian Circles in the North of England and the Midlands to move a number of picked men, some on the Sunday night and some early on Monday morning. His rather optimistic account speaks of 'the promptness and cheerfulness with which the order was obeyed . . . so that probably not less than two thousand men were by different routes converging on Chester.' The telegram to *The Times* had mentioned eight hundred.

But any optimism on the part of the raiding parties was entirely without justification. At first, according to *The Times*, no credit was given to the rumour of an attack when it reached Liverpool. There, fifty or sixty men were seen departing by train to Chester. Chief

Constable Greig immediately reported the fact to Chester and took precautions to prevent disturbances in Liverpool.

Meanwhile in Yorkshire, the *Leeds Mercury* reported large numbers of Irish leaving Leeds, Bradford, Halifax and other towns on the Monday, under circumstances which caused grave suspicion in the minds of the local authorities that they were Fenians moving to a common rendezvous. The Halifax correspondent reported seventy Fenians leaving Halifax.

A telegram was received by the Earl of Grosvenor, one of the MPs for the City of Chester, stating that five hundred Fenians had arrived from Manchester and had seized the Castle. The telegram was premature but all morning the trains from Manchester, Bolton, Warrington and elsewhere arrived, disgorging numbers of Irishmen who formed up in Chester, lounging about in small parties and seemingly awaiting others. Nothing so daringly unconventional in the way of insurgency had ever been seen before in England.

Chester was now the scene of a strange drama.

> The strangers were moving about the city last night in groups of about a dozen and knots of them were assembled at the corners of the streets apparently discussing the events of the day. Large numbers were parading the roads outside the city, and they appeared to be well-organized in their movements. [10]

And yet no battle took place. No jewellers shops were attacked; no citizen assaulted; an air of unreality and expectancy hung over Chester only to disappear like mist in a breeze. For the citizens of sleepy Chester 'the excitement seemed to be welcomed by many as an agreeable relief to the oppressive monotony of ordinary Chester life.' [11]

Indeed, the *Manchester Guardian* reporter joined a train at Manchester and found himself among a merry group of Irishmen singing the 'Lakes of Killarney' and other Irish melodies. But something strange happened at Warrington to these men, each of whom had two tickets, one to Chester and another through to Dublin. They were warned by someone on the platform to leave the train, and explained that 'a relation who had been for some years in the Wigan police' had been their informant.

Meanwhile, at Leeds, on the other side of the Pennines, an Irish boy called Fenton who had been seen on the Leeds railway platform was followed and found to have in his possession a parcel of 130 cartridges. There is no evidence as to his destination but no doubt he too was on his way to Chester. Those who arrived gave as their pretext the story that they had come to see a prize fight.

Among the groups standing on the railway platform at Chester were one or two better dressed men, presumably the Irish-American organizers. They conversed together earnestly, but immediately ceased when any official approached them. Jewellers shops were closed and volunteers and police went to their headquarters ready for action immediately. A Company of soldiers arrived at noon, while the Mayor of Chester and the Chief Constable were still trying to find out from the strangers who had arrived at Chester what their business was. They obviously did not accept the story of the prize fight, and with good reason.

It was rumoured that a gunboat had left the Mersey for Holyhead, but in Liverpool itself there was no sign of any disturbance though a large force of police were kept in readiness for an emergency.

> Suddenly the Chief Constable of Chester and the Colonel of the military received telegrams which must have taken their breath away. The guards of the Castle were instantly doubled; the police marched out; mounted expresses dashed off in all directions. Soon troops began to arrive from Birkenhead as fast as special trains could bring them. Very quickly the loitering groups were observed to disperse, on some whispered message reaching them. They poured into every train returning to the towns they had left in the morning. They had got word that the plot was 'blown upon' by some traitor. Some of them were observed to fling revolvers into the Dee. A large party took the train to Holyhead.[12]

> However, it was promptly discovered that information had been given to the police authorities almost at the last moment. Those, therefore, who had already reached Chester were sent back, and men were placed at the railway stations and on the roads leading to Chester to stop those who were coming. In this way the whole of the men forming the expedition dispersed as silently as they had come.[13]

Some curious scenes were enacted as the men dispersed around rural Cheshire. The quiet and peaceful town of Frodsham was 'much disturbed by the appearance of gangs of low, ruffianly looking fellows making their way to the railway station'.[14] By 5 p.m. no fewer than sixty to seventy had arrived, no doubt intending to go to Chester by the 5.30 train. Before the arrival of the train however, two men who had rapidly driven in a cab from Chester arrived. This resulted in a change of plan and the assembled men took a train to Warrington, in batches of five to twenty. Between 7 a.m. and 2 p.m. two to three hundred men in small parties passed through the town, many of them singing 'When Johnny comes marching home'. The song was curiously appropriate and there was no doubt a touch of Irish irony in its choice. The figures given in these reports may well bear out Denvir's estimate of two thousand men involved in the plan, but probably half of them never arrived at Chester as the word to return went around. The *Annual Chronicle* estimated four hundred reinforcing an original five hundred arriving in one batch from Manchester and Stalybridge. More significantly it recorded that:

The first intimation received in Chester of the intended raid was at 12.30 a.m. on the 11th, by Mr. Fenwick, from Mr. Superintendent Ryde and Detective Inspector Carlisle of Liverpool, and was to the effect that an ex-officer of the American Army, who produced his commission as an officer in the Fenian service, had revealed the whole plot to them.[15]

The Mayor of Chester lived outside the city so the deputy Mayor, William Williams, was contacted and the Adjutant General at Manchester was asked for reinforcements. Volunteers were sworn in as special constables. The element of surprise so necessary for the plan to succeed had been lost due to the defection of a leading Fenian whose name, John Joseph Corydon, was to become notorious as the leading police spy later used for the purpose of identifying Fenian leaders. Through his betrayal Chester was being patrolled by armed troops, and seventy seven Irishmen arriving from the Liverpool and Holyhead steamers were arrested at the quays on February 12 at Dublin. The plot had fizzled out without a shot fired in anger.

Corydon had in fact been supplying the English authorities with information since September 1866. It was one of the defects of the secret society that it threw up spies like Corydon and Le Caron who were able to betray the movement. It was a weakness understood by Michael Davitt, who was one of the men who marched from Chester on that day of failure. Corydon, Davitt and McCafferty are three remarkable sides of the Fenian panorama.

Corydon's part is described by Denvir in unflattering terms:

At first sight you might set him down as a third rate actor or circus performer. He wore a frock coat, buttoned tightly, to set off a by no means contemptible figure, and carried himself with a jaunty, swaggering air, after the style of a theatrical 'professional'. He was about the middle height, of wiry, active build, with features clearly cut, thin face, large round forehead, a high aquiline nose, thick and curly hair, decidedly 'sandy' in colour, and heavy moustache of the same tinge. His cheeks and chin were denuded of beard.[16]

At first it was thought that a man named Arthur Anderson, who strongly resembled Corydon, was the informer. Michael Breslin, a secret agent of the Fenians in the Chief Superintendent's office in Dublin Castle, had some time previously sent warning to Thomas Kelly, then Leader of the Fenian organization, that an Irish-American officer was betraying their secrets to the British Government.[17] On hearing this, Kelly had made arrangements for Breslin to observe and identify all the men who answered to the description given. A few had not yet passed the screening and among them was Corydon.

Corydon was brought to Manchester in order to identify Colonel Kelly and his aide, Captain Deasy, when they were arrested later in the year. There he was to throw off his mask and appear openly in identifying accused Fenians for the Crown. No one was hated more among the ranks of the Fenians at the time of the Manchester rescue.[18] Only stern discipline prevented an attempt to assassinate him. The freeing of Kelly was of more importance to the organization than an act of vengeance.

The veteran Fenian, John Devoy, confirms the object of the Chester attack and also the betrayal by Corydon:

> The plans were all upset by the spy John Joseph Corydon whom nobody suspected at the time. He was trusted by McCafferty and gave the Government timely information, which enabled it to frustrate the project. Troops were rapidly moved to Chester and many of them arrived before the hour set for the attack. The Fenians were at their rendezvous ready for action, but McCafferty did not arrive on time and they had no commander. They could not fight regular soldiers with revolvers and were puzzled by the absence of McCafferty. When he reached Chester several hours late he no doubt explained his delay satisfactorily, but the rest of the organization were left in ignorance of it for years. The awkward and maddening fact to him was that the train he was coming on from London was side-tracked to allow the troop trains to pass. Perhaps that was the supreme irony of the betrayal.[19]

It was not until 1874 that Devoy obtained this information from McCafferty and there is no evidence elsewhere to contradict the account. But McCafferty entertained some curiously bold if not hairbrained schemes which set him apart from more sober if equally daring Irish-American officers. He had a plan to capture the Prince of Wales and hold him as hostage to compel the release of Fenians still held in prison. It was typical of his almost larger than life, wild Southern temperament that when he heard, incorrectly it would seem, that Devoy had called him a coward over the Chester debacle, he approached Devoy and said in a cold quiet voice: 'Devoy, I am told you have called me a coward. Now I don't allow any man to call me a coward and live.' Certainly Devoy took him seriously although such a scene would now be a cliché in a Western film. But then few would have believed in the possibility of the Manchester rescue or the fantastic Catalpa expedition rescuing Fenian prisoners from Australia. Their social implications for Irish nationalist aspirations are, however, more significant and it is here that the one-armed figure of Michael Davitt, carrying a bag of bullets to Chester, unable to use a weapon and by inclination not particularly disposed to use one is of the greatest significance.

Michael Davitt (1846-1906) towers above the original Fenians not merely for his immense moral courage, which he shared with such men as O'Donovan Rossa in gaol, or indeed with his saintliness, which he shared with a few, but for his vision and his understanding of the strength and weaknesses of the Fenian Movement. It is not without significance that Sir Robert Anderson, the Assistant Commissioner of Metropolitan Police and Head of the Criminal Investigation Department, when he came to write his memoirs,[20] made the startlingly crude and yet sharp observation that 'in the "New Departure" Fenianism made no surrender to the Land League; it merely assumed its name.' In the sense that the Land League was the essential militant link between old-style physical force Fenianism and their successors in the Dublin Post Office, fusing national and social demands and for the first time placing greater emphasis on the latter in the agrarian problem, the police chief was right.

After Chester, Manchester and the subsequent arrest of the man whose name runs like a thread through all these events, Ricard O'Sullivan Burke, Davitt was to find himself procuring and distributing arms and was arrested at Paddington on 14 May 1870, and subsequently convicted of treason felony. Corydon not only identified him without ever having seen him before, not difficult in the case of a one-armed man, but swore to his having been at Chester. He had certainly not seen him there, but whether this was out and out perjury or based on hearsay it is not possible to know. The saint and the spy first met in the police cell.

The wild McCafferty, who had been to London to make final plans with Kelly only to have his return train shunted into a siding, was arrested when he arrived at Dublin on the *New Draper* to join the Irish uprising on 23 February. Sentenced to death, McCafferty was reprieved and became one of the prisoners for whom the Fenian Amnesty Movement was to agitate following the failure of the uprising

Back in Chester, there was an orgy of self-congratulation as a meeting of the Town Council on 13 February passed a vote of thanks to the authorities, the volunteers, fire brigade, police and others taking an active part in the prevention of the raid. Quantities of ammunition and cartridges were found in various places and Chester sent a memorial to the authorities praying that it might be provided with more soldiers for its defence. *The Times* estimate of the existing garrison was fifty-four efficient soldiers and two officers. The Fenians had chosen their target well. The evidence does not make it clear whether or not John McCafferty had the full support of the other Fenian military leaders in preparing to raid Chester Castle.[21] The exploit certainly bears his stamp but it is hard to imagine it planned in isolation and certainly McCafferty claimed to have been in London with Kelly. No one ever refuted this or accused him of acting without authority.

As cartridges were dragged from the River Dee and shillelahs and haversacks turned up in odd places, William Williams J.P., estimating 1,400 as the number of Fenians in Chester, complained that 'it was a perfect disgrace the city should be left in such an insecure state, there being 800,000 or 900,000 rounds of cartridges in the Castle . . . besides the large quantity of arms.' For the Fenians this would have been a remarkable haul. But it was Fenian cartridges that were being picked up not far from the city centre, on the banks of the canal and even on the roads outside the city. The Fenians had left as they had come, but they left some souvenirs and a footnote in history behind them.

The participation of McCafferty and Davitt in the Chester Castle raid illustrates the curiously diverse nature of Fenian support. Michael Davitt was born at Straide, County Mayo on 25 March 1846. His family shared the fate of many others in the terrible famine and, when he was six, took him to Haslingdon in Lancashire. There, at the age of eleven, he went to work in a cotton mill, and within a year he had lost an arm at work. He joined the Fenians at the high tide of their activity, in 1865 when he was nineteen. Captain John McCafferty had been an officer in the Confederate Army in the American Civil War and Captain Kelly had a good opinion of him, despite fighting on the other side. Born in Ohio in 1838 his parents were both emigrants and their feeling for Ireland was passed on to him.

An adventurer by nature, McCafferty had enlisted in the Confederate regiment chosen to carry out the most dangerous enterprises, Moseby's guerillas, for which surprise and audacity were the two characteristics most required. In the United States he had taken part in Fenian meetings but his attempts to set foot in Ireland seemed ill-fated. After escaping from Chester together with John Flood, he was arrested while leaving the *New Draper* in a small boat, and placed in the dock of Green Street Courthouse, Dublin. He was typical of the new breed of Irish-American soldiers equipped with a military experience hitherto denied to Irishmen. Natural commanders and leaders in battle, they were often impatient of theorists like Stephens.

'McCafferty had done some very daring feats in the Civil War of which Kelly has told me' Devoy wrote in his recollections. 'On one occasion he had got inside the Union lines with a detachment of Morgan's men, captured a lot of ammunition, loaded it on steamers or tugs which he had seized and brought his booty down the Mississippi, under the fire of the Federal batteries.'[22] There can be little doubt that here was the inspiration for the plan to take Chester Castle. Both at Manchester and Chester the chosen weapon, light and easily concealed and obtainable was the revolver. The sophisti-

On his way to the Castle he encounters some suspicious characters, —

Chester Castle, 1867. Ensign Smith of the Chester Militia spots the Fenians. A sketch from a contemporary Chester novellette. (Courtesy of Chester Public Library)

The Fenian stamp of 1866. Now known to be a forgery but the design was adopted for the official commemorative issued in 1967. Numerous forgeries of the forgery exist. (Author's collection)

cated techniques of modern guerilla warfare, demanding speed, surprise and the ability for the fish to disappear into the sea, are not very different from those used by the Fenians or McCafferty. The only trouble was that fish with Irish or American accents could sometimes be hooked by the authorities. But it was unusual in a cavalry man to prefer the revolver to the swashbuckling sabre. Certainly, in the conditions of Chester or Manchester the revolver was appropriate, but McCafferty as much as Kelly understood the need to capture more effective arms for the planned insurrection in Ireland. However, both his pronounced American accent and his unfamiliarity with the area were disadvantages.

It was in Portland prison that McCafferty met Devoy where they worked at stone cutting in the same group. That McCafferty was alive and in prison was due to a reprieve following sentence of death. It took a Court of Appeal of ten Irish Judges to dismiss important legal points, the most fascinating of which was whether a man who had been in custody since 23 February could be held responsible for the events of the Fenian rising in Ireland occuring on the night of 5 March.

McCafferty's reaction to sentence by Mr. Justice Fitzgerald is revealing. No Emmett or even O'Brien, he was clear, cold and calm; straightforward in manner and with that strange chivalry and courage associated with the romanticized idea of the Southern Gentleman. It is clear that he was a proud man in that tradition as his words emerge.

I do not deny that I have sympathized with the Irish people. I love Ireland. I love the Irish people. And, if I were free tomorrow, and the Irish people were to take the field for independence, my sympathy would be with them; I would join them if they had any prospect whatever of independence. But I would not give my sanction to the useless effusion of blood, however done; and I state distinctly that I had nothing whatever to do, directly or indirectly with the movement that took place in the County of Dublin. I make that statement on the brink of my grave. Again, I claim that I have a right to be acquitted of the charge against me by the language of the law by which I have been tried. That law states that you must have two independent witnesses to prove the overt act against the prisoner. That is the only complaint I have to make, and I make that aloud. I find no fault with the jury, have no complaint against the judges. I have been tried and found guilty. I am perfectly satisfied that I will go to my grave. I will go like a gentleman and a Christian, although I regret that I should be cut off at this stage of my life. Still, many a noble Irishman fell in defence of my Southern clime. I do not wish to make any flowery speech to win sympathy in this court of justice. Without any further remarks, then, I accept the sentence of the court.[23]

It is curious that in regard to McCafferty's earlier career two sources cite different guerilla groups but Michael Lennon's researches in the United States[24] do not reveal McCafferty's name in Morgan's guerillas nor any record of the incident described by Devoy. He had no known Southern associations and was a bartender in Atwater East on the Detroit-Milwaukee railroad, more than once figuring in the Magistrates court where he was compelled to make restitution of money won in a game known as Three Card Monte.

One wonders how much of the poseur, adventurer or genuine patriot there was in McCafferty. As colourful a figure as can be found in the annals of Fenianism, his role was small and his contribution to its philosophy non-existent. But his exploits almost rank with the James Brothers in the boundary now blurred between fact and legend; dashing hero or fake adventurer, certainly he is now regarded as the man most responsible for the later Phoenix Park murders. In a curious way he represents a tradition which still exists in the provisional wing of the IRA, one that finds an attraction in violent means with little social philosophy other than national sentiment, the hallmark of the romantic right. The more socially conscious and less violent Davitt personifies the reluctant conspirator forced to take up arms but preferring political agitation as a means to his end, a tradition perhaps personified by the SDLP or even some members of the official Sinn Fein today.

Of Michael Davitt, it would be presumptious to add more than a footnote to Sheehy Skeffington's classic biography.[25] But Davitt's career spanning the physical force movement of Fenianism, the dark days of pain and humiliation in prison and the re-emergence into the sphere of agrarian reform linked with Parliamentary and mass agitation, also spanned the schools of thought of Irish freedom movements. He added more clearly than any predecessor a social and indeed socialist, if agrarian, philosophy to the concept of national freedom. Perhaps most significantly of all within the context of this particular study he was the one man who epitomized the struggle of the English weaver and the Irish homesteader against the complacent establishment. He believed that Irish emancipation needed the understanding and support of the English worker and acted as a bridge between the two movements in later years; explaining the problems of Ireland in England and vice versa. In Haslingdon he enthusiastically supported the Labour movement. His dream of land nationalization was an advanced socialist concept. It is tempting to sketch the life of this man whose courage went beyond the military physical courage of McCafferty and resembled the stuff that saints are made of. His Lancashire and Irish backgrounds traversed the gulf between England and Ireland more than any other man associated with Fenianism and indeed Fenianism was no more than his introduction to the political scene.[26]

Davitt's career as a Fenian had two phases. There was first the stage in which he went quietly about his usual business at Haslingdon, awaiting the call for action from his leaders. The Chester Castle episode was the awaited call but already he was to display a potential for leadership, the confidence in his abilities shown by his chiefs when, in spite of the fact that his lost arm prevented him from handling a rifle, they committed to his charge the captainship of a detachment, was proved not to be displaced. To enable his companions to escape, he had to supply them with money, which they had deemed to be unnecessary; he did so by pawning his watch. Davitt had even arranged an alibi, so that, in case suspicion should fall on him, he would have been able to show to the satisfaction of any court of justice that he was at his work at Haslingdon all the time.

At that time there was no suspicion of his participation in the Chester raid. In the moment of defeat he flung himself fearlessly into the Fenian cause, dealing in arms under the guise of being a commercial traveller. He organized the scattered Fenians and shipped rifles over to Ireland. Davitt always maintained that the Manchester Martyrs were 'offered up as political sacrifices to the anti-Irish feeling in England.' Davitt filled the gap left by earlier failures and arrests.

Davitt's ability and energy, his whole-hearted devotion to the Fenian cause, and the rare combination of coolness and daring which he brought to its service, soon marked him out for promotion to a place of trust and danger in the councils of the organization. Soon after his first joining them in 1865 he became leader of his local Rossendale 'Circle'. When he left his employment under Cockroft, the Haslingdon postmaster and printer, in 1868, it was to take up the position of organizing secretary of the Fenian body for England and Scotland. In this position he was immediately under the Supreme Council of the IRB and received instructions from them . . . . His principal duties were those connected with the purchase of arms and the despatchment of them to various Fenian centres in Great Britain and to Ireland. He had, at the time of his arrest, a depot in Leeds, taken by him under the name of Robert Jackson, ostensibly as a storehouse for various kinds of groceries and dry goods. To this warehouse were forwarded the rifles purchased by Davitt. Thence they were despatched anew in smaller bales, to the local centres; another fictitious name other than Jackson being given as that of the consigner. Those sent to Ireland were mostly addressed to real persons unconnected with the Fenian organization, and intercepted at the railway station by Fenians purporting to come on behalf of the consignees. The rifles were packed in barrels, so as to appear as much like soap or some equally harmless commodity, and as little like guns, as possible. All this was excessively perilous work, involving constant travelling about the country and the assumption of a number of aliases, without the possibilities of disguise which one less unmistakenly marked by nature could have enjoyed. The slightest hitch in his arrangements would at any time by sufficient to set the police on the track of the whole complicated scheme. The extraordinary thing was not that Davitt should have been ultimately tracked down, but that he should actually have succeeded in baffling the British police for nearly two years after he took up the organization.[27]

Although a member of a physical force movement, violence for its own sake was contrary to Davitt's nature. He was no bold romantic like McCafferty. About Davitt's own original contribution we will have a word to say later. Inevitably the police closed in on Davitt and in March 1870 they were on the track of John Wilson, a Birmingham gunsmith from whom Davitt purchased large quantities of arms. These were traced to Leeds having passed through the Birmingham depot.

In six weeks, sixteen consignments of arms, in which Davitt acted as distributor, were thus tracked to different destinations; eight to Ireland, five to Newcastle-on-Tyne, one to Glasgow, and one to Manchester. The sixteenth was a consignment not from but to Davitt who was now in London. The police in Birmingham saw Wilson leave that city with the bag, and the London police, warned by telegraph, were waiting for him when the 10.40 p.m. train from Birmingham arrived at Paddington Station on the night of Saturday, 14 May 1870. Davitt was also waiting for that train. He was seized by detectives, questioned as to what he was doing there and for whom he was waiting and was finally taken into custody on the charge of loitering.

When arrested, Davitt had, it was stated, £150 in his possession. Wilson had in his possession fifty revolvers. The theory of the prosecution was that Wilson had come to deliver arms to Davitt, and to receive payment for them. The Crown Prosecutor, when Davitt and Wilson were brought up at the police court, dwelt upon this as a suspicious circumstance, and said, in urging the charge of treason-felony against both the prisoners, that he could show they had been connected and that the arms were to be ultimately sent to Ireland for treasonable purposes.

The result of the trial was that Michael Davitt and John Wilson were convicted of treason-felony. As sentence was about to be passed, Davitt made an earnest appeal to the judge, not for himself, but for the Englishman. He declared that Wilson never knew until he arrived at Paddington station that he, Davitt, was an Irishman, or that his name was not 'Jackson'. He would, he declared, cheerfully undergo any additional sentence that might be passed upon him, if Wilson would be spared and his wife and family saved from the workhouse; and he begged that the Englishman's sentence might be added to his own.[28]

Davitt was held at Clerkenwell Gaol and a press scare about a rescue attempt helped feed the fires of prejudice when he was eventually tried for Treason-felony. It was at this stage that Corydon's testimony in relation to the Chester raid was used against him. Above all, Davitt's failure to implicate another man in respect of a letter written by him in order to prevent a political assassination, went against him and he began his sentence of fifteen years penal servitude where he was the object of terrible humiliation. The unwanted interval in his activities marks the low tide of Irish insurgency as the waves of Fenianism receded from the shore until the swell of Davitt's Land League was to crash against the rock of the English and Irish establishment.

Today, one of Michael Davitt's guns from 1867 is on display in the Kelly House in Mount Bellew, but his real monument is the legacy of moral judgement and political tactical sense which he combined uniquely in a spirit that was unconquerable and selfless. Less the Fenian and more the Leader of a new political movement it is significant that a man of Davitt's stature saw Fenianism with all its weaknesses and its conspiratorial nature as the only means available to fight for his ideals at this early period of his life. Even that arch enemy of Fenianism, Sir Robert Anderson, admitted that[29] 'in Mr. Michael Davitt, the Fenian movement can boast no more interesting personality'. He quoted the aims of the Land League — 'the complete destruction of Irish landlordism, first, as the system which was responsible for the poverty and periodic famines which have decimated Ireland; and secondly because landlordism was a garrison which barred the way to national independence.'[30]

This conclusion was a far cry from the philosophy which took Davitt on the remarkable Chester Castle raid, but Chester was nonetheless the beginning of the road to the Land League and the alliance with Parnell which was to be the next chapter of Ireland's variegated struggle for national and economic independence, ends that are so frequently intertwined and confused.

## NOTES

1. *The Times* 12 February 1867.
2. Ibid.
3. F.L. Crilly, *The Fenian Movement*. 1909 pp. 50-51.
4. *The Times* 18 February 1867.
5. *Manchester Guardian* 14 February 1867.
6. *Annual Chronicle* 1867.
7. *Ibid.*
8. John Denvir, *Life Story of an Old Rebel*. 1910 pp. 81-85.
9. Article under pseudonym Owen Roe, quoted in *Cork Weekly Examiner* 5 November 1962.
10. *Manchester Guardian* 12 February 1867.
11. *Ibid.*
12. F.L. Crilly *op. cit.*
13. J. Denvir, *The Irish in Britain*, 1892.
14. *Liverpool Mercury*. February 1867.
15. *Annual Chronicle* 1867.
16. J. Denvir, *op. cit.*
17. Owen Roe, *op. cit.*
18. Paul Rose, *The Manchester Martyrs*, Chapter 5.
19. John Devoy, *Recollections of an Irish Rebel*. 1929 p. 188.
20. R. Anderson *A Great Conspiracy*. 1910 p. 87.
21. See Kevin Nowlan's essay in *The Fenian Movement*, ed. T.W. Moody 1968.
22. John Devoy, *Recollections of an Irish Rebel* 1929, p. 65.
23. A.M. Sullivan, *Speeches from the Dock*, 1968 p. 171.
24. *Irish Independent* 10 October 1956.
25. F. Sheehy Skeffington, *Life of Michael Davitt*. 1908.
26. See T.W. Moody's chapter on Davitt in *Leaders and Workers*, ed. J. Boyle.
27. F. Sheehy Skeffington, *op. cit.*
28. F.L. Crilly, *op. cit.*
29. R. Anderson, *op. cit.*
30. See Michael Davitt's *The Fall of Fendalism in Ireland*. F.L. Crilly, *op. cit.*

# Chapter 4

## *The Murphy Riots*

While English reactions to Fenianism included sympathy with the plight of Ireland and even the tragedy of Clerkenwell helped to produce a new understanding of Irish aspirations on the part of Gladstone, one particularly sordid series of incidents illustrates the backlash that Fenianism produced in many English towns. These were provoked by the appearance on the English scene of an Orange firebrand by the name of Murphy.

Demagogues directing popular anger and resentment against easily identifiable minorities in their midst have been a phenomenon throughout history. And the cry of 'no Popery' has had a special appeal in Britain since the reformation.

The rise of Fenianism was accompanied by a reaction reflected in the editorials of *The Times*, horrified at the apparently innate ingratitude of the Irish. They reflect the level of popular prejudice directed against all those remotely connected with Fenianism. To many of the most deprived inhabitants of the industrial slums, the Irish in their midst were the object of their prejudices.

Between 1864 and 1870 contemporary journals reveal the activities of the Orange demagogue, William Murphy, agent of an organization called the Protestant Electoral Union. In the Midlands, North-East, London and the North-West, his activities were to provoke riots and a reaction on a scale reminiscent of Mosley's marches through London's East End or what Andrew Boyd recently termed the 'Holy War' in Belfast.[1] Just as Paisleyism was directly linked to the phenomenon of the civil rights movement, so Murphyism reflected the reaction to Fenianism at grass roots level. Interestingly the strange, if familiar figure, of Murphy, made its first significant appearance in the Midlands. For as John Denvir recalled:

> In the chapters on Fenianism it will be seen that Birmingham was one of the most active centres of the movement and there cannot be a doubt but that a considerable number of Irishmen there were enrolled in the

revolutionary organization. It is probably this that raised against the Irish and Catholic population of the town, whether Fenian or not, a feeling of enmity. This was exactly the inflammable condition that suited the purpose of the no Popery firebrand, Murphy, when he made his appearance at Birmingham in the summer of 1867.[2]

In fact he had made his appearance in Wolverhampton three months before when the *Manchester Guardian* reported on his activities followed by *The Times*.[3]

Long before the serious riots in Birmingham hit the headlines the perceptive reader might have forseen the pattern described in the Wolverhampton Riots of 25th February. These occured before the Clerkenwell and Manchester events provided any pretext for Murphy's provocative campaign. In the face of provocation, the Irish did not stand aside, although ultimately in some areas they suffered on a scale far beyond anything they inflicted upon Murphy's followers.

*The Times* and *Manchester Guardian* both reported that:

> The announcement that Mr. Murphy, the agent of the Protestant Electoral Union, would on Friday night 'unmask' the confessional to the people of Wolverhampton produced the greatest excitement amongst the Irish Roman Catholics of the district, and the magistrates deemed it necessary to obtain the assistance of two troops of Hussars from Coventry. The yeomanry were also called out, and special constables were sworn for duty. The state of affairs is thus described in a telegram which we received from our correspondent:- Altogether 70 regular troops, 40 yeomanry, 140 police, and 250 special constables were on duty in the town. They have been patrolling the streets. Ten thousand people were outside the hall, and threats of firing property have been made. A rush at the hall was defeated, and bludgeons taken from the Irish. There were three thousand persons present at the lecture. The town was cleared at 10 o'clock. Father Kelly was sent for by the stipendiary, and has gone among the Irish.

On the eve of Sunday 15 June 1867 a large mob collected around a wooden building, specially built in the middle of Birmingham to house an audience for Murphy's lecture on 'Romanism'. Stones were thrown at the building and three ticket collectors were seriously wounded. Only three or four policemen were on the spot initially but were later joined by a large force armed with cutlasses. All the streets in the neighbourhood of the building were cleared but the crowd continued to increase. Meanwhile Murphy held another lecture session and the 8th Hussars stood by in readiness for the anticipated riot and the crowd was held back by a large force of police.

Then, following a lecture on the 'Errors of Roman Catholicism' on the Sunday night, a very serious riot took place. The Town Hall had been refused him as a result of the Wolverhampton events but his 'tabernacle' in Birmingham became the focal point for speeches which *The Times* correspondent described as 'in every way in singular bad taste.'

But Murphy was undeterred, delivering a long address on Monday afternoon followed by a sermon on Monday evening. Lectures, speeches or sermons, the single theme was hostility to Catholicism and Catholics intermingled with references to the Irish. 'Popery is the same today as it was in days gone by. If she had any power . . . what wouldn't she do to you? What wouldn't she do to me? Why she would roast me as she did Ridley, Cranmer and Latimer.'[4]

Provoked by his sermons, perhaps foolishly, Irishmen and Irishwomen surrounded the tabernacle and its applauding audience only to clash with the police wielding cutlasses. Policemen were 'roughly handled' and injured rioters taken to hospital. Mr. Thomas Aston, a prominent member of the Protestant Association had his shop broken into and the window panes smashed while priests exhorted the crowd to be peaceable. Rioters were remanded in Court while the Riot Act was read and the military called out. Two streets were sacked by rampaging Protestants who also attacked and damaged a Catholic church. One soldier and several policemen were badly injured by the end of Monday evening's rioting. A detachment of infantry of the 82nd Regiment arrived from Weedon at 11.30 p.m. Meanwhile G.H. Whalley, M.P., an ally of Murphy, demanded freedom of speech for Protestants while the Mayor and the Stipendiary Magistrate, Mr. Kynnersley, required Murphy to leave the town.

Special Constables were sworn in as the total arrested on Monday had mounted to a hundred. Even pensioners under Major Smythe were called out while rifle volunteers under Major Ratcliffe stood at the ready. By Tuesday morning the rioting had been momentarily checked and the crowds still thronging the streets were a little more subdued. Some rioters had already received sentences of up to six weeks and others were sent to Quarter Sessions for trial. More soldiers arrived on Tuesday night, this time a hundred men of the 81st Regiment from Manchester.

As Birmingham became quiet on Wednesday, Park Street was in ruins and 'The utter wreck in that locality is indescribable . . . the mob carried away every moveable article . . . This street was inhabited almost exclusively by the poor class of Irish.' A local report described how, having sacked the houses, the 'Party of Order' marched up and down the street armed with fragments from window shutters wainscotting, chairs and tables, singing 'Glory, Glory Hallelujha'.

Murphy's attack on the Catholic Mass, on the 'magical' power of priests and on the Pope had done its work all too thoroughly.

But even after Wednesday Murphy continued, claiming that the Virgin Mary was a married woman and attacking uninspected nunneries . . . 'and I ask you, my friends, what happiness had the sisters of misery who were locked up in the prison cells of Rome.' He was still busy unmasking the confessional on Friday by which time the riots were a spent force and the law was busy dealing with those arrested.

Most apposite was the comment which reflected the revulsion of the organized labour movement at the riots. It said that it was ironical that they were not caused by the bug-bear of the press, the trades unions, and expressed the hope that Birmingham would investigate their cause with as much thoroughness as it was examining 'trade outrages' in Sheffield. It saw the riots as evidence of an internal condition of social rottenness and analyzed the malaise of the class ridden society in which they were spawned:

> . . . Protestants blame the Catholics, and Catholics Protestants . . . perhaps they are all to blame. But what lies at the root of all this social derangement? And what is to cure the cause of evil? These are questions much more easily made than solved. We believe that the great cause of evil among us is the truth that Baron Talfourd died declaring — viz, 'The lack of real sympathy between class and class.' For years we have been growing up capitalist and labourer in isolation. Every day separates wider and makes the distinction more marked. Poverty and wealth goes side by side, and there comes a time when the attraction of social cohesion cannot stand the strain . . .[5]

It was an analysis which James Connolly and James Larkin would have understood only too well and which is as relevant today as it was in Birmingham in 1867.

Murphy's subsequent progress was less than noteworthy although by the end of May 1868 his visit to Oldham and the tenor of his lectures created a riot and a mob pelted police with stones seriously injuring two of them while 'The Irish were said to have kept within doors, and remained very quiet during the whole of the evening.'[6] The military in Ashton were placed on alert and the following day the streets were crowded with young men decorated with Orange favours. Following an attack on Oldham's Catholic Chapel, the Baptist Chapel in Hollinwood (about a mile from where the Manchester Martyrs memorial now stands) was attacked in retaliation while the next day the Catholic chapel in Failsworth nearby, was ravaged. Violence bred desire for revenge and inevitably the Irish responded by stoning the Independent Chapel in Osborne Street and St. John's Church, Miles Platting. From a sociological point of view it is worth noting that all these areas lie on the north-east side of Manchester characterized at that time and even today by rows of dull terraced houses and the 'Dark Satanic Mills'

The Irish Frankenstein. An English view of Fenianism. From *The Tomahawk* of 18 December 1869. (Author's collection)

The English Frankenstein. An Irish view of British rule formenting bigotry and sectarian violence. From *The Weekly Freeman* of 6 May 1893. (Author's collection)

depicted so grimly by Blake and more recently, if more nostalgically, in the paintings of L.S. Lowry. For today the Manchester connurbation takes in all these administratively separate municipalities stretching from the heart of the city to the foot of the Pennines.

But it was from Ashton-Under-Lyne that we get the most graphic story of Murphy's impact upon the North-West, no less a centre of Fenian activity than Birmingham whence the Irish had settled, spreading from Liverpool in the search for employment in the most impoverished urban areas of the cradle of industrialization. Denvir's account, is however, backed up by the recently published *History of Ashton-Under-Lyne* which spares one page of its vast volume for the events. But first Denvir, who is always worth reading in the original and whose works are almost impossible to obtain other than in specialist libraries. His use of the term 'firebrand' perhaps sheds a little light on the character of Denvir, almost spoiling for a fight where the honour of Ireland was concerned, but without any deep appreciation of the real implications of more thoughtful Fenians. To Denvir, unlike many of the Fenian Leaders, such as Stephens or O'Leary religion and nationality were closely identified, perhaps the result of living in the environment of Irish ghettos in Protestant urban England.

Murphy's appearance in Rochdale caused an attack on the Catholic Church, the school, and the priest's house, and also on the Irish houses in Mount Pleasant. He was the instigator of still more serious rioting at Ashton and Duckinfield. The mob, after his harangue, broke into the Catholic Chapel of Astley Street, Duckinfield, split up the crucifix, tore down the ornaments, and did considerable other damage. At Bury his followers got rather roughly handled by about eighty or a hundred militiamen who were up for their annual training at the time. The Lancashire militia is largely recruited from the Irish neighbourhoods of the large towns, and though some of these poor fellows may not be the most edifying Catholics, they feel bound to make up for any shortcomings in that direction by being ready to fight to the death for creed or country, should either be insulted. The climax of the Murphyite riots appears to have been reached at Ashton-Under-Lyne, on May 10th and 11th, 1868. When attacked the Irish fought with great heroism, but as they were a handful compared to their opponents, they were in the end overpowered, and their houses, as usual in such cases, plundered and gutted, and young and old subjected to the most brutal treatment, of which one Irishman afterwards died. Altogether, about one hundred houses and two churches were destroyed by the mob before the authorities put forth any real effort to deal with the reign of terror that prevailed in Ashton. As usual the Irish were made the victims of the law as well as of the mob, and the Catholic body could not even get any redress for the destruction of their churches. It was no wonder, therefore, that Murphy was emboldened to carry the Civil War into other towns, the most serious consequence that happened to him being that from time to time he was bound over to keep the peace, which obligation he as regularly set at defiance. Riot and bloodshed everywhere followed in his track. Ultimately, in one of the disturbances he created, the wretched man received such injuries as caused his death.[7]

The development of Ashton-Under-Lyne is fairly typical of the Irish impact on Lancashire's mill towns which were to produce Chartism, Fenianism and Murphyism before workers closed their ranks in the Trades Union and Labour Movements and the descendants of Irish immigrants acquired a social mobility which today makes them acceptable in every walk of life.

It must be remembered that the rise of national consciousness in England was associated with the reformation and the struggle under Elizabeth I against Catholic powers like Spain. The Catholic religion therefore implied an alien intrusion just as the Protestant plantations in Ireland provoked the same response among Irishmen. Thus national and religious feeling were intertwined through historical events. In 1717 the number of Roman Catholics in the parish of Ashton-Under-Lyne was returned as 'none'. The need for the British to fend off foreign interference led to continual anti-Catholic propaganda, easily exploited against the English catholics, and, even more so, the Irish Catholics in their midst. This fact, like the 1717 return, may well have reflected the fear and need for protection of what was initially a small minority. However, as immigration from Ireland swelled the numbers of Catholics, their later arrival on the scene would have led to their being crowded into the poorer 'ghetto' areas of industrial towns and cities emphasizing their separate identity. Catholic churches tended to be built in back streets.

In 1767, *An Account of Papists within the Diocese of Chester* recorded only four persons of the Catholic faith in the Parish of Ashton-Under-Lyne, but gradually the community increased so that by April 1856 work had already begun on St. Anne's Roman Catholic Church when St. Mary's Church was opened and the former was eventually completed three years later.[8]

Murphy advocated the hanging of all Catholic Priests. After the Birmingham riots, he had moved north and appeared in Stalybridge, not far from Ashton on 13 January 1868. There, at the Forrester's Hall he announced that every Popish Priest was a Fenian Head Centre. 'I am going to Ashton to lecture in a cotton mill near the Catholic Chapel [St. Mary's] and it will not take us long to drive the Popish lambs back to Paddy's land.'

In this he followed his traditional pattern of rabble rousing oratory under the guise of a religious lecture, brandishing a revolver and amid the wildest enthusiasm from the audience declaring 'I'm a queer lad, as you'll find out' and after his initial attack, waxing more eloquent, inciting his audience to violence . . . 'If people once break out in Lancashire they will first seize the Catholic Priests, then the Sisters of Mercy, and afterwards the lambs, and send them all afloat, neck and crop back to Paddy's land.' The Catholic Church was described as 'the baby house yonder' while references to the 'Popish Dogs' were interspersed with crude prejudice against the confessional . . .' A Roman Catholic could murder his baby or his young wife by paying £26.2.9. to the priest and confessing his crime to him.'

It was all the more remarkable therefore that in the House of Commons G.H. Whalley, M.P. for Peterborough was able to describe him thus:

> a more honest, truthful and I might say a more careful man in his statements has never appeared as a public lecturer than Mr. Murphy.

But from the Parsonage in nearby Dukinfield the Unitarian Minister John Page Hopps attacked Whalley's defence of Murphy in a letter to *The Times*, exposing Murphy through his own words and blaming him as the direct cause of the riots at Birmingham, Bury, Ashton, Stalybridge and elsewhere. On the very day his letter was published, 28 May 1868, an Irish mob stoned the Independent Chapel on Osborne Street and St. John's Church, Miles Platting.[9] Anger and violence had taken over in the wake of Murphy's advance and the voice of reason and conciliation was not to be heard above the mob. Belfast 1970 had its precedents in England a century earlier.

Outbreaks of riotous trouble occurred over many weeks. Murphy gained a number of followers.

> On Sunday, May 10th 1868, five hundred of these misguided souls marched to Ashton to pull down the old Cross, their number increasing to two thousand before they reached the town centre. More than a hundred of the town's Irish population helped to swell the ranks of the excited mob, bringing with them weapons of every kind available, such as scythes, bludgeons, pokers, a few swords and bayonets, and even revolvers. Reaching Cavendish Street, the band marched up here to Old Street, then turned towards Henry Square where a crowd waited to oppose them. One of the mob leaders, named Flynn, led an attack of Irishmen against this hindering group. Police had gathered at this end of the town and raised a barrier of their men across the bottom of Stamford Street, moving at the double into Cavendish Street to meet the returning mob. Thence the constables were forced into Hill Street in broken ranks, and here the Irish took up a firm stand against them. Women and children, with aprons and pockets laden with stones took part in hindering the force, the police being obliged to use their truncheons in self-defence. By a deft move, the Irish rioters slipped away into Bentinck

Street, massing there on some waste land known as 'Thacker's Ground', and attacking houses in Charles Street and another portion of Cavendish Street. Others went via Portland Street, breaking windows and causing much general destruction. By some means another mob reached Flag Alley but were defeated by the masses of onlookers in that area, after the doors of many houses and shops had been forced open and food and furniture thrown into the road! The Cavendish Street crowd made its way to Burlington Street breaking up Father Crumbleholme's residence to the best of its power and attacking St. Anne's Church with great resultant destruction! An attempt to fire the building having failed, the mob moved on from there to St. Mary's Church in Wellington Road. Here, on this Sunday evening Father Beesley received word of the attack on St. Anne's. He interrupted his service to send home the women of the congregation. Then, with the remaining twenty male worshippers, for two long hours he and his little group fought off the attacking mob. How insecure was still the position of the Roman Catholic Church in Ashton-Under-Lyne is evidenced by the fact that the police apparently made no attempt, in this area, either to quell the mob or give assistance to the besieged few. Although it has been said that two thousand special constables had been sworn in by the official guardians of the law, in preparation for anticipated trouble, there appears to be little doubt that this account is in error. The number is greatly in excess of what would, in any case, have been likely to be called, and all other records and evidence point to the priests and congregations of the churches concerned having fought their defensive struggle unaided. A more reliable account appears to be that which affirms that it was only at the last, when the chairman of the Watch Committee, Hugh Mason, had been brought to the scene, had read the Riot Act, and had sent for the assistance of the Hussars and the 70th Infantry Regiment from the Ladysmith Barracks, that the police finally became active in giving their assistance to the churches suffering under the onslaught.[10]

After the rioting at Ashton and as the memory of Manchester and Clerkenwell became dulled, the waves of Murphyism receded but not before Murphy's ambition took him into the electoral battle. In Hanley County Court on 4 June Patrick Macarthy received two months imprisonment for an attack on Murphy. He had knocked him down and when Murphy chased his attacker, three Irishmen set upon him. On his way to the police station Macarthy was alleged to have said he was sorry he did not kill Murphy. There is little reason to doubt that he felt this whether or not he informed his captors of his feelings.

But on 15 July the arrest of Murphy himself was announced. The Mayor of Bolton, apprehending a Breach of the Peace, issued a warrant, preventing him from delivering his lecture on 'Freedom' but no charge was ever made.[11] There was no riot at Bolton. Following the Bolton example Murphy was taken to Bell-Vue Gaol (the same prison that housed Colonel Kelly and Captain Deasy) and released only on condition that he did not lecture. But a week later he spoke at Chorlton Road in the City. Murphy then proposed himself as a candidate for election to Parliament and called a public meeting. A Mr. Teare moved a resolution condemning the Magistrates of Manchester for the unconstitutional arrest of Murphy. A Mr. Leatham chaired the meeting which was joined by a 'formidable phalanx of Irishmen'. Plainclothes police were in evidence among the 'great number of orangemen' and others who made up a crowd of about five to six thousand.

Inevitably, fighting broke out, Orangemen and Irishmen having come armed with sticks and stones. Heads were broken and pistols were fired and thirty-one arrests were made. As Murphy arrived, the fighting subsided and following his speech a vote of confidence adopted him as 'a fit and proper person to represent the Protestant in Parliament'. And yet as three cheers were being given for the Crown another three for William of Orange, followed by three groans for Popery, Murphyism was approaching its end 'not with a bang but a whimper'[12]

Scenes of violence were subsequently enacted at Jarrow, Walker and Willington Quay, North Shields. Shots were fired and windows smashed as Irishmen stormed the hall only to be stopped by the police as Murphy and his audience escaped by the back exit, having first broken up their chairs in preparation for their defence. If the lecture was entitled 'The Confessional Unmasked', Murphy's own mask was slipping by this time — March 1869. By the 17 June 1869 the wheel had turned full circle as Murphy appeared before the Stipendiary of Birmingham. Arrested while trying to enter the Town Hall to attend a meeting, the riots of 1867 had not been forgotten by the Mayor, Mr. Holland, who forbade the meeting. Murphy was discharged and there was no repetition of the incidents of two years before. It is significant that as the menace of Fenianism diminished, the authorities began to act with a little more vigour in curbing Murphy's incitement to violence.

*The Times* reported Murphy at Birmingham on 30 July and the following April at Woolwich. His last recorded appearance seems to have been on 20 April 1870 at Greenwich. From Plymouth to Wolverhampton and Birmingham and on to Ashton, up to North Shields passing through Birmingham to Plymouth, Murphyism left a trail of division and bigotry and not a few broken heads and gutted ruins; but its impact was superficial and the passions it awoke have gradually evaporated in all but two or three centres in Britain. Yet Murphyism as a phenomenon was not unique nor was it to end in the British Isles where in one corner it is just as prevalent today, though armed with greater and more sophisticated weapons, and feeding from the same bigotry that divided working man from working man, as it was in the mean streets of Birmingham or Ashton-Under-Lyne in the eighteen-sixties.

## NOTES

1. See Andrew Boyd, *Holy War in Belfast.* 1969
2. J. Denvir, *The Irish in Britain.* 1892.
3. The first record of a Murphy Riot relates to Plymouth, 8 June 1866.
4. *The Times* 18 June 1867.
5. *Beehive* 22 June 1867.
6. *The Times* 29 May 1868.
7. J. Denvir, *op. cit.*
8. G.F. Foster (Ed.) *History of Ashton-Under-Lyne.* 1947.
9. *Ibid.*
10. Ibid. see chapter 6. The Faith of Our Fathers.
11. *Manchester Examiner* 15 July 1868.
12. *Ibid.*

# Chapter 5

## *The Manchester Rescue*

*(1) The Smashing of the Van.*

Thomas Kelly (1833-1908) and his aide Timothy Deasy were arrested in the early hours of 11 September, in Oak Street, Shudehill, not far from the centre of Manchester, where they had apparently gone to clear up a complaint by one of the members of the movement. Two of their colleagues managed to escape and at that time the police, unaware of the identity of their captives, merely charged them under the Vagrancy Act and remanded them in custody. Meanwhile, communications with the Irish police revealed their probable identity.

Kelly, a native of Mount Bellew in Galway, was a farmer's son. It was intended originally that he should train for the priesthood, but young Kelly was ill-suited for this kind of life and instead became an apprentice in the printing trade in Loughrea. Like so many young Irishmen with ambition and enterprise, he was to leave his impoverished native land for new opportunities across the Atlantic.

In the United States, having been active in the Emmet Monument Association and the New York Printers' Union, he became involved in Fenian activities in its earliest days in 1858, taking the Fenian Oath which bound him in allegiance to the cause.

By 1865 he himself was a senior officer, having already founded a newspaper in Nashville, Tennessee. Caught up in the civil war, he rose to the rank of Captain, and was severely wounded in the service of the Union forces. For America he fought with great skill and courage, winning rapid promotion; but he was to remain true to his oath of allegiance to Ireland. Thus, although forced to abandon the newspaper when civil war broke out, his service with the 10th Ohio, an Irish Regiment, and his military experience during which he was for a time Chief Signal Officer with General Thomas, were to equip him for the struggle closest to his heart.

At the time when Kelly came to Lancashire, the organization of the Irish Republican Brotherhood in Great Britain was under the leadership of three Irish-American officers. They were Colonel Ricard O'Sullivan Burke; Captain James Murphy (1836-1891), in charge of activities in Scotland, and Captain O'Meagher Condon, in charge of the Northern Counties, who was to play a leading role in the Manchester affair.

Prior to the arrest, Kelly and Deasy together with Captain Michael O'Brien, soon to be a central and heroic figure in the trials to come, had been staying with Condon in Shudehill. Although this account of the matter is challenged by some of his contemporaries like Neary and even Devoy, it would seem that it was Condon who was responsible for organizing the rescue under the direction of Ricard O'Sullivan Burke.[1]

Kelly's position at the centre of the Fenian movement was one of the highest responsibility, with *de facto* control of the movement. His incarceration would have been another hammer blow that the movement could not afford in the wake of the Irish disaster earlier that year, making his release a matter of the utmost urgency.

In a contemporary account[2] the following assessment was made of Kelly, whose arrest was a major coup for the British authorities:

> Col. Kelly is said to be an Irish-American, a man of great talent, and has had considerable military experience, having held commands of importance in the Southern States. He was the trusted friend and adviser of Stephens when that person was at the head of the Movement, but perhaps the head centre himself had not more influence among the brotherhood or stood higher in the confidence of his countrymen than did Kelly. They had unlimited faith in his integrity; they relied on his military skill for the planning of expeditions that were to be undertaken, and he was consulted in all matters of importance connected with the conspiracy. Not only was he the chief adviser but he was looked upon as the principal fighting man of the Brotherhood and was known among the Fenians by the high sounding title of 'Kelly the Soldier'. When Stephens (the Fenian leader), was busy in Dublin in perfecting the plan of the Fenians, Kelly was his right-hand man. Stephens was arrested while in the midst of his work, but Kelly succeeded in eluding both spies and detectives. He did not leave Ireland although a price was set upon his head, and it was impossible for him to move about without running the risk of detection. His friend Stephens was in prison and he determined to effect his release. The wonderful manner in which Stephens escaped from Richmond gaol is now a matter of notoriety, and it is also well known that the escape was planned and carried out with much daring by Kelly.

Deasy was widely described in the British Press as Kelly's aide-de-camp. Although less renowned than Kelly, he too had displayed great bravery in battle during the American Civil War, in which he was wounded. A County Cork man, he was to return to his county in September, 1865. He was soon a marked man and spent a short period in prison before his appearance in Manchester. When Kelly arrived with about 150 Irish-American officers in 1867 to help arrange plans for the uprising he was joined by Deasy. It was their common American background revealed in their speech which, more than anything, led to their identity being discovered after their arrest.

After the split in the movement, Stephens was not alone in being the object of criticism; Kelly himself was under attack for his position on the '67 rising and estranged from some of the Fenian circles in Dublin. Kelly had displaced Stephens against whose reluctance to strike in 1865 he had rebelled and was the *de facto* leader of the movement in 1867. It was Kelly more than any other leader except Devoy who thirsted for action against the English; he wrote in *The Irishman* of 1 March 1866 in optimistic terms: 'All is well for Ireland yet. Next Christmas I have confidence I will dine with you as a free and independent citizen of the Irish Republic.'

Kelly had accused Stephens of cowardice while Stephens called upon the Irish people to follow Kelly's leadership. The revolt went off at half cock with few arms, little money and a fair amount of betrayal. Stephens had remained silent, realizing that revolt would mean disaster. But Kelly, the man of action, was there and in command when the disaster happened. If his judgement was in question his courage and military skill were not.[3]

Two important actors in the drama that was to unfold were Edward O'Meagher Condon who had fought with the famous Irish American Corcoran Legion in the American Civil War and who headed the Manchester District, and Captain Michael O'Brien (1836-1867) who had served with Ricard O'Sullivan Burke in the Civil War and now again in England. Burke was chosen by Kelly as the best man to purchase arms in England and there can be little doubt that Burke was looked upon as the essential link in the command chain from Colonel Kelly to the English Fenians.

Kelly and Deasy, who had given their names as Martin Williams and John Whyte, were about to be released by the magistrates when a detective officer decided to apply for their remand on suspicion of connection with the Fenian conspiracy. But the news of their arrest and of the arrangements for their transport was filtered out to Fenian sympathizers among the Irish population of Manchester.

More than a tenth of the population of Manchester at that time was Irish, living in areas that resembled the Negro ghettos of North American cities today, and often known as 'Little Ireland'. In Little Ireland, Engels had observed, 'the Irish have discovered the minimum necessities of life, and are now making the English workers acquainted with it.'[4] It was among these teeming wretched streets that the news of Kelly's and Deasy's arrest was to pass from mouth to mouth, and among them there lived many ready to join in any attempt to rescue their leaders.

Edward O'Meagher Condon and Michael O'Brien had, of course, worked closely with Kelly, and there is little doubt that he was also well known to a young man called William Philip Allen who lived in Manchester at that time. Condon, in a remarkable account of the rescue published in the *Irish World* of 4 January 1908 was bitter about the circumstances of the arrest, and its background:

> On going to Manchester, I found Captain O'Rourke, an old comrade of the Corcoran legion during the Civil War, in charge of the National Organization in Northern England. It was then arranged that he should come back here, and endeavour to secure, if possible, sufficient resources to enable us to begin practical operations.
>
> This was done. Captain James Murphy, formerly of the 20th Mass., was then in charge of the body in Scotland, and Col. R. Burke in control of the men of the South of England. Captain Deasy, formerly of the 9th Mass., was living in Manchester. He was a splendid soldier, but his retiring disposition rendered him indisposed to take part in the work of organization. At the Convention there were present nearly sixty delegates from my district. Captain Murphy brought twelve with him from Scotland.
>
> I was entrusted with the control of the Organization in that section in Manchester, the organization had become so weakened that it seemed proper to reduce the number of circles from nine to three. By dint, however, of incessant exertion I had within a few months effected a complete reorganization throughout the district, and then, in order to inspire the members with renewed confidence and take concerted measures from the future, I recommended to Colonel Kelly, who was at the head of the I.R.B., that a convention of delegates from the whole Organization throughout Britain be held without delay.
>
> I was walking down a street in Manchester one night in September of the year mentioned, and unarmed, when I saw approaching from the opposite direction two tall men, evidently Irish peelers, with a small individual between them. I stepped aside in order to observe them without being noticed, and, as they came closer recognized the middle party as Corydon, the informer.
>
> Retracing my steps, I followed the three, meeting with a friend on the way who came with me, and saw that they entered a police station not far off. Warrants were out, we knew, for the arrest of the Irish-Americans who were believed to be still in Britain or Ireland, and it was evident that Corydon had come to assist the police in ferreting out those who were supposed to be in Manchester.
>
> Kelly and Deasy went to a house in Shudehill Market, where I had formerly lodged and where communications were still received, in order to get any of these that might have arrived. Soon after leaving the house, a little before midnight, they were arrested.[5]

Devoy's recollections[6] quote a letter from Ricard O'Sullivan Burke naming the men who volunteered for the rescue — 'James Lavery, John Neary, Thomas O'Bolger, Peter Ryan, William Melvin, Michael Larkin, Timothy Featherstone, Charles Moorehouse, Peter Rice, William Philip Allen, Patrick Bloomfield, John Stoneham, Joseph Kelley, John Ryan, James Cahill, and the two American officers, Michael O'Brien and O'Meagher Condon.'

He claimed that he had selected Thomas O'Bolger and Peter Ryan to undertake extra hazardous duty, and advised on the conduct at and after the rescue, in particular that no life was to be taken unless necessary to the success of the rescue, when it was to be taken without an instant's hesitation.

O'Brien was to cover the retreat, presumably one of the reasons for his capture. Burke named James Cahill as killing one of the horses and commends Lavery, O'Bolger, Ryan, Rice and Cahill for their energetic action. Burke drove near to the scene in a cab after the event and was modest enough to say that the credit was due only to the Manchester I.R.B. 'who actually accomplished it', adding 'I only gave form and direction to that force'.

After their identification as Fenians Kelly and Deasy were removed to Bellevue Gaol on the other side of the City for their remand. Telegrams from Dublin Castle and the Home Office warned the magistrates of a possible attempt to release them, and it still remains a mystery why greater precautions were not taken by the authorities in Manchester. Nevertheless some extra precautions were in fact taken and the two men were conveyed in a Victorian Black Maria — a horse-drawn prison van driven by a policeman. Police Constables Shaw and Yarwood with Detectives Bromley and Taylor were positioned on the box: Constables Knox and Connoll were behind. Inside the van was another officer holding the keys.

Whatever the accuracy of the following account given by Condon, the result was a startling success and a severe blow to the prestige of the British authorities which they could not forgive.

All present favoured an attempt at release, but John Nolan strongly urged that I should procure men for the work from other cities, to which they would depart when it was accomplished. I thought that it would be a slight on the Manchester men to ask others to take their places in an affair of the sort, and it was soon decided that they only should participate . . .[9]

The van which conveyed prisoners to the gaol had to pass under the arch of a railway bridge on Hyde Road, beside which was a vacant lot, whence egress could be had to the railroad yard and the country beyond. When I enquired of the Centres what resources were available, I found that, except for £1, held by Nolan, there were no funds in the possession of the Manchester Circle, nor any revolvers. This was certainly a very unsatisfactory state of affairs, but it had to be dealt with.

It was, of course, necessary to have arms, and I despatched Daniel Darragh to Birmingham to purchase ten revolvers, in order to avoid any suspicions which might be excited through an attempt to buy them in Manchester. I had decided also to take Kelly and Deasy, when released, first to Ashton-Under-Lyne to obtain a change of clothing and other disguises, and then convey them to Newcastle, or an adjacent town, whence we could procure passage to some Continental port.

When all arrangements were practically completed, in order not to leave the organization without a head during my absence or in the possible case of my capture, I wired Captain Murphy and Colonel Burke to come to Manchester, so that they might fill my place.

Kelly had passed for my uncle at the house where he stopped and my message merely said: 'Uncle is dying, come immediately', signing the name which I employed in correspondence with those addressed. Captain James Murphy was then absent from Glasgow organizing as usual, and didn't get my telegram till too late, but Colonel Burke received the message sent him, and reached Manchester on the day before the affair took place. It was not necessary for him to do anything but wait, and he took no part in the rescue.

Darragh reached Manchester on the evening of the 17th with the arms which I had sent him to purchase, and Colonel Burke and Captain O'Brien came with me to the place where I distributed them in accordance with the recommendations of the centres, who, of course, knew more about the qualities of their men than I or any other stranger could possibly know.

One of these was Daniel Reddin of Dublin, one of the bravest and coolest men I have ever met. He was arrested after the rescue, in which he had done his whole duty, and suffered five years' penal servitude, but became paralyzed in prison from punishment, while the alleged doctors pretended to believe that he was shamming, and prodded the soles of the helpless man's feet with large needles. He died soon after his release.

After I had distributed the arms, Colonel Burke and Captain O'Brien returned with me to my lodgings. The next morning O'Brien accompanied me to a house on Oldham Road, where the intended rescuers were to gather, while Colonel Burke went to the Police Court. I never met him again till I reached New York from Portland Prison eleven years later.

The men selected, ten in number, assembled promptly at the place indicated. Before they started for Hyde Road I distributed some money among them, and directed them to keep off the street and escape observation as much as possible. There were several saloons in the vicinity into which they could go.

It appeared, then, only necessary after stopping the van to take the keys from this man, and release the prisoners. If the authorities became aware of our project, or suspected that one was on foot, they would undoubtedly have sent a cavalry escort to guard the prisoners on their way to the gaol, and our hopes of effecting a rescue would be frustrated. It appears clearly evident that until a fuss occurred at the van door, to which I will refer presently, there was not the slightest suspicion in the minds of the authorities that any interference whatever would be attempted with the van.

When the examination of the prisoners was concluded at the

Courthouse, they were again remanded to Bellevue, Kelly on the testimony of an inspector from Scotland Yard, and Deasy on that of an official from Dublin. Evidently rumours of an intention to effect a rescue had been heard in certain quarters, notwithstanding all my efforts to preserve secrecy, for groups of people gathered around the van when the prisoners were being placed in it, and one of them drew a long knife, and muttered some threatening words. The police promptly seized the idiot who had the weapon, and threw him into the van with the other prisoners. This incident evidently alarmed the court officers, and induced them to send four men in a cab behind the van, which carried six more, while the policeman who had charge of the conveyance stood inside instead of outside, as he had invariably done before. Not one of these policemen was, however, armed, a fact which proved that the officials had no suspicion whatever that a rescue would be attempted.

The policemen who accompanied the van were a miscellaneous lot, apparently embracing the long and short and the fat and lean of the Manchester force, and they were utterly helpless to make any resistance against us. The van was stopped, the off-horse shot, and the other held as soon as the conveyance reached the vacant lot beyond the bridge.

The policemen sprang off, appeared dazed, and hastened out of range as soon as possible, and though some of the English crowd which gathered threw stones, not one of our men was touched. James Lavery, sought to break in the roof with a large stone, but, this method involved too much delay, Rice fired at the lock, and just at this moment the officer in charge, who had been crouching down, raised his head to look through the louvres of the ventilator in the door, and received a bullet wound which proved fatal. The keys were then handed out by one of the ordinary prisoners, and the door opened. If those keys had not been promptly forthcoming, some scaffold poles lying near an adjacent house would have been used to batter in the door. The prisoners were both handcuffed when released. On seeing this I ran into a house and got some knives, with which, using a brick for a hammer, I attempted to cut the links of Deasy's handcuffs. They were too strong, however, and I then told him and Kelly to start off, saying that we would keep the crowd back, until they were at a safe distance. We then followed. At this time friends and foes were mixed, all running towards the wall, and getting over it at various points. When we reached and crossed it, a train coming in from somewhere passed slowly across the route which the released men had taken, and cut us off from them. Brennan, however, knew the locality, and guided me to the house of a friend some distance off, where I exchanged my coat and hat for others, cut off my moustache, and then, notwithstanding the urgent remonstrances of Brennan, started out again to go to the house in Ashton to which I had arranged that Kelly and Deasy were to be conveyed. Condon, Allen and Larkin were caught by the pursuing mob but Kelly and Deasy were safely on their way to Ashton.

In spite of their being in handcuffs Kelly and Deasy were never recaptured. Speculation in the press as to their whereabouts continued for weeks. A chain of friendly hands spirited them away in spite of the strenuous efforts of the police.

The police suspected that Kelly and Deasy were hidden in

Ancoats, regarded as the main Fenian district of Manchester. Several anonymous letters were received by the Mayor, one of them alleging that the fugitives were in a house at Evey Street, Ancoats. At 11.30 a.m. fifty constables arrived at the house. The shutters were drawn and an eager crowd watched with excitement as the police surrounded the house, armed with revolvers. Two City Magistrates, Messrs. Kennedy and Clarke, accompanied them and Inspector Garner ordered the door to be burst open. Only one man and two women were in the house, but there was some evidence that it had been occupied by others who had probably made a hasty retreat leaving behind correspondence. Several hats of different sizes, Irish newspapers and a portrait of Stephens were found but no trace of the wanted men.

The last that was seen of Deasy after the two parted company at Taylor Street was when he entered a house in Beswick, still handcuffed, and emerged with another man, the handcuffs having been struck off with a hatchet upon the sink stone in the kitchen. The lady of the house identified the stranger, as speaking with an American accent. He left at 4.20 p.m. along Wellington Road towards Bradford. Allen ensured Kelly's escape before falling into the hands of the pursuing crowd.

A £300 reward was offered for information leading to the capture of the two fugitives who were described in the following terms:

Colonel Thomas J. Kelly, aged 36, 5' 6", hair (cropped close) whiskers, and beard brown, eyes hazel, flat nose (large nostrils) stout build, one tooth deficient next to double one in right top side, scar over right temple, small scar inside of right arm, large scar on inside of belly from an ulcerated wound. Dress brown mixture suit, coat (with pockets at sides) deerstalker hat. Captain Timothy Deasy, age 29, height 5' 10", complexion swarthy, eyes hazel, hair and moustache dark brown, whiskers shaved, of proportionate build, long face, sickly appearance, speaks with strong American accent. Dress dark pea jacket, dark grey trousers, deerstalker hat.[7]

On 24 September it was reported in one of the Liverpool evening papers that two men closely resembling Kelly and Deasy had entered Liverpool on foot while the detectives were watching railway stations and had succeeded in getting on board the *Hibernia* and leaving for America. There was some speculation as to whether they would be arrested at Londonderry.[8]

On 26 September a man called Clinton claimed to have seen Kelly making for the Irish quarter of Nottingham. On 1 October a Scotsman suspected of being Deasy was roused from his bed by the Mayor of Bristol.

On 14 November it was reported that 'Deasy is said to have

crossed the Atlantic in the *City of Paris*, joining the ship at Liverpool and being assisted by Kelly who was disguised as a porter.'[9] On 15 November it was reported from 'reliable sources' that Kelly was in Belgium. Summing up the speculation one contemporary writer wrote: 'It has been hinted as is feared, that they are both across the wide Atlantic Ocean or have escaped to France.'[10]

It should be added as a postscript that Kelly was lucky to escape from the van with his life, a shot having passed through the van four inches from his head. But even this should throw some light on the circumstances in which Sgt. Brett met with his unfortunate and tragic death. The poignancy of the drama lay not so much in the daring rescue as in the events which were to follow as Imperial Britain prepared to make an example of those unwise enough to challenge her authority in Ireland and take up arms against her laws. As the police combed out the Irish quarter of Manchester for suspects, Kelly and Deasy were making their way to freedom.

It was reported by the *New York Irish People* on 16 November that Captain Deasy had arrived in New York. Soon afterwards, the following letter was published in the same paper:-

My Dear . . . I have arrived here safely, and here I intend to remain. To obtain liberty for a people, risks and sacrifices are necessary. I am willing to take my share. The devotion of those around me proves their earnestness in the same direction. With that never ceasing hope of freedom beyond, we can bear to struggle on for a great cause, trusting to posterity to do us justice in our efforts to obtain liberty . . . You know how we stand here. If Irishmen in America but do their duty, we shall not be wanting in ours when the day of trial comes, the machination of some who must still insist on raising the slogan of party to the contrary notwithstanding. This is not the place to refer at length to the events in which I have recently played a part, nor to the circumstances which have brought that event about . . . I can never forget your persistence in the course decided on. Let us but pursue it, and we shall yet arrive at the end of the goal. Our sacrifices are nothing compared with the objects in view. Ever yours faithfully,
  Thos. J. Kelly.[11]

It would seem that Deasy boarded a ship at Liverpool while Kelly, was concealed at the house of Dr. T.M. Kelly, a dentist, in Oxford Road, Manchester. The house was raided several times by the police but Kelly was either spirited away or hidden in the water cistern on the roof of the house. It is said that he spent some time in the Cheetham Hill area, where on one occasion he escaped from the police by changing clothes with a Father Tracy, before being taken to Liverpool by a Fenian who drove for a wine and spirit merchant. Concealed among the cases of wine he was delivered into friendly hands who assisted him to board a ship bound for America. It is strange to think that this man of action and adventure died in 1907 in America, where he worked as a Customs official of the New York Custom House, having himself been smuggled to America in a cabin specially constructed by a ship's joiner foreman called Egan. One story is that Kelly having himself posed as a ship's porter carrying Deasy's baggage and pretending to haggle over a shilling tip, attracted so much attention that an unwitting policeman helped the 'gentleman' on his way, admonishing the 'porter' for his impudence.[12]

Meanwhile the Irish quarters of Manchester were raided and searched and dozens of suspects, selected almost at random, were brought before the Magistrates. 'In their zeal to capture all suspected persons the Manchester police . . . summarily apprehended on suspicion a highly respectable young gentleman, a land surveyor resident in Stockport who bore a strong resemblance to Colonel Kelly. For this unfortunate coincidence he spent thirty-six hours in a police cell.

The police were naturally more than anxious to save face. In their zeal the innocent and the guilty were dragged off to the cells, where some of them were the victims of a certain amount of private vengeance on the part of their captors.

One such unfortunate innocent was a Royal Marine on leave, who happened to be in the vicinity of the rescue and whose only sin was that he shared the same nationality as the Fenians and carried the name of Thomas Maguire. His arrest was to become an important element in the case.

On a lighter note, one man with a strong Irish brogue turned up at Court a few days later and surrendered to the Magistrate 'as the only means I have of saving myself from being arrested over and over again wherever I go, as a Fenian.' An Irish accent was not exactly advantageous at that time. Indeed it became almost a badge of Fenianism, as the authorities tried to compensate for their negligence in allowing Kelly and Deasy to escape. The names of the first batch of twenty-two prisoners were listed when they came up for remand — some of them still under assumed names. Guarding the Police Station was a group drawn from the same Cavalry Regiment that had cut down men, women and children of their own nationality in the Peterloo Massacre of 1819. Manchester still retains the memory of its own martyrs who were killed at the assembly at Peter's fields and with whom the 'Manchester Martyrs' are frequently confused.

Meanwhile more arrests followed, and by 21 September fifty suspects were in custody while arrests were still continuing. One of those arrested was Condon's colleague John Nugent. Ten prisoners were, however, discharged on that date for want of satisfactory identification. At the same time the police were still hunting for Kelly. The neighbourhood of Eccles was raided and searched in a vain attempt to find the two wanted men. The police in the Manchester area were armed with cutlasses and every police station was supplied with revolvers. The precautions that should have been taken earlier were being taken too late.

When the prisoners came before the Magistrate, all except William Allen and Michael Larkin said that they had witnesses to prove they were elsewhere when the van was attacked; but all were remanded in custody. As the prisoners rose in a body to leave the Court, a murmur of sympathy came from the women's section of the Court creating a moment of tension as it mingled with audible hisses from the public gallery, particularly as young Allen was being removed by the Constable-in-Charge. In the eyes of the press and the public he was already regarded as a guilty man.

Examination before the Magistrates to establish a *prima facie* case against the accused started on Thursday, 27 September. The prisoners presented a formidable list and a formidable problem for the Court which would have to be satisfied that there was sufficient evidence against each individual to justify sending him for trial before a judge and jury.

Twenty-eight men faced the Court to hear the evidence against them. William Allen, Edward Condon and Michael O'Brien were defended by Ernest Jones, barrister and champion of the working man. As a Chartist leader fighting alongside the redoubtable Feargus O'Connor, he himself had known the inside of an English gaol for two years and was a symbol of the common interest of radicals and Fenians which is examined in a later chapter. Unfortunately his disdain for the establishment almost immediately led him to clash with the Court and deprive the accused of a sturdy and able defender.

Michael Larkin along with five others was represented by Mr. Cottingham. Mr. W.P. Roberts was instructed by subscribers to a defence fund and represented nine of the men; Thomas Maguire and five others were defended by Mr. Bennett.

Almost immediately battle was joined by Ernest Jones, the Chartist leader, over the handcuffing of the prisoners. 'It appears to be discreditable to the administration of justice that men whom the law presumes to be innocent until they are found to be guilty should be brought into Court handcuffed together like a couple of hounds.' Mr. Jones supported by Mr. Roberts and Mr. Cottingham asked that the handcuffs be ordered to be taken off. The Magistrate, Mr. Fowler, insisted that the prisoners were in the charge of the Police Authorities and that he had no power to make such an order, but would only concede larger handcuffs if a prisoner was suffering.

In spite of Mr. Jones' insistence that the Magistrate was the superior authority in the Court and that there was adequate police protection, Mr. Fowler refused to interfere.

Mr. Higgins, for the prosecution, outlined the circumstances of the attack on the van. He admitted that there was doubt as to whether one or more shots were fired but 'it was certain that one shot was fired by the man Allen through the ventilator. It was fired with deliberate aim, and it took effect in the head of Brett, entering the skull on the right-hand side and coming out on the other.' But the real outcome was never in doubt, for as Mr. Higgins pointed out: 'If a number of men associated themselves together for the purpose of making an attack upon the Police Officer when that Officer was in the execution of his duty, according to the law of the country it was not only wilful murder in the man who fires the shot but it was wilful murder in the case of the others who were there, and taking part in that transaction, and assisting in that unlawful act.'

Constable Shaw testified that he saw Allen put his pistol to the keyhole of the ventilator and fire once, and that in the affray not less than one hundred shots were fired; he had Allen impressed on his memory from the first because of his daring behaviour. After the evidence of Constables Yarwood and Shaw and a short adjournment, Mr. Jones repeated his application for the handcuffs to be taken off. He objected also to the presence of part of a military force on the bench with the Magistrate. Mr. Cottingham insisted that the Magistrate had power and authority 'to direct that the prisoners may be relieved from the pressure of these manacles'. Mr. Fowler remained adamant, whereupon Mr. Jones astounded Court and spectators alike by a daring, courageous and dramatic exit' from the Court.

> As a member of the English Bar I decline to sit in any Court where the Police over-ride the Magistrate. I will not lend myself to any such violation of the ordinary course of justice. This is your Brief, Mr. Roberts, I am sorry to return it, but I cannot disgrace the Bar by proceeding with the defence.[13]

Handing over his Brief and gathering up his papers and umbrella, Mr. Jones marched dramatically out of Court to the accompaniment of loud hisses from the public gallery.

The demonstration had some effect, since ultimately the Magistrate retired to consult with police officers as to the necessity of the prisoners remaining manacled. After twenty minutes he returned only to announce that it would not be prudent to remove the handcuffs. His reply was greeted with applause from the public gallery. As the proceedings continued, Mr. Roberts exploded in anger with words comparing the events to those which are now remembered as the trial of the Tolpuddle Martyrs. 'Recollect we are in Manchester, we are not in Dorsetshire,' he said. But Manchester was shortly to have its Martyrs too. The dispute continued angrily. Condon and another defendant refusing to be represented by any other than Ernest Jones.

Perhaps the most vivid picture was painted in court by one of the women prisoners in the van who testified:

> I was in the Police van on the 18th of this month. I was in the alley. There were five more besides myself. Sgt. Brett was there. I remember the van being stopped. I heard a sound like a large stone being thrown at the side of the van, and then a pistol fired, like as it were at the horse's head in front of the van. Then someone came to the back of the van, at the outside and the trap door was opened . . . someone came and began to knock at the back of the door. Brett looked through the ventilator and said 'Oh my God, it's those Fenians!' The women began to scream, and said they should all be killed. The man outside then asked Brett to give him the keys. The trap was then shut, Brett was doing his best to keep it shut. When the man asked for the keys Brett said he would not give them up. I could not see who the man was. He asked for the keys again, and said that if Brett would give up the keys they would do him no harm, but let two men out of the van. Brett said 'No, I will stick to my post to the last.' Someone then got on top of the van, got a large stone, and beat a large hole in the van over where Brett stood. Two of the women seized hold of Brett and tried to pull him out of the way of the stone falling upon him. The stone did not fall through. The women said to Brett as they were pulling him back, 'you'll be killed.' A stone was then forced into the trap and Brett could not close it again. A man then put a pistol through the trap. Brett was looking through the higher part of the ventilator. I was looking lower down, and saw the pistol and I pulled Brett away and I said, 'Oh Charlie, come away, look there.' I took hold of his coat and tried to pull him away, as I did so his head came on a level with the trap, and the pistol was discharged. Brett fell into a stooping position against the door. I could see the man who fired the pistol. I have seen him since at the City Gaol. The man with the light coat and blue necktie was the man who fired. Allen came to the door and asked for the keys, but we said we dare not give them to him. He threatened to blow our brains out if we did not give them up. A woman then got the keys out of Brett's pocket and handed then through the opening . . . the door of the van was then opened and the women came out, I among the number. Brett fell out.[14]

The witness then said she could pick out two men in the crowd, she only heard three pistol shots and saw nothing more as she fled to the security of the City Gaol where she had been originally sent for stealing.

Indeed, it was one of the features of the trial that so much of the evidence came from prisoners who had much to gain from their testimony at the trial. There was a long procession of witnesses to identify the men in the dock. One of them advanced his views on Fenianism, 'I believe they are a lot who want to upset the country, and murder everyone they come near who resists them.' This man identified Edward Condon. Proceedings also followed against a further six men arrested after the others, while three accused, Nugent, Lynch and Moore, were released for lack of evidence.[15]

The trial of the men was held by a 'Special Commission' and prosecuted by the Attorney General, evidence of the extreme seriousness with which the Government regarded the incident and the Fenian Movement which instigated it.

In this situation, before evidence had been given, the issue was virtually prejudged, particularly in view of the evidence given at the committal proceedings before the Magistrate, and by reason of the address to the Grand Jury giving the alleged account of the offences. Mr. Justice Blackburne described to the Grand Jury how Brett refused to give the keys up and 'in consequence of his refusal he met his death by a shot in the head'. He went on to say: 'The evidence goes to show that Allen was the person who fired the shot.'

In the course of the first day the Grand Jury returned 'true bills' against all the prisoners for murder, felony and misdemeanour and the five 'principal offenders' were joined in one indictment. They were Allen, Larkin, O'Brien, Condon and the curious outsider the Marine named Maguire.

On the second day the stage was set for the trial of the five men. As the judges took their seats at five past nine the crowd outside the Court was kept back by a wooden barrier specially erected outside the building. A military force of nearly 2,000 men assisted a large body of armed police in guarding the route and approaches from the Gaol to the Assize Court, and escorting the van containing the prisoners. This time there was to be no possibility of a repeat performance of the rescue.

The *Freeman's Journal* reported that Daniel O'Donoghue, Member of Parliament for Tralee, had pressed the Home Secretary for postponement of the Special Commission which was to try the prisoners as they had not had time to prepare their defence. Whilst most of the English press, and in particular *The Times*, strongly supported an early trial, the radical *Reynolds News* (a weekly journal of Politics, History, Literature and General intelligence) described the Manchester trial as a 'deep and everlasting disgrace' to English government.[16]

*The Nation* (Dublin) had commented that there was 'no hope of a fair trial for the prisoners given the present state of the English people'. A public effort was sponsored by the newspaper to collect money for the defence of those on trial. But the trial of Allen,

Condon, Larkin, O'Brien and Maguire was to take its predictable course. The verdicts were a foregone conclusion. The Attorney General (Sir J.S. Karslake), Mr. Higgins and Mr. Hannen were Counsel for the Crown; Mr. Digby Seymour, Q.C., Mr. Sergeant O'Brien, Mr. Cottingham and Mr. Ernest Jones were to appear for the defence. Popular feeling ran high against the men in the dock and the Attorney General's closing speech for the prosecution was greeted with applause.

Had they been Italian and used the same means to win a free Italy, they would have been deified in London as Garibaldi was. Irish Garibaldis were transported or hung.[17] Indeed the nation that gave shelter to Kossuth and watched the struggles of Poles, Hungarians or Italians with sympathy had a blind spot where Ireland was concerned. It is perhaps difficult today, unless one looks at the situation in Northern Ireland, to grasp the depth of anti-Irish feeling among many sections of English society from Queen Victoria down to unemployed penniless labourers. Contempt, fear and hatred were emotions that guided the actions of governments and brutalized mobs alike. The attitude, while having a basis in the cry of 'No Popery', was akin to racialism.

Not for nothing was Lord Salisbury at a meeting four years later to proclaim in all seriousness that 'you would not confide free representative institutions to Hottentots for example', in a clear reference to Ireland. To his ilk, democratic institutions worked admirably when 'confided to people who are of Teutonic race'. It was this sort of attitude with which men like Mr. Roberts and Mr. Digby Seymour had to contend. To make matters worse, the trial was held in an atmosphere of exaggerated fears and rumours, adverse comment in the press and public hostility in the locality.

*Reynolds News* attacked the Home Secretary for refusing Roberts' petition to postpone the trial or move it to London.

Mr. Roberts, solicitor for the accused, was saved by the intervention of Mr. Digby Seymour from being committed for contempt of Court by the presiding Judge, Lord Blackburne, when he objected to all the jurors living in the neighbourhood of Manchester. Mr. Digby Seymour himself asked for the removal of the trial to the Central Criminal Court due to the 'excited feeling which has not subsided since the lamentable occurrence'.

The case was opened for the Prosecution by the Attorney General, who emphasized the legal rule under which several men could hang for the murder of one man by another — that when men combined together with a common design to rescue, were prepared to use violence if necessary, and death ensued, the crime was murder committed by all engaged in the rescue. In the Attorney's words, 'all those who were aiding and assisting in enabling Allen to carry out the common object were equally guilty of the crime of wilful murder.'

First to give evidence was Constable Yarwood, who testified that as the van was proceeding along Hyde Road, which was crossed by a railway arch, Larkin rushed towards the horses' heads, shot the horses in the neck and fired up at the officer in the box — although not taking deliberate aim. The Constable knocked Larkin's pistol up and it went off over his head. He then threw a stone which cut Larkin on the lip. Larkin fired and pursued him, and then fired a third shot.

He identified Allen and O'Brien and said that he saw Thomas Maguire among the men in the embankment. The repeated identification of Maguire, who was later to produce a cast-iron alibi, is one of the curious features of the trial which casts grave doubts on evidence that on the surface sounds accurate and reliable. Yarwood had at the commital proceedings identified O'Brien as having shot the horse and he then referred to the presence of another man. This shadowy figure crops up on more than one occasion and remains one of the real mysteries for those examining the case dispassionately. Yarwood, curiously enough, saw no revolver in Allen's hand.

Constable Shaw then identified all the prisoners but, to be fair to him, expressed himself less than certain about Maguire, saying that he thought Maguire was there helping to break the van but that he did not get a clear look at him. Condon subsequently confirmed in his later account what should have been apparent to the Court, that Maguire was in no way connected with the rescue operation. Nevertheless, Shaw's willingness to testify even in this limited way against Maguire and the fact that he was vague in the extreme casts doubts on his certainty on the one crucial question — his identification of Allen. He repeated the evidence he had given before the Magistrate. He testified to seeing Larkin and Condon throwing stones, but again could not swear to seeing revolvers in the hands of Condon and O'Brien.

His evidence above all points to the real reason for the firing of the fatal shot. It was Police Constable Shaw, not a witness for the defence, who said: 'My impression was that Allen fired to break the lock of the van.' Whatever Allen's culpability, the motive was clear and logical.

Then came Thomas Patterson, a puddler, who showed his unreliability by telling the Court that he identified Maguire as having thrown up stones to Allen who went up to the door and placed his revolver to the ventilator.

George Pickup, a brickmaker, took the stand and told the Court he had seen Larkin hammering at the door with a hammer and 'saw another man' fire at the door. He did not refer to Allen except that he recalled him saying to Kelly — swearing emphatically to this part of his evidence — 'Kelly, didn't I tell you I would die and lose the last drop of blood for you?'

A hairdresser, John Griffiths, gave evidence that he saw Allen point his pistol 'as I thought at the lock of the van', but he also identified Maguire as being among the men who were attacking the van. He recalled that Maguire had on an old fashioned hat. Maguire was also identified by a youngster of twelve, George Mulholland, who told the Court that he saw Maguire get on the roof and break it open with a big stone. He was not able, however, to say whether Allen or Larkin fired at the horses, although before the Magistrates he had sworn that it was Allen. His testimony seems somewhat suspect in view of the way it fitted in with previous evidence in spite of the initial contradiction before the lower Court. The last witness to testify on the second day, a railway clerk called John Beck, again identified Maguire as throwing stones.

When the proceedings opened on the third day the first witness was John Knowles, a grocer, He, too, testified to having seen Allen fire through the door of the van, but said that a man who got on top of the van was not one of the prisoners. Again, William Hughes saw Maguire handing up stones but stated that 'I saw a man hammering at the ventilator, and then he fired at it, that man was not one of the prisoners either.'

Edward Ridgway admitted that one of the prisoners not in the docks (Ryan) reminded him forcibly of the man who fired the shot at the back of the van.

In addition to these two references to another man, Frances Armstrong was to refer to 'one man who came to the ventilator' who 'had a slight moustache and another with a dark coat on'. Allen was clean shaven and wore a light coat.

On Thursday, 24 September, *The Times* had described in its columns a suspect 'of rather special importance' who was not apprehended. It went on:

> He is a man stoutly built, over the middle height, who took a leading part in attacking the rear of the van while others were assaulting it in front. Some bystanders saw him present a revolver at Police Constable Knox and Constable Connoll, those being the two policemen stationed on the footboard behind the van. He was also heard to say, 'turn up the keys and let the prisoners out'. The constables making no answer to the demand he and another fired at them, but neither of the shots took effect.

Certainly no such evidence on this score was adduced at the trial, and the 'other man' remained shrouded in mystery. It is, however, to this day popularly accepted by most Irishmen familiar with the event that Allen did not fire the fatal shot. The historian cannot look the witnesses in the eye and cross-examine them. Only print remains to record their testimony which undoubtedly weighs heavily against Allen. But O'Hegarty[17] describing the trial as a farce, attributed the plan to Ricard O'Sullivan Burke and names Peter Rice as having fired the fatal shot. This may well be based on Devoy's view. He wrote:

> Then they found that Edward O'Meagher Condon, who had been ordered to bring a sledge-hammer, a crowbar, and a set of burglar tools with which to open the prison van, had failed to bring them, and while they were trying to batter in the door with stones and pieces of timber, one man, Peter Rice, thought he would shoot out the lock and he fired a shot through the keyhole. The policeman (Brett) inside the van had, at the time, his eye to the keyhole unfortunately, and the bullet killed him.

The same view is accepted by Jules Abels[18] who states that a sledge-hammer and crowbar had inadvertently been left behind. His version[19] may well be based on the earlier account, but both conflict with Condon's denial and are obviously based on Bolger's report.

As to Allen, the evidence in his favour may at first seem unconvincing, but the correspondent of the *Cork Herald*, in a letter dated 13 November 1867, reported the arrival in New York of seven of the men who attacked the van; one of the party admitted in his presence that he was the one who had fired the shot which killed Brett. He spoke with a Lancashire accent and gave no name. This would add substance to Condon's and subsequent versions.

What adds significance to this is that in giving his evidence Hughes described the other man who had fired as being five foot seven or eight in height wearing an overcoat with a velvet collar. Was he perhaps also the man described by Frances Armstrong or the man referred to in *The Times*, or was he Peter Rice or the man in New York? Or were all these four the same man?

Three witnesses at the trial made specific references to someone other than Allen as having been closely involved in the shooting incident. Hughes and Ridgway actually went so far as to refer to another man as having fired into the back of the van.

Add to this the alleged admission to the American correspondent of the *Cork Herald* and the notice in *The Times*, and the doubts begin to mount. It would seem from these points alone that someone else was at the back of the van who may well have fired the fatal shot, and all this goes to make Allen's persistent assertion of his innocence more convincing, even to the most sceptical reader. It must also be considered in the context of the subsequent breaking down of witnesses and the acquittals in the trials following Allen's and the recognition of Maguire's innocence. In both cases, the same witnesses had given evidence, and Maguire had been convicted on the same indictment and the same evidence as that which sent Allen to the gallows.

But above all, Condon's subsequent reference to Rice forty years later, when there was nothing to hide, raises a strong possibility that the shadowy figure at the back of the van, mentioned in *The Times* notice and in New York a short time later, may well have been Peter Rice, and that Allen was after all not the man who killed Sergeant Brett.

On the other hand other witnesses had no doubt that Allen fired the shot, although Thomas Barlow, who saw Allen pursued, stated that 'Allen fired his pistol in the brickfield (where he was caught) at the ground, so as not to hurt anyone.'

Thomas Sperry, employed by the Midland Railway Company, described how Allen was caught, while a cab proprietor, Henry Wilson Slack, was yet another of the long procession of witnesses to identify Maguire as being on top of the van. The third day finished with less vital witnesses, although the injured policeman, Sgt. Bromley, identified O'Brien as having fired at Constable Trueman, grazing his back.

On the fourth day Detective John Taylor described how he had seen Allen with a pistol in each hand, making a rush across the archway at the people on the right hand side of the arch, before running away. Constable Trueman saw Allen, with one foot on the cab's step, fire through the ventilator, heard a woman's voice cry out 'he's shot' and then saw Allen look through the ventilator.

The cross-examination of witnesses was itself a revelation of the prejudice among many of the witnesses, and only the most salient features of the trial have been quoted in this necessarily much abbreviated account.

As to the van itself, a gunmaker named Thomas Newton who had examined it gave evidence that a bullet had gone through the side and struck against the door of a cell. Another had pierced the Royal Arms and another just at the corner of the rim. There was another hole on the roof, but there were no marks in the door either inside or outside.

At this stage, evidence was given of warrants against Kelly from Manchester and Deasy from Ireland, and the case for the Crown was concluded.

Mr. Seymour then submitted that if Kelly's and Deasy's detention was unlawful through excess of jurisdiction or other irregularity, such as want of a proper warrant, then he and his friends would have the right to do their utmost to escape and therefore if a death were accidentally to ensue the offence committed would not be a capital one. He argued from Hawkins' *Pleas of the Crown* that this would reduce the charge to manslaughter.

Mr. Justice Blackburne, however, after a long and involved exchange of argument, did not regard this as applying to strangers who were not in custody; and although there was a warrant from Ireland which was not backed at the time of arrest, he was of the opinion that the Magistrates were perfectly entitled to remand them.

Witnesses were then called for the defendants. Mary Flannigan, governess, said that on 18 September, the day of the attack, she was taking a walk in the Hyde Road and was speaking to a person named Wilson when she saw O'Brien talking to some friends at ten minutes to four opposite the gaol gates on Hyde Road. However it turned out that Wilson himself had been charged and that Kelly and Deasy had been to his home, so that this evidence was of no assistance.

Isabella Fee, who kept a public house on Rochdale Road, and her son both confirmed that Shore (Condon) was in their house at a quarter to four on the day of the attack, which occurred three miles away at four o'clock.

Neither of these witnesses really covered O'Brien and Condon, but such was not the case in relation to Maguire.

First to the witness stand came Elizabeth Perkins of Preston Court, Salford, a widow and sister of Maguire: 'On the 18th he did not get up until half-past three in the afternoon because he was not well. My brother did not go out until near seven o'clock that evening. My house is about 2 miles from Hyde Road.'

Mary Ingham, a next door neighbour, said: 'I saw Maguire on that day. He spoke to me through his bedroom window and asked me if he could come with me to a party. That was half-past three exactly.'

Elizabeth Ingham, also from next door, saw him crossing the yard at four o'clock, and this was backed up by James Grant and Elizabeth Blackburn, none of whom had any connection with Fenianism and who had seen him at various times between 3.30 and five o'clock.

Maguire had served ten years in the Royal Marines, spending most of the time at sea. He told the Magistrates: 'I never had no correspondence with no one and there was never one of my people connected with Fenianism. I never was near the place, nor would I know my way about Bellevue. I never was out in that direction in my life'[20]

It was only after the conviction that Maguire would be able to testify under the remarkable rules that then operated: 'The witnesses against me have sworn falsely, I was not there. It was the third time I had been on furlough since I was in the Royal Marines, I had been three years in India, China and Japan. I was paid, and came to see my friends on furlough. Having been for years to sea, and not much in England, I thought I would enjoy myself when I came here.' His senior officers also gave him a good character — but this was to come later, and the Jury did not have the benefit of hearing it until they had passed judgement on him.

They did, however, listen to the speeches for the defence, which underlined the atmosphere in which the case was heard.

Mr. Seymour charged the Jury to say 'I will never surrender to personal fear or to popular prejudice the keys that control my conscience'.

Mr. Sergeant O'Brien next addressed the Jury for the prisoners Larkin and Maguire, to be followed by the Attorney General who hoped the conviction of the five men would have the effect of showing those who were foolish enough to believe that they could upset the British Constitution by Fenian conspiracy that they were very much mistaken. Prompt justice would deter others.

Summing up, Mr. Justice Blackburne emphasized that the use of dangerous violence in the rescue made the offence murder, and included those assisting in the violence of others.

Strongly leaning towards the prosecution, he hardly dealt with the case of Maguire except to point out that 'Mulholland, who was a sharp lad, spoke positively to seeing Maguire at the attack on the van'.

Ignoring Constable Shaw and the evidence from inside the van, he advised the Jury that 'there was very strong evidence that the shot which killed Brett was not merely fired in such circumstances that it would be likely to kill him, but there was strong evidence that it was intended to kill Brett'.

After a summing up which lasted two and a quarter hours the Jury retired at 6.15 p.m. on the fifth day. At 7.30 they returned to give their verdicts — Guilty in every case. The only punishment for murder was death by hanging.

On 13 November the proceedings of the Special Commission ended, having extended over sixteen days from 9 a.m. in the morning to 6 p.m. in the afternoon, and frequently much later. Of the twenty-six prisoners named in the calendar, twelve are convicted, the five for murder and seven for riot and assault. The seven men were sentenced to penal servitude; they were John Brennan, John Carroll, Timothy Featherstone, Charles Moorehouse, William Murphy, Daniel Reddin and Thomas Skelly. Eight were released without any indictment being pressed against them; one was acquitted of murder. Two prisoners who had been found not guilty of murder, upon evidence almost identical with that given in the first trial, were convicted of riot and assault by another jury.

William Hogan, who lived in Birmingham and was a Director and Manager of an Insurance Company, had helped Condon's men to obtain revolvers for the attack on the van. Daniel Darragh and others had brought the arms to Manchester. Both Hogan and Darragh were later tried for their part in the supplying of weapons. Hogan was acquitted; he had a copy of one of the revolvers made. The gunsmith who made the originals swore it was one of his and his evidence was nullified by this remarkable stratagem. Darragh, however, was convicted and he died in Portland Prison within a year. After much effort on the part of some Members of Parliament the Government allowed the body to be disinterred and taken by William Hogan for burial in Ballycastle, County Antrim.

As soon as the verdict was given, the thirty to forty members of the English press who were present at the trial put their heads together. It was clear to them that Maguire's alibi was not merely credible but true. In spite of the verdict, the representatives of the press were convinced of Maguire's innocence and acting upon this conviction they drew up a petititon addressed to the Home Secretary:

> We conscientiously believe that the said Thomas Maguire is innocent of the crime of which he has been convicted, and that his conviction has resulted from mistaken identity. We, therefore, pray that you will be pleased to advise her Majesty to grant her most gracious pardon to the said Thomas Maguire.

And indeed, faced with the all-pervading doubt about Maguire and the spreading conviction as to his innocence, the Home Office on 21 November announced that he had been given a 'free pardon', the traditional if unsatisfactory method of acknowledging a miscarriage of justice in England.

But if Maguire was innocent and pardoned, there was perhaps hope of magnanimity from British Justice, in respect of the other four men, found guilty upon the evidence of the same witnesses whose testimony had convicted the pardoned man.

The *Freeman's Journal* on 15 November 1867 devoted its editorial to the acquittal of Maguire. It asked if it had not occurred to the Home Secretary 'that the witnesses, who made such a palpable mistake in the case of Maguire, might not have made mistakes about the other four?' It was fair to say that evidence should not be relied upon in other cases when it broke down so completely with regard to Maguire. 'The passions and emotions of the jury were aroused at the first trial. The witnesses were not sifted until subsequent trials, when some completely broke down, resulting in the acquittal of the second batch of prisoners.'

The prevailing view at the time was that after the pardon, and bearing in mind that the offence was fundamentally political, the executions would not take place. It was a fair assessment to say that this was generally concluded that, notwithstanding the abandonment by the Crown of the verdict on which they had been sentenced.

This posed a difficult problem for the authorities. So many witnesses had sworn to seeing Maguire playing an active part in the smashing of the van that to admit error in his case was to admit the possibility of error in the cases of the other four men. A jury sworn to give a true verdict according to the evidence had found Maguire guilty, while a large number of trained pressmen with no axe to grind had been so outraged that they took the unprecedented step of petitioning the Home Secretary.

On 4 November 1867 the *Freeman's Journal* carried an editorial against the carrying out of the sentences, pointing out that no malice was present as the men had no knowledge that Brett was in the van; the *Manchester Examiner*, for example, commented that 'we do not for a moment imagine that the capital sentence will be carried out in either case, but we none the less wish that the verdict had commended itself on more satisfactory grounds to the confidence of the public.'

All over Britain, for a variety of motives, ranging from the humanitarian opposition to a public hanging for a political offence by the Manchester Radical John Bright to the calculatingly scientific analysis of Karl Marx, there was widespread opposition to the executions.

*The Times* which as the mouthpiece of the establishment, called for firmness in exacting the ultimate penalty, and the depressed and deprived mobs which were always available to intimidate radical and advanced thinkers, reflected only part of the popular mood. Prejudice against Irishmen in 1867 might well be compared to prejudice in England a century later against coloured immigrants, although it was national and religious rather than racial in character, and there existed many pressures against it. Edward Thompson's description of their relationship prior to the Fenian period illustrates the positive side.

> . . . there were many reasons why English Radicalism or Chartism and Irish Nationalism, should make common cause, although the alliance was never free from tensions. Antagonism could scarcely take racialist forms in the Army, Navy or in the northern mill-towns, in all of which the Irish fought or worked side-by-side with English fellow-victims. From the days of the United Irishmen — and the time when the Irish with their shillelahs had helped in the defence of Thomas Hardy's house — a conscious political alliance had been maintained. English reformers

generally supported the cause of Catholic Emancipation; for years, Sir Francis Burdett was its foremost parliamentary champion, while Cobbett furthered the cause. The London Irish formed an Association for Civil and Political Liberty, which had Hunt's and Cobbett's support, which co-operated closely with advanced English Radicals, and which was one of the precursors of the National Union of the Working Classes (1830) — itself the forerunner of the Chartist Working Men's Association (1836) There is thus a clear consecutive alliance between Irish Nationalism and English Radicalism between 1790 and 1850, at times enlivened and confused by the fortunes of the O'Connor family.[21]

When Fenian prisoners were facing death it was primarily the middle-class radicals and the organized working men of the cities who pressed the Home Secretary and petitioned the Queen for their reprieve. On 21 November John Bright wrote in his diary:

Home Office talk with Mr. Hardy in favour of Fenian convicts at Manchester; without avail, I fear Tories know little mercy, terror is their only specific.

On the same day a large meeting of from twenty to twenty-five thousand London working men was organized as a result of the strong feeling against the executions. It was held at Clerkenwell Green to adopt a petition to the Queen for clemency, addressed to Sir John Cavell, a master of the household.

The Radical working-class newspaper, the *Beehive* of 19 October 1867 commented in its editorial on Fenianism that it was the offspring of injustice and misrule. 'There is, however, no doubt of one thing, that the gross injustice inflicted on Ireland for so many years by the British Government and Legislature, has created a deep-rooted hatred of English rule in the hearts of all true Irishmen, and that the perpetrators and abettors of this unjust Irish policy are now reaping the fruits of their bad legislation.'

A meeting of the International Working Men's Association (now famous as the organization in which Karl Marx first put forward his theories)[22] throws some light upon this difficult relationship. Discussion was sparked off by a letter from the President, Mr. Beales, condemning Fenian tactics while supporting their objectives. Mr. Lucraft, who thought no good would come of using physical force, commented that he 'thought it strange that the Irish of London had not made common cause with the English and Scots in the reform agitation'. The point was taken up by Mr. Weston, who commented that 'centuries of oppression and the hatred engendered by it could not be cured by the concessions of reform which the English demanded for themselves'. Perhaps this is the key to any lack of sympathy in methods if not in aims which may have existed between the Radicals in England and the Irish Republicans.

Prejudice and bigotry had their part to play in no little measure but none could accuse the Fenians of being an arm of the Catholic Church in spite of the fact that the mass of Fenians were Catholics and the mass of Irish Catholics in England sympathized with Fenianism: *The Times* noted 'It is gratifying to record the consistent firmness with which our Roman Catholic clergymen at least have discounted all sympathy with Fenianism.'[23]

Mr. Herman Jung, Secretary for Switzerland, recognized the Irish problem in its complexity in a discussion of the I.W.M.A.

> I am no abettor of physical force movements but the Irish have no other means to make an impression . . . while they are denounced as murderers Garibaldi is held up as a great patriot; and have no lives been sacrificed in Garibaldi's movement? [It was perhaps the authentic voice of radical opinion in England when he went on to say] I may not agree with the particular way the Irish manifest their resistance but they deserve to be free.

The differences were of means, not ends, and the same thread goes through most of the dialogue between English and other radicals with the Irish Nationalist Movement right up to the Battle of the Bogside which was to bring out British troops and interfere with the holidays of Britain's Prime Minister in August 1969.

At the same meeting of the I.W.M.A. Mr. Lessner pointed out the appalling population figures in relation to Ireland:

> In the course of twenty years the Irish population has dwindled down from eight to five and a half million, and this decline is in consequence of British rule.

Mr. Eugene Dupont, Secretary for France, described Fenianism as 'the vindication by an oppressed people of its right to social and political existence . . .'

> . . . what is the use of talking of legal means to a people reduced to the lowest state of misery from century to century by English oppression — to people who emigrate by thousands to obtain bread.

At the famous meeting of the Working Men's Association Mr. Dupont had pointed out that 'the English working class who blame the Fenians commit more than a fault . . . they have the same enemy to defeat — the territorial aristocracy and the capitalists.'[24]

This was basically the attitude of the early Marxists to the Irish question. Marx, who drafted the memorandum to the Home Secretary, did not approve of Fenian tactics. Engels, whose wife was a Fenian who had played some part in sheltering those involved in the Manchester affair, described their tactics as 'foolishness which is to be found in every conspiracy'. Mr. Morgan commented that

'Englishmen applauded insurrection abroad, but denounced it in Ireland. The Irish had every reason to have recourse to physical force. Where they [the English] treated in the same manner by a foreign power they would revolt sooner than the Irish.'

'The crime of starving the Irish', added Mr. John Weston, 'was far greater than the accidental killing of one man in trying to rescue the Fenian prisoners.'[25]

At a public meeting on 20 November, at Cambridge Hall, Newman Street, London, the Referend H. Solly, organizer of the Working Men's Club and Institute Union, addressed a densely crowded meeting of working men. He stressed the political nature of the offence and the fact that far from seeking plunder or exacting revenge, the Manchester prisoners had believed they were acting on behalf of their country. He laid great stress on the need for the Government to see as its duty not so much the punishment of a crime as the removal of its cause. The implications for Ireland were only too apparent.

Charles Bradlaugh, the implacable radical and atheist whose refusal to take the oath of allegiance was to precipitate a remarkable parliamentary storm made an appeal for mercy: 'If the Government is strong let it pardon, if it is weak and cowardly let it hang the men who are condemned.' Bradlaugh was later to advocate a Commission of Englishmen and Irishmen to look into the problems of Ireland with a view to legislation.

The attitude of Charles Bradlaugh and John Stuart Mill to Ireland, like that of Marx, is of particular significance for a generation that has rediscovered the Irish Question. Nigel Sinott's article published in the *Journal of the Cork Historical and Archaeological Society* January — June 1972 is an up-to-date analysis of Bradlaugh's approach. Foreshadowing, Arthur Griffith, he could see no reason why, if Hungary's people could have a parliament, an analogous course might not be pursued. Colonel Kelly had been to him for advice and Bradlaugh was connected with the drafting of the 1867 Fenian Declaration. He did not, however, believe Ireland to be ready for Republicanism and criticized the Fenians for copying the violence of Governments. He did not believe that an enduring revolution could be effected by revolvers in his century. In joining the appeals for the Manchester Martyrs and the later Amnesty Movement there can be little doubt that he was following the dictates of his view expressed in the *National Reformer* of 17 March 1867 that:

> The men who are the real criminals and traitors are not those who risk their lives and liberties in what must from the army opposed to it, be an unsuccessful and terribly unsatisfactory appeal to force.

Charles Bradlaugh (1833-1891). English Radical, Member of Reform League, Member of Parliament. Advised Fenians on drafting of 1867 Declaration of Irish Republic. (Courtesy of National Secular Society)

"THOROUGH"

CHARLES BRADLAUGH.
BORN SEPT. 26, 1833.
DIED JANY 30, 1891.

M.P. FOR NORTHAMPTON 1880-1891.

FOUR TIMES ELECTED TO ONE
PARLIAMENT, IN VINDICATION OF
THE RIGHTS OF CONSTITUENCIES.
INDIA, TOO, CHOSE HIM HER
REPRESENTATIVE.
A SINCERE FRIEND OF THE PEOPLE.
HIS LIFE WAS DEVOTED TO
PROGRESS, LIBERTY, AND JUSTICE.

The Charles Bradlaugh statue in Northampton. (Courtesy of National Secular Society)

The trial of the Manchester prisoners inspired him to write 'A Plea for Ireland' in the *National Reformer* of 20 October 1867, in which he laid the blame for Ireland's woes quite clearly at the door of those who were her rulers. He attacked the military occupation which had done nothing to plant the empty fields; he railed at the land laws and the established Church and asserted that: 'It is not the Fenians who have checked cultivation. Those who have caused the wrong at least should frame the remedy.'

At the November Clerkenwell Rally he questioned whether the three men were criminals at all while his future colleague and co-editor of the *Nation Reformer* Annie Besant was moved to write that 'evidence of the most disreputable kind was admitted.' The trial and subsequent execution of the Manchester Martyrs and the later struggles for amnesty thus acted as a catalyst not only upon Parnell and his countrymen, but upon all the more enlightened forces in England, with the sensitivity to see cause rather than effects, for as Bradlaugh had observed: 'How could they take those lives with the consciousness that if we had governed Ireland better these things would not have happened.'

The Birmingham disturbances took place on 20 November. There was scant support in this area for members of the Reform League who tried to elicit sympathy, and a rival mob of several hundred held a meeting in favour of hanging the Manchester prisoners. Even *The Times* disowned this group, describing them in scathing terms: 'They were,' it wrote, 'of a class who are always ready for any kind of mischief or depredations.' Only a force of armed Irishmen prevented the mob from sacking the Roman Catholic Cathedral.

Similarly, the deputation to deliver the Clerkenwell memorandum was followed by a hostile crowd groaning and hissing 'with such vigour that the demonstrations must have attracted the notice of Her Majesty herself'. This rival faction was, however, led mainly by subordinate members and officers of the Royal Household itself. Now just as the Irish had joined in the defence of Thomas Hardy's house against such a mob, Englishmen were defending the liberty of Ireland and the lives of Irishmen against the same mindless hatred and violence. If Lord Salisbury could compare Irishmen with Hottentots and the Queen of England could look upon them as a 'shocking abominable people — not like any other civilized nation', it was not surprising that this outlook was reflected at the other end of the spectrum of Mid-Victorian English Society.

Meanwhile, John Stuart Mill was to add his illustrious name to those who interceded for the condemned men, personifying the tradition of individual freedom and conscience which is one of the positive legacies of this period.

A somewhat isolated but remarkably eminent group of intellectuals including Frederick Harrison and Professor Beesly supported Mill and Bright, as did George Odger of the Reform League.

At another level, action was taken by eminent Counsel William Digby Seymour, Ernest Jones, James Cottingham and Lewis Cane; they submitted a long and complex legal memorandum for early consideration by the Court for Crown Cases Reserved. It was sent to the Trial Judges and was based on the allegation made at the trial that the wrongful detention of Kelly and Deasy altered the nature of their rescue. Lords Justices Blackburne, and Mellor rejected it and declined to put it before the other judges.

On 22 November *The Times* announced commutation of Edward Condon's sentence:

> We have very great pleasure in announcing that upon the recommendation of her Ministers, Her Majesty has been graciously pleased to respite the capital sentence upon the convict Shore (Condon) in whose favour it may be remembered that he was unarmed when apprehended and that he was not proved to have been armed during the fatal affray.

This provided an excellent but hardly plausible pretext for what was a far more compelling reason, namely Condon's American citizenship and the fear of antagonizing American sentiment. Sympathy was expressed in various ways. An old lady turned up at Salford Gaol with a pint of beer 'a little luxury' for Allen; the Dowager Marchioness of Queensberry wrote to the condemned men enclosing £100 for Larkin's family. When Larkin read this letter he was overcome with tears. John Bright's Diary records: 'The Marchioness of Queensberry's letter to them is beautiful; my eyes filled with tears as I read it.'

Hope remained to the very end, encouraged by the news of Maguire and Condon. Father Charles Gadd expressed this feeling in his reminiscences:

> Two days before the date appointed for the execution, Edward O'Meagher Condon — an American subject — received his reprieve. (It was not however till eleven years later that he was set at liberty on condition of his being banished for twenty years). Then we began to think that, after all, the dread penalty of the law would not be carried out to its fullest extreme. There was hope and a strong one, that the remaining prisoners if not pardoned, at any rate would receive a reprieve.[25]

Meanwhile, after the failure of the petition, preparations were made by James Finlen of the Clerkenwell protestors to demonstrate by a funeral march. Some objected, as it would bring them into conflict with the authorities.

As the last-minute attempts to secure a reprieve were rejected, and as 22 November 1867 came to its close and the harrowing farewell of Larkin to his family had passed, the three men drew up their final declarations for posterity.

On the night of Friday 22 November 1867, a strange sight would have greeted the casual passer-by at Salford Gaol, Manchester. About thirty feet above the ground a part of the prison wall had been removed to provide a platform with access from behind. Upon this platform, barely visible through the gloom was the ghastly shape of the cross-beamed gallows hung around with black drapery. The crowd was dense, well supplied by the gin palaces of Deansgate and the portable beer and coffee stalls. The crowd laughed, sang, smoked, scuffled, drank and fought. Throughout Manchester and Salford, silent congregations with tear-stained faces and hearts throbbing with emotion assembled in the various churches to pray for the eternal welfare of the young Irishmen doomed to die that morning.

Indeed this was to be no ordinary execution. The whole might of authority seemed to be determined that the extreme penalty should be exacted. By morning, the area from which any view of the spectacle might be obtained was protected by strong barricades, six or eight on the Manchester side alone. The civil authorities, acting on the instructions of the Home Office, had taken possession of New Bailey Street the day before and under the command of a Captain Sylvester it was policed by five hundred men drawn from the Manchester, Salford and County forces. The Manchester side of the river, Stanley Street, Albert Bridge and a short distance along New Bailey Street, was occupied by the Manchester police force under Captain Palin.

Five hundred soldiers in and around the prison were augmented by 2,000 ordinary and special constables occupying the surrounds of the Prison and the area between the spectators. The band of specials, distinguished from the crowd only by their white sleeve badges and short truncheons, performed their duties with gusto.

But this was not all: a large detachment of troops from the 72nd Highlanders was on duty at the prison and a squadron of the 8th Hussars was stationed at the front in Stanley Street with another battery in reserve within the prison walls. During the night a strong body of infantry had occupied the railway viaduct overlooking the north side of the prison. This was the only point from which the specially constructed scaffold might reasonably be attacked. Salford railway station was occupied by the reserves of that force and all the traffic in and out was stopped. 'In short, between midnight and six o'clock this morning, a walk through the streets produced the impression that the city was in a state of siege.'

Probably not more than 2,000 saw the hanging and among the

8,000 to 10,000 present there was no demonstration of feeling for or against. In contrast to the previous night and early morning there was a 'decorous silence' induced by the horror of the occasion. The crowd which had gathered around the well-guarded scaffold melted away as the night wore on and only the 2,000 'specials' filled the space in front of the drop and the prison wall.

As the day dawned a slight November mist began to thicken into a yellow murky fog and the number of spectators swelled rapidly. Like a huge fortress, the dim outlines of the massive prison loomed through the gloomy fog with an air of unreality. Inside the prison a couple of children played on the Judges' benches of the sessions house, oblivious to the drama being enacted outside, and their laughter was the only sound which broke the stillness of the silent interior.

On Friday night the condemned men had bid farewell to their relatives. Only Allen was refused the consolation of seeing the girl he loved, and after writing letters and drawing up their declarations they spent their last evening in prayers and meditation. Only the raucous noises of the crowd outside disturbed their religious observances, in which they were comforted by three Catholic clergymen, Father Gadd, Father Cantwell and Father Quick.

A double flight of steep wooden stairs of about 35-40 steps awaited their last journey to the hangman's noose. Still nervous to the end, the authorities placed stout ladders against the towers on the prison walls, so that in the event of an attack the troops could easily reach the platform and defend the building.

When the condemned men were awakened at their own request at five o'clock, the gallows outside were shrouded in darkness. After Mass, the prisoners partook of Holy Communion and each man in turn denied having shot Brett. Until the last they wanted to make a final statement from the scaffold, but they were induced to forego this final demonstration by the priests. As the crowd outside riveted their eyes on the scarcely perceptible gibbets the three men remained in prayer until their last breakfast at 7 o'clock.

At about a quarter to eight the hangman, William Calcraft, and his assistant entered the cells and each of the prisoners was pinioned in his own cell. They were bound with strong leather straps passing round the waist and smaller thongs binding their elbows to the back, and others fastened down the wrists in front of the stomach. They remained unflinching throughout and their priests stood beside them exhorting them to courage and firmness, which they displayed throughout their ordeal.

Meanwhile the tramp of soldiers was heard through the fog in the Gaol yard, and a company of Highlanders drew up with fixed bayonets beneath the scaffold on either side. Two smaller detachments of eighteen or twenty men ascended the platform built on a level with the scaffold. Simultaneously the heads of a line of soldiers arose above the parapet of the railway viaduct. By this time the fog was so dense that objects could only be faintly distinguished at a distance of thirty yards. For a few fleeting moments, absolute silence prevailed.

Then just after eight, came the ritual processions as the human sacrifices were led to the scaffold. First came Father Cantwell repeating the litany of the Catholic Church. By his side was Allen, desperately concealing any outward appearance of weakness, ghastly pale, uttering the response 'Lord have mercy on us' in a firm voice. As he ascended the staircase he seemed to summon all his courage, and he succeeded so far as to be able to confront the crowd with an unshrinking countenance. 'O'Brien,' reported *The Times*, 'stout and powerfully built, looked perfectly resigned, anxiously and fervently looking at the crucifix, repeating in firm accents "Christ hear us, Christ graciously hear us." By contrast, the small undersized figure of Larkin needed support as he also prayed on his way to the scaffold, but as he neared the head of the stairs he gave one hasty glance at the black beams overhead and seemed to stumble or faint.

Only a partition separated the victims from the platform outside, and at about five minutes past eight the door was flung open and Allen, clasping his crucifix, appeared. As this happened almost every head in the crowd was uncovered. Immediately the executioner, Calcraft, assisted by one Armstrong, placed the noose around Allen's neck and pulled a thin white cap over his ashen face before stooping to tie his feet together. Through all this Allen continued in fervent prayer.

Then followed O'Brien, with remarkable courage. He turned to Allen, shook his head, and kissed his right cheek through the thin white cap, speaking a final word that will never be known. Then he himself was capped, his feet bound and he was placed alongside Allen on the drop.

Last came Larkin, who was led directly to O'Brien's left. He seemed to stumble and regain himself and after the white cap was placed over his head he fell against O'Brien who turned to him firmly and spoke a few words of encouragement. For a moment the hangman disappeared from view and, as the three men stood before the crowd, their words "Lord Jesus, have mercy on us" rang out. Suddenly the bolt was drawn by the hangman and the men dropped. A subdued hum of terror and surprise ran through the crowd.

Almost at that very moment a loud explosion shook the air and the riflemen stood ready to use their arms, but it was only a fog warning on the nearby railway. The rear portion of the crowd rushed back upon the barriers and a series of rushes followed that could well have resulted in serious injury to the spectators. The obscene spectacle was over for them, but there remained a postscript. 'Allen was dead in about a minute; but the death of his fellow criminals was more painful, both Larkin and O'Brien appearing, from the vibration of the ropes, to struggle. O'Brien was next to yield, and about two minutes later the stillness of the rope showed that Larkin had ceased to live.'[26]

Allen died instantly as did O'Brien, but 'Larkin's suffering was very great and it was nearly two minutes before he ceased beating the air in ineffectual struggle.' *The Times* blamed this on clumsy adjustment of the rope.

But the gruesome truth was not disclosed until some years later when Father Gadd told the full story of those last terrible minutes in an account reported by John O'Dea.[27]

Young Allen died instantaneously. His neck was broken. The other two ropes, stretched taut and tense by their breathing, twitching burdens, were in ominous and distracting movement. The hangman had bungled! For Larkin and O'Brien the drop was too short. Canon Cantwell and Father Quick had retired as soon as the bodies fell. So had the Governor and the other prison officials. None remained but Father Gadd, old warder Kirdkland and the hangman. Calcraft then descended into the pit and there finished what he could not accomplish from above. He killed Larkin.

Then he turned his attention towards O'Brien, but O'Brien was in the Monsignor's charge and he forbade the hangman to touch him. Poor O'Brien's hands were clasped within the Monsignor's own. His fingers touched the crucifix the chaplain held. For three-quarters of an hour he breathed, and for three-quarters of an hour the good priest knelt, holding the dying man's hands within his own, reciting the prayers for the dying. Then the long drawn out agony ended.

O'Brien the last of the three was dead. After a while the bodies were cut down and Father Gadd saw them buried in quicklime within the unhallowed precincts of the city.

## NOTES

1.   See Anthony Glynn: *High on the Gallows Tree.* and Paul Rose: *The Manchester Martyrs.*
2.   C.G. Smith: *The Manchester Fenian Outrage* 1867.
3.   Desmond Ryan: *The Fenian Chief* 1967.

4.  F. Engels: The Condition of the Working Class in England (1969) p. 124 quoting J.P. Kay *The Moral and Physical Condition of the Working Class in Manchester*, 1832.
5.  Reproduced in full in F.L. Crilly: *The Fenian Movement*. 1908.
6.  See *Devoy's Postbag* and *Recollections of an Irish Rebel*, Chapters XXXV and XXXVI.
7.  *The Times* 19 September 1867.
8.  *Ibid.* 25 September 1867.
9.  *Ibid.* 14 November 1867.
10. C.G. Smith, *op. cit.*
11. *Freeman's Journal.* 30 November 1867.
12. *The Manchester Examiner* November 1867.
13. See *The Times* 17 June 1929: Obituary of Judge Atherley Jones.
14. *Ibid.* 12 October 1867.
15. *Ibid.* 16 October 1867.
16. *Reynolds News* 3 November 1867.
17. Sir Shane Leslie: *The Irish Tangle*. 1946 p. 117.
18. P.S. O'Hegarty: *History of Ireland Under the Union*. 1952.
19. Jules Abels: *Parnell*. 1966.
20. T.D. A.M. D.B. Sullivan: *Speeches from The Dock*. 1945.
21. E.P. Thompson: *The Making of the English Working Class*. 1963.
22. Minutes of I.W.M.A., also reported in *The Times* 21 November 1869 and *Reynolds Newspaper* 24 November 1867.
23. *The Times* 3 December 1869.
24. *Ibid.* 21 November 1869 and Minutes of I.W.M.A.
25. Recalled in J. O'Dea: *Story of the Old Faith*. 1910.
26. Annual Register 1867.
27. O'Dea *op. cit.*

# Chapter 6

## *The Clerkenwell Explosion*

In England the Fenian disturbances, the Murphy riots,[1] the demonstrations by working men, and the bread riots in several towns, produced a feeling that serious disorder was imminent. The long drawn-out political crisis of 1866-68 coincided with a period of great economic tension and distress. It has been shown that the economic crisis chiefly affected the political one by stirring the working class and radical middle class into more vigorous action than they had demonstrated for a long time or were to again in the future. Unemployment affected large numbers after the financial crisis of 1866, but the rise in prices hit everybody.[2] The police and military were called out in town after town to quell disturbances. The mood of excitement and rebellion grew fiercer in Ireland as clerical opposition to the Fenians weakened.

Priests who had denounced the criminal folly of secret societies now denounced the English politicians and the Manchester trial and executions. Even Cardinal Paul Cullen of Dublin, a bitter opponent of the Fenians, referred to the responsible English statesmen as 'that brood of vipers'. The most moderate of nationalists took the view that justice in England should have been done with a less obvious display of haste, hatred and perjury.[3] In the major cities of England and America, in Australia, Canada, South Africa and in Europe protest meetings were held. Even in far off New Zealand hundreds of demonstrators marched at Hokitika and erected a memorial to the Manchester dead; the authorities armed the police and enrolled hundreds of special constables.[4] Among those arrested was the parish priest Father William Larkin and a hotel owner named John Barrett. As news of the world wide support reached Ireland Fenian morale improved and from many counties the police reported that a rising seemed likely. A dramatic incident might tip the balance from demonstrations to revolt, from words to blows. The Manchester executions had created a situation more favourable to the Fenians.

At this critical moment Ricard O'Sullivan Burke was captured. After the Manchester rescue he had returned to his guise of businessman in Birmingham. The need for arms was even more urgent as the mood in Ireland changed. The British police net around him had been closing even before the Manchester rescue and executions. The Home Secretary had written to the Mayor of Birmingham asking him to make enquiries about the sale of arms in that city. It was found that a certain Mr. T. Winslow, apparently acting for the Chilean Government, had been buying arms on a large scale from Kynochs Arms Manufactory. It was also found that a certain Mr. George Barry had bought a large number of revolvers and that both Mr. Winslow and Mr. Berry resembled the Fenian leader, Ricard O'Sullivan Burke.

In November Burke went to London and stayed at 7 Tavistock Street, near Tottenham Court Road. A police spy, John Devany, who was living in the same house identified Burke to Inspector James Thompson of Scotland Yard. On 27 November when Burke was walking with his assistant, Joseph Theobald Casey, he was followed by Devany and Thompson. In Woburn Square Inspector Thompson saw P.C. Benjamin Fordham and called on him to assist in detaining Burke.[5] Burke claimed to be a medical student named Barry and demanded to see the warrant for arrest. When Thompson said he would show the warrant at the proper time a fight developed. Burke managed to break away from the two policemen. Inspector Thompson drew a revolver and shouted 'By God, Burke, if you don't stop I will fire on you.' Burke is said to have replied 'Don't do anything desperate.' Thompson called on bystanders to assist him but no one was willing. The two policemen got Burke to a cab and drove to Bow Street Station while Casey followed in another cab. Curiously enough, Casey seems to have made little effort to help Burke to escape or even to escape himself. He followed the police to Bow Street Station and later on was arrested and charged. Casey's part in the arrest and trial of Ricard Burke remains strange. It is hard to explain why he went voluntarily to Bow Street. Possibly he wanted to support any statement made by Burke. As the police had obviously recognized Burke it is difficult to see what good could have come from Casey's support. When he was arrested Casey said he had been Assistant Station Master at Gleethorpe, Lincolnshire, in the employ of the Great Northern Railway, and that he had recently come to London. This was denied at the trial by Inspector Thompson who said Casey had been a porter at Gleethorpe and before that an employee of Messrs. Pickford & Company. Casey was born in Kilkenny and was a nephew of the Fenian leader, James Stephens.[6]

At Bow Street on 28 November Burke and Casey were formally charged and remanded for trial. While awaiting trial they were sent to the Clerkenwell House of Detention.

Inspector Thompson was awarded £10 for the capture of Ricard Burke and promoted to the rank of Superintendent.[7] P.C. Fordham received £2 for his help. While the police were celebrating their awards the Fenians in London were meeting to discuss the situation and to plan the rescue of Ricard Burke. A dramatic rescue in the heart of London would stir Irish feeling and perhaps provide the stimulus for insurrection. While the Fenians planned, the British Cabinet decided to meet the dangerous situation in Ireland by proclaiming martial law and forbidding all public meetings, demonstrations and parades. The new law was to take effect on 12 December, the very day chosen by the Fenians for their rescue attempt.

The prison to which Burke and Casey had been sent was in the parish of St. James and St. John, one of the five administrative vestries of Clerkenwell and today part of the London Borough of Camden. The parish originally grew up around the Convent of St. Mary and the Priory of St. John of Jerusalem. The area is rich in historical associations with civil commotions, assemblies, executions, riots, and working class movements. Wat Tyler was an early disturber of the peace in Clerkenwell and was killed there in 1381. In Elizabethan times public executions took place in Clerkenwell Green. In the seventeenth and eighteenth centuries the area was completely built up.[8] John Wilkes was born in Clerkenwell and it was on Clerkenwell Green that he made his great speech after expulsion from the House of Commons. It is probable that Thomas Paine wrote *The Rights of Man* when he was living in the Old Red Lion in St. John's Street, though this is disputed. At the time of the French Revolution there was a Corresponding Society in Clerkenwell.[9] In 1816 came the Spa Fields Riots and in 1833 the 'battle' of Coldbath Fields when the police and National Union of the Working Classes clashed. In 1848 the district was a centre of the Chartist organization and several demonstrations were held there including one in favour of Irish political prisoners.

In 1867 the Irish were numerous in the parish of St. James and the surrounding districts. For over 400 years Clerkenwell has been a centre for Irish emigrants. As early as 1563 the Vicar of St. James recorded the burial of a certain Patrick Kelly while O'Briens, O'Donnells and O'Neills abound in the seventeenth century registers of the parish. Not only Irishmen favoured Clerkenwell. The parish registers show the burial of Channel Islanders and Welshmen. Many Welsh settled in Finsbury and even today seem to control the milk trade. Probably they first went there for the Annual Welsh Fair held in Clerkenwell. By the eighteenth century enough had settled in the parish for a Welsh school to be opened in Clerkenwell Green.

The *Clerkenwell Census of 1677* for the parish of St. James shows a strong concentration of Welsh names though included among the Lloyds, Jones, Owens, and Thomases are names like Bolster, Collins, Larkin, Macken, Neal, Pearce, Riley and Walsh. The census shows only house-holders. Thomas Macken was a house-keeper and it is noted that labourers lived with him. George Walsh was a brewer.

By 1867 the population had become much more variegated. So many Italians had settled in the adjoining Holborn area that it became known as 'Little Italy' and an Italian Catholic Church was erected there. Even today the annual Italian parade in Clerkenwell on the Feast Day of Corpus Christi is one of the sights of London. The 1861 census shows hundreds of Germans and Russians lived in the area and even fifty-six Americans. Of the total population of 65,000 no less than 1,135 had been born in Ireland.

The English clock making industry was centred in Clerkenwell and in the 1860's had not been ruined by Swiss and German competition. The 1861 census showed that 877 men were employed in clock or watch making, while another 725 were employed in the goldsmiths and jewellers. The only other large industry was printing which gave employment to 720. A total of 188 occupations in Clerkenwell were listed in 1861. They included 116 police, forty soldiers, twenty-five authors, editors and writers, 113 cow keepers, two fishermen, one Roman Catholic priest and one vermin destroyer. Sixty-three occupations for women were listed, ranging from the 1,233 dressmakers to the seven pew openers. The district boasted 110 school mistresses and ninety-eight governesses as well as thirty 'women of the criminal class' and 239 with 'no stated occupation or condition'. The census report also notes four actresses and five 'artists' women'. No less than 1,688 inhabitants were in prison and 547 were in the workhouse. The district was dominated by two large prisons and the workhouse. The Coldbaths Fields Prison (Middlesex House of Correction) was the largest but Burke and Casey were put in the second gaol, the Clerkenwell House of Detention. This prison was built between 1845 and 1846 on the site of the former Clerkenwell New Prison and incorporated part of the seventeenth century gaol.

The House of Detention was used mainly for prisoners awaiting trial at the Middlesex Sessions House a few yards south-west of the prison. A brick wall, 3 feet thick at the base and 25 feet high, surrounded the prison and enclosed an exercise yard just over 100 feet long and 60 feet wide; the exercise yard was about 3 feet below the surface level of the street pavement outside. The entrance to the prison was on the south-east side, the other boundaries being Rosoman Street on the south-west, Corporation Lane on the north-west to its junction with Bowling Green lane, and Woodbridge Street on the north-east. Corporation Lane was a narrow street with the prison wall on one side and a row of three storey tenements on the other. Opposite the centre of the wall was a narrow court, called St. James's Passage, running into St. James's Place, which was parallel to Corporation Lane, and ran into Rosoman Street. The shabby tenements in Corporation Row were typical of the slums surrounding the prison; they were let to poor people, and some were used as workshops by jewellers and cabinet makers. Ten of the houses commanded a view of the prison exercise yard.[10]

Conditions in the prison were grim but no worse than in other English prisons of the time and prisoners awaiting trial were permitted certain privileges. They were allowed to order meals from outside if they had money and were permitted visits by close relatives. The Prison Act of 1865 had provided for certain improvements but the Act was a dead letter in most cases. Permission to hear Mass in the prison had been granted to Roman Catholic prisoners by the Middlesex Magistrates by 61 votes to 60 in July 1867.[11] The privilege of paying for food was important for the wealthier prisoners as the prison diet was one pint of oatmeal gruel for breakfast, one pound of bread for dinner, and one pint of oatmeal gruel for supper. Silence day and night had to be observed by all prisoners and any breach of this rule was punished by the stoppage of a meal or a reduction in quantity.[12]

While Burke and Casey were in Clerkenwell Gaol they must have heard some of the demonstrations taking place in Clerkenwell Green. The Reform League was particularly active in Clerkenwell. In 1867 the League had over 100 London Branches and over 300 provincial branches. It was a working class organization helped by some middle class individuals and was a rival of the National Reform Union. The latter organization was middle class and wanted reform of the British parliamentary system; it wanted a gradual extension of the power to vote. The Reform League, demanded manhood suffrage, one man one vote, and secret ballot as well. In 1867 such demands were considered revolutionary and even treasonable. While the League members were unanimous in wanting political freedom for all Englishmen they were divided about giving the same freedom to Irishmen. The League leaders had stormy sessions about Fenianism and Irish Home Rule. After the Clerkenwell

Explosion Fenianism split the League and it was broken by the results of the 1868 election when the English working class (with certain exceptions), at last given the vote, returned Conservative members. In 1866 and 1867 the League was very active and many branches were dominated by pro-Fenian sympathizers. The League was closely linked with the First International of Karl Marx and Friedrich Engels. The Council of the First International included among the English representatives Blackmore, Buckley, Cremer, Fox, Gray, Hartwell, Howell, Leno, Lucraft, Odger, Shaw and many others who were also active members of the Reform League. Several of these were to play a part in the Social Democratic Party and in the formation of the Labour Party in Britain; the older members had served in the Chartist Movement in the 1840s.

The economic crisis in England in 1866, the widespread poverty and unemployment, the obvious need for parliamentary reform and the difficult trade union situation brought increasing support to the League. At some of the meetings in Clerkenwell Green over 20,000 persons were present. Several English working class leaders were uneasy about reform in England becoming entangled with reform in Ireland. The spirit of English nationalism could be easily unleashed as the Liberal Party and the Conservative Party were to find to their cost when the Home Rule Bills were fought to the verge of civil war.

On 17 November 1867 over 3,000 persons had attended a public meeting at Clerkenwell Green. The Chairman, Mr. Glegg, said it had been called by the working men of Clerkenwell, who while not approving of the manner in which the Fenians sought to free their country, yet felt that they had been goaded into rebellion by the way their country was governed. He denounced the execution of Irish prisoners in Manchester. A local man, James Finlen, a former member of the Chartist Executive, moved a resolution that the prisoners in Manchester should be treated as political prisoners and not as ordinary criminals and that capital punishment should not be carried out. The motion, seconded by Charles Bradlaugh who dealt with legal points, was carried unanimously. James Murray had called for a memorial to the Home Secretary and a petition to the Queen and these also were carried unanimously. The following day a deputation of working men went to the Home Office where the Home Secretary refused to see them. The deputation was large and pushed its way into the Government Buildings and proceeded to hold a protest meeting. Eventually the police were called and the intruders ejected. In Parliament on the same day the Prime Minister, Lord Derby, derided the idea of Irish independence and added 'the very idea of an Irish Republic is ludicrous and entirely ridiculous . . . there is no possibility of any such scheme in any circumstances being carried into effect.'

On the following day another demonstration was held in Clerkenwell Green. Among the speakers were James Finlen who claimed he had done his duty as an Englishman, and Thomas O'Halloran who said he had been elected by a meeting of Irishmen in Notting Hill to express their thanks to their English fellow workers. He trusted that English and Irish working men would go forward hand in hand until the entire freedom of the people in both lands was accomplished.

Two days later, on 21 November, yet another demonstration was held. Despite the cold weather over 4,000 were present. They welcomed sympathizers from Liverpool and America. Again James Finlen spoke, this time to report that he had been dismissed from work for his political opinions.

The demonstrations did not cease with the executions in Manchester but rather increased. Feeling became more bitter and the police had difficulties in controlling the crowds. After Burke's arrest extra police patrolled the prison area but their task was made difficult if not impossible by the flow of demonstrators, many of whom, as the local paper reported 'had an Irish look about them'.

The two Fenian prisoners on remand were allowed to buy food and to have visitors. Burke was visited by his sister, Mrs. Cathleen Barry, while Casey was visited by Mrs. Ann Justice. Scotland Yard detectives in plain clothes kept watch on these visiors and followed them in the hope of tracing and recapturing Colonel Thomas Kelly. Unknown to Scotland Yard Burke was in direct communication with the London Fenians. He wrote often to his lawyer, Dr. Edward Kenealy, who passed some of the letters to Mrs. Barry. The letters appeared to be of trivial importance and dealt with family affairs. On the back of the pages were instructions and notes in invisible ink. It is not certain if Dr. Kenealy knew of this subterfuge but he was sympathetic to the idea of Irish independence.

Edward Kenealy (1819-1880) was a lawyer of ability. He was one of the large number of Irish doctors, lawyers and writers who appeared when restrictions on catholics receiving education and professional training were relaxed by the British Government. He had emigrated from Cork to London after giving up priestly ambitions and even christianity to concentrate on languages and law. He wrote *Brallaghan, or the Deipnosophists* in 1845. In this highly successful book he described his friend, fellow Corkonian and fellow emigrant, William Maginn (1793-1842) as 'theologian, historian, metaphysician, mathematician, philosopher, phrenologist, stenographist, fencer, boxer, orator, linguist, political economist, newspaper editor, wit, joker, duellist, translator, antiquarian and tory'.[13]

Kenealy produced a vast quantity of poetry and claimed that his poems were translated from Arabic, Bengali, German, Greek, Italian, Latin, Persian, Portugeuse, and Russian as well as from Irish. His interest in the Irish language was matched by his interest in politics. He joined the London Irish Confederation in 1847, took part in chartist activities and became President of the Davis Club. Two members of the club were arrested in August, 1848, and charged with sedition; they were among the hundreds of chartists arrested at the time. Arms were seized in many parts of London and ammunition was found hidden in St. James's Churchyard, Clerkenwell. The majority of the arrested men were English but there were a number of Irish prisoners who had links with the revolutionary movement in Ireland.[14] Kenealy defended his two fellow club members in court but was unsuccessful. William Dowling was transported to Australia and Francis Looney got two years hard labour.[15] According to his daughter, Kenealy intended to go to Ireland to take part in the 1848 rising but was dissuaded by his friend, Charles Rosenberg.

Kenealy was an obvious choice as a lawyer for defending Fenian prisoners; the American ambassador to Britain, prodded by U.S. politicians, had arranged for him to take over the defence of Ricard Burke. Until the day of the explosion Kenealy was a frequent visitor to the gaol. He was given several letters by Burke to pass on to Cathleen Barry who gave them to James Murphy. It is possible but not certain that Kenealy was aware that the letters included messages written in invisible ink. His speedy withdrawal from Burke's defence saved him from a difficult position.

Burke's sister, Cathleen Barry, took an active part in political matters. She wrote to the press on Burke's behalf and raised funds to pay his legal expenses. At the time of the trial she lived in Harriett Street, Lambeth. The 1861 Census shows her living at 7 Harriett Street, and gives her age as forty-five; at the same address was her husband, William Barry, and two children, Ellen and Mary.

Ann Justice remains a mysterious figure. When she visited Casey she claimed to be his aunt. Montague Williams, her sympathetic counsel, described her as plain looking, poorly dressed and about forty to forty-five years old.[16] A hostile paper was more flattering and said she was good looking with 'Bold dark gleaming eyes which rove unabashed'.[17] The British press generally gave her age as around thirty while the court report gives it as twenty-two.[18] She lived at 7 Pulteney Street with her husband who was a tailor and a member of the Fenian Movement.

The escape plan suggested by Burke was straightforward and relied on surprise and speed. He had noticed a weak point in the prison wall. It had been breached by workmen laying pipes in the road. Burke suggested that an explosive charge be placed in the cutting and fired after a signal had been given to the prisoners. In the confusion after the explosion Burke and Casey were to race to the breach in the wall where friends would be waiting with horses to get them away from the area quickly. There was much controversy afterwards concerning the amount of gun-powder used and the responsibility for using too much. It is probable that Burke overestimated the amount needed. From the inside of the gaol the wall appeared much higher than from the outside owing to the low level of the exercise ground; the appearance of the wall gave an impression of much greater thickness than was really the case. Burke had intended the explosive to be placed in the recess below ground level; the break in the wall was repaired on 10 December only two days before the first rescue attempt.

At the subsequent trial of those alleged to have caused the explosion, the informer, Patrick Mullany, claimed to have seen a letter from Burke giving details for the placing of the gunpowder. He said the letter was written in invisible ink and with the aid of water and copperas had been deciphered. As far as he could remember it included the lines:

> There is a house here called the 'Noted Stout House' and at that house there is a sewer and a weak part of the wall. If you get a barrel of gunpowder and place it there, you will be able to blow the wall to hell. Get the men to buy it in small quantities. The job must be done, and done at 3.30 or 4 o'clock.[19]

Many years later Jeremiah O'Sullivan who claimed to have exploded the charge said that 548 lbs of gunpowder had been used on the instruction of Colonel Burke and that at the time it had been considered an excessive quantity and dangerous to nearby housing.[20] Besides being a surprising amount of powder to get into one barrel it sounds as though the writer was writing with the knowledge of hindsight.

Meanwhile, the increased support for the Fenians at the end of 1867 failed to heal dissension in the leadership. The Fenians in America were split into two sections. One group wanted to concentrate efforts on attacking Canada. The leader of this group was William J. Roberts. He believed that it was more practical for the Fenians to attack Canada, where nearly one fifth of the population were of Irish birth or descent; the French-Canadians were hostile to British rule, British sea power could not be used effectively, and the American Government would maintain an attitude of benevolent neutrality; there was a strong chance that a successful and prolonged raid would lead to an Anglo-American conflict. American sea-power would then be available for landing troops in Ireland. It was a practical scheme but nullified by the fact that the British Secret Service had penetrated the leadership; all three Fenian raids ended in defeat. The leading spy was Thomas Beach of Colchester. He played the part of Henry Le Caron, a Frenchman of Irish descent, to perfection and rose to be an Inspector of Fenian Forces. In this position he was able to report in detail to the British Government almost every movement of the Fenian Forces on the Canadian border.

The second group, led by John O'Mahony, kept to the original aim of helping the Irish Republican Brotherhood and working for a rising in Ireland. The split in policy was intensified by personalities and bitter arguments over funds. Supplies to Ireland dwindled as the argument grew. Indecision spread among the officers in England and Ireland. The element of surprise had been lost, and there was no longer any chance of large scale help from Irish Regiments in the British Army. Two years of defeat and waiting had sapped morale and numbers. Many were in favour of a return to America where they could work without the constant fear of arrest. The London Fenians were divided in their allegiance though most supported Richard Burke, On his arrest the leadership of the O'Mahony wing of the London Fenians went to James Murphy, a former Captain of the 20th Massachusetts Infantry Regiment.[21] He made the arrangements for the rescue attempt. Murphy was normally in Glasgow where the Fenian movement had strong support. In November Murphy and Michael Barrett, a Fermanagh Fenian, travelled to London in high hopes of freeing Burke. James Stephens had been rescued in Dublin, Kelly had been rescued in Manchester, a successful rescue of Burke in London would go down in Irish annals.

James Murphy made most of the arrangements for the rescue attempt. Gunpowder was purchased and brought to Clerkenwell. Some of the money for the explosive was collected at a public meeting ostensibly held to collect funds for a new church. The purchase of the gunpowder was made in small quantities so as to avoid suspicion. The making of these purchases brought more people into the scheme and an informer obtained exact details of the plans. The information was sent to Superintendent Ryan of the Dublin Metropolitan Police, a curious decision as Scotland Yard would have been the obvious choice.

Superintendent Daniel Ryan acted quickly and sent the following message to Governor Rowland Codd at the Prison and to Superintendent Mayne at Scotland Yard:

'Immediate and Confidential. I have to report that I have just received information from a reliable source to the effect that the rescue of Ricard Burke from prison in London is contemplated. The plan is to blow up the exercise walls by means of gunpowder — the hour between 3 and 4 p.m. — the signal for all right, a white ball thrown up outside when he is at exercise.
>        Daniel Ryan
>            Superintendent'[22]

Immediate action was taken to increase the security of the prison. The official reports of the time stress that an informer in Dublin gave the information to Superintendent Daniel Ryan; they go into some detail and throw suspicion on a Dublin woman. The reports do not explain why a London Fenian should bring or send such precise details to Dublin hours before an attack on the gaol. At the time the British Government had two agents in London well placed to gain details of the rescue attempt, they were Thomas Beach and General F. Millen.

Probably the reports that the information came from Dublin was a cover story to protect the agents; as Millen kept his double dealing a secret all his life it seems likely that he gave the information to the Government. Thomas Beach would certainly have claimed credit for the report if it had come from him. The accuracy of the information points to someone high in the Fenian leadership yet not directly involved with the plan as the day was not given. In fact the message would have been too late if the first rescue attempt had not been foiled by a faulty fuse.

The first attempt to rescue the two prisoners was made on Thursday, 12 December. James Murphy and two companions wheeled a barrow through the streets of Clerkenwell. On the barrow rested a thirty six gallon beer cask filled with gunpowder and covered by a tarpaulin. Beer casks being no novelty in that part of London the watching police took no notice of the men, not even when they rested the barrow against the prison wall. A white ball was tossed over the prison wall as a signal to Burke who was slowly circling the prison yard with the other prisoners. The warders saw the ball and presumed a child had thrown it over accidentally; one of the warders picked it up to take it home to his child and later it was produced in evidence. Burke pretended to have a stone in his shoe and leaned against the wall in a well protected area. He fumbled with his shoe and held his breath, waiting for the explosion and a desperate race to the wall in the confusion.

Outside the wall Murphy lit the fuse and hurriedly retreated to a safe point. The fuse spluttered and went out. Murphy returned to the barrel, relit the fuse and hurried back to his companions. For the second time the fuse went out. Once more Murphy returned and lit

Not Belfast 1981 but London 1867. Houses in Clerkenwell shattered by blast from the explosion of 13 December. (Courtesy of Islington Public Library)

The scene of the Clerkenwell Explosion. The original photograph is in the possession of the Islington Central Library. It must have been taken on the morning of Saturday, 14 December, 1867, as the gap was reported to have been sealed on that day. The photo was taken from an upper storey window in the Gaol. Part of the circular exercise path can be seen in the lower foreground. (Courtesy of Islington Public Library)

the fuse, now dangerously close to the barrow, and again the fuse went out. After a hasty consultation with his small group Murphy gave the order to wheel the barrow away. The police were still unsuspicious but one or two bystanders were glancing curiously at the barrel and at any moment the alarm might have sounded.[23]

In the exercise ground a warder ordered Burke back into the line of men slowly circling the area. He delayed as long as possible but finally had to rejoin the circle. Only the sound of horse traffic and the shouts of playing children could be heard. Soon the prisoners were taken back to the cells. The attempt had failed.

The Fenians held a meeting and decided to try again the following day at the same time. On Friday afternoon Ann Justice visited the prison to make known the change of plan. Apparently Burke was then unaware that the Governor had decided to cancel the normal period of exercise for the prisoners, had put extra guards on duty and had taken other precautions against a surprise attack on the prison.

Friday, the 13th, was a cloudy day, the temperature a little above normal for December. Soon after 3.30 James Murphy, Michael Barrett and Jerimiah O'Sullivan wheeled the barrow to the prison wall. The cask was lifted from the barrow and set against the wall. The fuse was lit and the group retreated hastily to shelter after making sure that the fuse was well alight. But this time both Burke and Casey were in cells on the opposite side of the prison.

The barrel exploded. James Joyce in *Ulysses* writes of a flame of vengeance hurling the walls of Clerkenwell upward in the fog.[24] There was no fog but smoke and dust filled the scene blotting out all details. A hole was blown in the wall but most of the blast effect went across the road. Slum dwellings in Corporation Lane collapsed and fires broke out. Shattered glass and rubble filled the street. Women and children screamed and thousands of excited and terrified Londoners poured into the streets.[25]

In Farringdon Station the telegraph needle danced wildly. Every chronometer in Mr. Benson's shop on Ludgate Hill stopped. Horses bolted in all directions.[26] People as far away as Brixton were alarmed by the sound and even forty miles away in Ewhurst a man heard the explosion and felt constrained to sit down and write to the *Standard* about it.[27]

The hole in the prison wall was twenty feet wide at the base and sixty feet wide at the top. Barrett and O'Sullivan raced to the prison wall and peered in. They saw that the exercise ground was empty and that armed warders were already taking up guard positions. When others ventured to enter the prison yard a volley of shots was fired over their heads.[28]

At the very moment of the explosion John Moore, Chief Warder of the House of Detention, was telling Governor Rowland Codd that a number of men were hanging around the prison. Earlier in the day Moore's attention had been drawn to Jeremiah Allen who had been loitering outside the prison and refusing to go away. Allen had later been seen talking to Ann Justice and to a group of men on the top floor of a house adjoining the prison. Governor Codd was inclined to discount the possibility of an attack; he had just had an acrimonious discussion with Inspector Thompson and among other things had said that he hoped he would live until the attack was made and that he would live to a good old age.

Immediately after the explosion Allen was seized and beaten by P.C. George Ranger and then accused of causing the explosion; an unexpected turn of events for him as he was acting as a police spy and had hoped to claim a reward for information.

Timothy Desmond was a forty-six year old tailor from 10 Cross Street, Regent Street. He was arrested by P.C. Ambrose Sutton of the police reserve division who had been employed on special guard at the prison from the time of Burke's arrest.[29] Desmond was described as poorly clad and miserable looking.[30]

The third person arrested immediately after the explosion was Ann Justice who had been seen running away in the direction of Clerkenwell Green. She was arrested by P.C. Sutton who had been watching her for some time because of her frequent visits to the prison.

From the very beginning eyewitness accounts[31] of the man who lit the fuse varied considerably. Some witnesses even said Ann Justice fired the barrel but the weight of evidence was against this.

John Abbott, a boy of thirteen, who was near the spot where the explosion took place described the man who fired the barrel as 'dressed something like a gentleman', with light hair and whiskers and wearing a brown overcoat and a black hat.

An elderly woman, Joyce Anne Woodford, of 19 Peartree Court, Clerkenwell, was on her way to pawn some clothes when she saw the man standing by the barrel. She described him as being respectable looking, and dressed in a black frock coat and light trousers.

Another eye-witness, a newspaper boy named Frederick Dimmock, was passing through Corporation Lane on his way to deliver parcels of newspapers. He saw the actual explosion and said the fuse was lit by a man in a light coat.

The policeman, Ambrose Sutton, said he saw a man with red hair and an American style goatee beard run away after firing the barrel.[32] This description fits Jeremiah O'Sullivan who claimed in later years that he fired the fuse and eluded the police. O'Sullivan reached America safely and died there in 1922 at the age of seventy-seven. His story as told by his grand-niece has no doubt improved with the years. It contains many melodramatic details such as those of his struggle with a big corpulent man who seized him and had to be knocked down with a heavy blow of his revolver butt, this was followed by a five mile chase by armed police and a desperate leap across a stream when under fire. O'Sullivan blamed Burke for the loss of innocent life in the explosion and said it was due to the excessive amount of gunpowder used.[33]

In Clerkenwell there was confusion and panic until police armed with revolvers and cutlasses cleared the streets around the prison. Police Commissioner Richard Mayne of Dublin directed the special force of policemen in the district; at one time during the evening the number of police present rose to over three thousand.[34] The newly formed London Fire Brigade under the Command of Captain Eyre Shaw from County Cork was quickly on the scene and won much praise for its efficiency.[35] The fires in the 'Noted Stout House' and the shattered tenements were quickly put out and bulwards placed in position to guard against collapsing walls. Fifty firemen with picks and shovels set to work to clear the debris and search for victims.

The parish medical officers soon arrived and rendered first aid. Some of the casualties were rushed to the nearby St. Bartholomews Hospital, some to the Royal Free Hospital, and some to the workhouse.[36] Mr. White, the Treasurer of St. Bartholomew's Hospital, said that in his fifteen years as Treasurer he had never seen such fearful wounds or so much blood 'all the sufferers presented the appearance of having been drawn up a chimney'. He sat down that evening to write to the Prince of Wales to report that the resources of the hospital had been severely strained.

At the Royal Free Hospital the injured were attended by the Head Surgeon, Dr. de Meric, assisted by the three house surgeons, Doctors Jefferson, Hill and Lloyd Owen. The patients did not have the use of anaesthetic while their wounds were being treated.

A detachment of Household Guards under the command of Colonel Labalmondiere was sent to mount guard over the prison and immediate surroundings. They were relieved later by two companies of Scots Fusiliers under the command of Colonel Johnson.

As night fell the street pavement was pulled up and the gas mains tapped to provide light for the scene.

At the weekly Reform League meeting in Holborn that evening Mr. Mote was to have moved 'that the hanging at Manchester was neither more nor less than a judicial murder by the Government for political reasons'. The proposer agreed with the Chairman that the motion should be withdrawn.

The bars in the neighbourhood did a lively trade that night as the crowds swarmed around trying to get a view of the damage, and at that time Jameson Dublin Whiskey was available at two shillings per pint. Late that night a mob came out of a beershop with a long piece of rope and shouted 'Where's Finlen? Let's hang the . . .' James Finlen, the ex-chartist leader and member of the Reform League, at a recent meeting had carried a resolution in favour of Fenianism. He had also led the deputation to the Home Secretary to protest against the execution of Fenians in Manchester.[37] An unfortunate man who vaguely resembled Finlen was roughly handled by the mob and it required strenuous efforts by the police to rescue him from a perilous position.[38]

When the damaged houses had been searched and cleared it was found that three persons had been killed and over one hundred injured, of whom thirty-seven were detained in hospital. The dead were Minnie Julia Abbott, William Clutton, and Sarah Ann Hodgkinson.

Minnie Abbott was a seven year old child from 5 Corporation Lane, a house immediately opposite the scene of the explosion. The Abbott family was the worst hit in the area as five other members of the family were injured.

Sarah Hodgkinson was a thirty-six year old married woman, wife of a tailor named Henry Hodgkinson, and sister-in-law of a policeman.[39]

William Clutton was a forty-seven year old married man. His home was in St. James's Square, Clerkenwell, and he was a brass finisher by trade. He was found dead by a stable in Davies Street soon after the explosion. His chest had been smashed by a heavy blow[40] and it was presumed he was killed by a piece of flying debris. It is possible that Clutton was the man who tried to stop O'Sullivan's escape. The descripion of Clutton is the only casualty reported that fits in with O'Sullivan's report that he gave a killing blow with a revolver butt to a would-be captor.

The next day sixty-five year old Martha Evans died of injuries. She had received a deep cut at the back of the neck and had head and face wounds. She was one of the thirteen persons living at 3A Corporation Lane.

The four dead were buried in the same grave in Finchley Cemetery on the following Monday.[41] Later on two more explosion victims were to be buried there.

Soon after the explosion Allen, Desmond, and Ann Justice were taken to Bow Street Police Station. A rumour went round that Anne

Justice had tried to commit suicide. This was an unlikely event as she was handcuffed and had two warders stationed in her cell.[42] The prisoners were escorted by armed police. A huge crowd outside Bow Street Station blocked the road and stopped all traffic. Reserve police had to be called out to clear the way for the prison van and escort. As the three prisoners left the van they were met by a yell of execration, but following this initial outburst the crowd remained sober and serious.

After a few questions the three prisoners were remanded. At this first hearing Allen, who appeared to be of low intelligence and shaken by the explosion, claimed he was merely helping Timothy Desmond who was drunk. Ann Justice strongly denied a police report that she had run away with Allen. To this denial Allen retorted the explosion was enough to make anyone run.[43]

An inquest on the four dead was held and the jury recorded a verdict of wilful murder against Jeremiah Allen, Timothy Desmond and Ann Justice. The jurymen were critical of policeman Edward Moriarty. He had seen the fuse burning and in his own words 'had stepped back from eight to ten yards to see what would happen'. One juror accused the policeman of being paralyzed with fear but Moriarty denied this and said he had run down Woodbridge Street called for a fire engine 'but nobody seemed to take notice'.

Soon after the jury had recorded their verdict of wilful murder against him, Jeremiah Allen was released. He had at last been able to convince the police that he was at the explosion scene on their behalf and at the request of a police officer.[44]

On the morning of Saturday, 14 December, Clerkenwell was like a popular fair and a great moving crowd surged in the street. Even before the explosion the number of people in the district was unusually high. Twenty thousand were reported to have attended the nearby Smithfield Market Fair on the previous day, the tailors were on strike and thus many local men were free, while the vestry return for the week showed over two thousand in the workhouse.[45] The enterprising occupant of a house at the prison end of Rosoman Street did good business with the crowds; his house had been damaged and offered a good view over the scene in Corporation Lane so he charged sixpence for admission to see the ruins.

Besides the destruction in Corporation Lane buildings had been damaged in Bowling Green Lane, Coburg Street, Plumber Place, Rosoman Street, St. James's Walk, St. James's Buildings, Seckforde Street, Short's Buildings, and Woodbridge Street.[46] The whole area was strewn with broken glass and a small army of glaziers worked to repair the damage. Over four hundred houses were damaged in all.

The explosion did not delay the trial. On Saturday morning

Burke and Casey were taken to Bow Street Police Station. Three sergeants and ten policemen rode inside the van with the prisoners and they were escorted by thirty-eight mounted policemen under the charge of Superintendent Derkin. All the police were armed with revolvers and cutlasses.[47]

Sir Thomas Henry was hearing evidence against Burke and Casey and the committee proceedings had taken some time to complete. Immediately the Court opened, Burke's Counsel, Dr. Edward Kenealy rose and withdrew from the position of counsel for the defence. He said the 'dreadful proceedings' of the previous day had so influenced his mind he could not bring to the case that attention a counsel ought to give to so important an investigation. He described the explosion 'as a deadly blow at the very primal elements of civilised society.' He did not wish to impute that the prisoners had any part in the explosion but he felt their friends who had instructed him might have sympathies with the action; they had not satisfied him that they were not involved in the rescue attempt and he accordingly wished to withdraw from the case. Kenealy added that he thought the Government had been acting in a just and impartial manner and had even made documents available to him to which he was not strictly entitled.

The lawyer successfully extricated himself from the case and from the danger of being linked with the attempt to free Ricard Burke. In the following years he gained even greater publicity, particularly when he became leading counsel in the Tichbourne case which went on for years and brought him world notoriety. He was elected M.P. for Stoke, founded a newspaper entitled *The Englishman*, founded the Magna Carta Association, and even found time to father eleven legitimate children.[48] His sudden departure from the case left Ricard Burke without legal representation but the magistrate gave Burke permission to speak on his own behalf.

Burke told the court he deeply regretted that circumstances had deprived him of a learned counsel and had branded him a criminal. He expressed his gratitude to Dr. Kenealy and went on to deny any responsibility for the explosion.[49]

Evidence was then given about Burke's activities in Birmingham. William Day from Birmingham stated that Burke had used the name of Edward Charles Winslow and had claimed to be the representative of a firm of merchants in New York. Burke had told him that the firm had branches in Paris, Manchester and Liverpool and wished to start business in Birmingham. Day let a house at 10 George Street Parade, Birmingham, to Burke for £25 a year and Burke put up a zinc plate with the inscription 'E.C. Winslow, Commission Agent' on the door. Day had taken back possession of

the house after a year and had called in the police when he found
certain suspicious things left by Burke, including a door shaped like
a target and perforated with bullet holes.

Miles Lambert, who ran a commercial hotel at 41-42, Lord
Nelson Street, Liverpool, swore that Burke had stayed at his hotel
with Timothy Deasy and other Fenians. Lambert's wife swore that a
Mr. Winslow had stayed at the hotel but could not swear that Burke
or Casey had ever stayed at the hotel, she did not believe that Ricard
Burke was the same man as Edward Winslow and she did not
recognize his voice. A Liverpool police inspector gave evidence that
he had seen Burke at the hotel. It is interesting to note that in those
days a detachment of Irish police was stationed in Liverpool, a
custom that dated back to 1848 and the Chartist co-operation with
members of the Irish Confederation. Parts of the city of Liverpool
was so Irish that an Irish Nationalist M.P. was elected regularly.

Various other witnesses were called to identify Burke and Casey.
Burke questioned some of the witnesses and reserved the right to
cross-examine them when he had obtained counsel. The two
prisoners were remanded. As Casey was being escorted from the
dock he stood up and said 'I must here ask leave to declare my entire
abhorrence of the crime that was committed yesterday. I cannot find
words to express what I feel to convey my horror that such a crime
should be committed by any person whomsoever, and for any
purpose whatever.'[50]

All the Fenian prisoners were later removed to Newgate Gaol as a
safer place than Clerkenwell or Bow Street. The *chevaux de frise* were
replaced on the Newgate walls and a special guard of the City Militia
stationed inside.

# NOTES

1. H.J. Hanham *Elections and Party Management* 1959 p. 304.
2. J. Vincent *The Formation of the British Liberal Party* 1972 p.300.
3. T. de V. White *The Road of Excess* 1946 p.233.
4. R.P. Davis *Irish Issues in New Zealand Politics*
5. *C.C.C. Sessions Papers* Vol. LXVII, 1867/8 p. 543.
6. D. Ryan *The Fenian Chief*, 1967 p. 2.
7. D.G. Browne *The Rise of Scotland Yard*, 1956 p. 141.
8. W.J. Pink *History of Clerkenwell* 1860.
9. A Rothstein *A House on Clerkenwell Green* 1966 p. 26.
10. *Illustrated London News* 21 December 1867.
11. *Clerkenwell News* 17 July 1867.
12. M.C.C. *Regulations for the Gaol* 1860 p. 81.
13. H. Herd *Seven Editors* 1955 p. 69.

14. F.C. Mather in *Chartist Studies* (Ed. A. Briggs) 1962 p. 394 see also D. Gwynn *Young Ireland and 1848* 1949 p. 167.
15. R.C. Gammage *History of the Chartist Movement*, 1976 (reprint of 1894 issue).
16. M. Williams *Leaves of a Life* 1890 Vol. 1, p. 183.
17. *Irish Times* 25 April 1868 quoting London Express.
18. *C.C.C. Sessions Papers* Vol. LXVII (1867/8) p.486.
19. M. Williams *Leaves of a Life* 1890 Vol. 1, p. 185.
20. *Irish Press* 13 December 1938.
21. J. Devoy *Recollections of an Irish Rebel* 1969 (reprint of 1929 New York issue).
22. *Minutes of Visiting Justices*, Middlesex House of Detention, 1867. The message itself is marked in the minutes as 'Dublin 11 December 1867'.
23. *Irish Press* 13 December 1938.
24. J. Joyce *Ulysses* 1937 p. 40.
25. *The Times* 14 December 1867.
26. *Clerkenwell News* 14 December 1867.
27. *Standard* 22 December 1867.
28. *The Times* 14 December 1867.
29. *Observer* 22 December 1867.
30. M. Williams *Leaves of a Life* 1890 Vol. 1, p. 183.
31. *Observer* 22 December 1867.
32. *Illustrated London News* 21 December 1867.
33. *Irish Press* 13 December 1938.
34. *Durham Chronicle* 20 December 1867.
35. *Clerkenwell News* 14 December 1867.
36. Ibid.
37. *Essex Standard* 3 June 1868.
38. *Clerkenwell News* 14 December 1867.
39. *Times* 16 December 1867.
40. *Observer* 15 December 1867.
41. *Clerkenwell News* 17 December 1867.
42. *Clerkenwell News* 14 December 1867.
43. *Observer* 15 December 1867.
44. *Clerkenwell News* 17 December 1867.
45. *Clerkenwell Vestry Minute Book*, 1868.
46. *Register of Claims*, C.E.R.F.C.
47. *Clerkenwell News* 16 December 1867.
48. *DNB*, Vol. XXX, p.410.
49. *Observer* 15 December 1867.
50. Ibid.

# A COPY OF VERSES

## ON THE PARTIAL

# BLOWING-UP

### OF

# The House of Detention.

*1867.*

On the 13th of the month of December,
About four in that same afternoon,
Those villains with a barrel of powder,
The result will be known very soon.
A wretch in the form of a female,
With two men was going by the way,
He set light to the barrel of powder,
All in one moment was fear and dismay.

Sixty houses in one mass of ruins,
People they fled from there in fear;
The children ran from the shop doors,
Crying, "Where is my poor mother dear?"
The murderous villain absconded,
But this was their treacherous plan,
To blow-up poor innocent people,
To rescue but one single man

Oh, what a danger to the nation,
To a country that strove to be free,
Every true Irishman will curse them,
Its not Fenianism but treachery.
Mothers cry out for their children,
Fathers seek wives in despair,
Their forms are so mangled and blacken'd,
"Oh where are my children or dear."

An example of the verses, songs and pictures sold in London streets after the Clerkenwell Explosion. (Courtesy of Islington

# Chapter 7

## *Reactions and Relief*

The explosion caused a flood of rumours all over the country. No story was too fantastic to be disbelieved and the fear of further Fenian action produced a situation amounting to panic in many quarters. In the House of Lords a member declared terror 'had seized society'.[1] Richard Anderson was summoned from Dublin Castle to be special adviser on Fenian matters to the Secretary of State. He recorded his amazement at the alarm and lack of restraint in England.[2]

The Fenians were rumoured to be dynamiting the gasworks, attacking armouries, taking up the railway lines, and indulging in incendiarism with 'Fenian Fire' (phosphorus). Manchester was reported fired in several places[3] and stories of wide spread incendiarism in London were circulated. Plots to blow up the Crystal Palace and the iron works at Erith were reported, as well as attempts to cut the Atlantic Cable, and to put the street water plugs out of action by filling them with cement or by placing bombs in the water mains.[4]

A strong rumour swept Clerkenwell that 150 Fenians with two pieces of artillery were to make a fresh attempt on the prison despite the fact that the Fenian prisoners had been removed.

A plot to attack Brixton Prison was widely rumoured and the fact that this was a women's prison only lent picquancy to the idea.[5]

The Paris police were reported to have found correspondence from English Fenians containing plans for the destruction of the British Fleet and had forwarded the letters to Scotland Yard as a New Year Gift.[6] The Admiralty was reported as 'preparing for any eventuality' and it was noted that H.M.S. *Gladiator*, H.M.S. *Medusa*, and H.M.S. *Cromer* had been ordered to sea to search for Fenian privateers.[7] Fear of Fenian privateers caused the Jersey Militia to man the martello towers and take other precautions. From

Jersey to the Home Office came a message that the Fenians were tampering with the troops[8] and from Guernsey came the news that Thomas Simon, the Sheriff of Alderney, had been suspended from duty and charged with Fenianism.[9]

All leave was cancelled as the Army and Police stood by to face the expected Fenian attacks. A nation wide call was made for volunteers to act as special constables in the emergency and no less than 166,000 were enrolled.[10] This number has never been exceeded, even during the two world wars and with a much increased population.

Instructions were issued to the troops on rendering aid quickly to the civil power in time of Fenian attack. The Railway Companies were officially warned that the railways might be damaged.[11] At the Home Office tanks were prepared for chemical compounds to deal with phosphorus attacks and revolvers were carried by private secretaries.[12]

The Commander in Chief of the British Army, the Duke of Cambridge cancelled several social engagements. He wrote to Police Commissioner Mayne that he was seriously perturbed by reports of coming raids on the Tower and Woolwich Arsenal;[13] the Commander of the Arsenal had already reported that most of the Irish workmen there were Fenians. The Duke would have been even more perturbed if he had known that a key man at the Arsenal, a sergeant of Engineers, had volunteered to blow up the most vital parts of the arsenal. Colonel Kelly had agreed that this was a legitimate act of war but James Stephens, then in command, had vetoed the idea as he believed it would shock the whole civilized world.[14]

In York the Mayor and military authorities received telegrams that York Minster was to be attacked. Troops and artillery units were called out.[15] In Banbury alarm was caused when men were seen storing barrels under the town hall; the men turned out to be members of the local co-operative storing firkins of butter and lard in the cellars but it was noted 'they were chiefly working men and ardent radicals . . . regarded by some people as nothing better than, if not Fenians.[16] An attempt to blow up the Town Hall at Worcester was noted in some papers.[17]

The scare was strongly aided by newspaper accounts of Fenian raids, a few true, some highly coloured, and most highly unlikely. *The Times* called the Clerkenwell Explosion 'one of the most heinous, most reckless, and most foolish outrages that are to be found in the records of crime'.[18] The *Observer* referred to the explosion as an 'atrocious Fenian outrage' and as 'a daring scheme'.[19] An Irish paper wrote of Clerkenwell 'of all the fiendish ferocities ever perpetrated in any country, none exceeds that recently committed in the heart of London',[20] while another Irish paper referred to it as 'the most frightful crime of modern times'.[21] The *Spectator* called for stern measures to make the nation secure 'by the bayonet if necessary'.[22] The *Daily News* was restrained and only referred to 'a supreme effort in villainy'.[23]

The news of the casualities caused by the explosion came as a crushing blow to the Fenians and their supporters. The great demonstrations in sympathy with the prisoners executed in Manchester stopped or were very much reduced. Only five days before the explosion 20,000 had marched in the Dublin funeral procession commemorating the Manchester Fenians, while 50,000 had lined the streets.[24] On the same day 10,000 had formed a procession in Limerick and priests had led the prayers to God for the mercy which had been denied the men on earth. All over Ireland the demonstrations had been increasing in size and feeling and incidents were reported from many quarters. The Catholic clergy in general had lost their hostile attitude to the Fenians and were offering masses for the Manchester dead. On Thursday, 12 December, the British authorities issued proclamations banning further public demonstrations. The question of the hour was would the general population clash with the military and police authorities? The Manchester executions had swung the sympathy of the country behind the Fenians, a revolutionary situation had been created in Ireland and only a starting primer was needed. A successful rescue at Clerkenwell could have been the signal for open revolt. The news of the dead civilians swung opinion violently back, just as the Birmingham bombs over a century later swung public opinion violently against the Irish cause. The clergy refused further requiems and attempts at processions became half-hearted. Bombing, apart from the moral issue, was counterproductive.

In America the news of Clerkenwell caused confusion and increased dissension among the Fenian Brotherhood. Some condemned the action while others agreed with the speaker who said 'What if twenty died at Clerkenwell? We have killed a million for the negro'[25] The *New York Herald* condemned the rescue attempt and added that the best policy for the disaffected in Ireland and England was to wait for manhood suffrage which would cure the problem. The *Boston Advertiser* with a large Irish readership said 'It is difficult to conceive a more stupendous act of folly than this affair at Clerkenwell Prison'.[26] An Irish success at Clerkenwell would have provided a fillip to Fenian efforts in the United States at a time of strong feeling over the Alabama Claims. These claims loosely embraced all American grievances against Britain. The U.S.

Government demanded damages from Britain for losses inflicted by the *Alabama*, a warship built in Britain for the Confederate States during the Civil War. There are also claims for damage inflicted by privateers and raiders from Canadian bases. In the Senate a member had already suggested that Irishmen should equip and man Abyssinian privateers to raid British shipping;[27] as Britain was at war with Abyssinia at the time the idea was not so fantastic as it might seem.

In the months following the explosion the police force was strongly criticized for failing to stop the rescue attempt when they had received detailed information in advance. Police Commissioner Mayne, who had done so much to establish the British police force, was a tired, sick man. In 1829 as a young Irish barrister, he had been appointed with Colonel Charles Rowan as joint head of the new police force. His brilliant career of nearly forty years as Police Commissioner ended in bitterness and sadness. He had been strongly attacked over the rioting in Hyde Park in 1866 when a radical political demonstration developed into a riot with many casualties; there were many demands for Mayne's resignation. After the Clerkenwell disaster he offered his resignation to Spencer Walpole, the Home Secretary. The Under-Secretary is reported as saying 'We told Mayne that he had made a damned fool of himself, but that we weren't going to throw him over after his long public service.'[28] The Home Secretary gravely informed the House of Commons that the main reason the police had failed to stop the explosion was that they expected the prison walls to be blown up whereas they were blown down.[29] This extraordinary explanation was accepted with little comment in the House. In the months following Mayne was hounded by newspaper attacks, he worked under great difficulties with the Assistant Commissioner, one of his Inspectors took a libel action against him and harassed him with proceedings. His daughter died, and his health declined rapidly. Before the year ended the strain became too much and the Commissioner died, an embittered and unhappy man.

During Mayne's last year at Scotland Yard his staff were overworked trying to deal with the Fenian scare. Hundreds of letters arrived offering information and reporting possible Fenian plots. Mayne offered £400 reward for information concerning the attack in Clerkenwell. Parliament authorized a big increase in the police strength in London and two new divisions were created. Every clue, letter and rumour had to be checked. The police records contain details of many curious searches, like that for 'M.J.W.' who asked for an answer in the advertisement columns of the *Morning Star*, or that for the Rev. S. Brereton, Organizing Secretary of a non-existent Clergy Aid Assurance Society. An anonymous letter had suggested

Thomas Billis Beach/Henry Le Caron (1841-1894). Leading British Secret Agent against Fenian Movement. Born in Colchester, Essex. (Author's collection)

that the Rev. Brereton was connected with the explosion but it is far more likely he was wanted by his landlady for not paying the rent.

Assassinations, explosions, and incendiarism were prophesied for the Christmas period but the holiday passed peacefully, except for Frederick Baker who was executed at Winchester on Christmas Eve for the murder of sweet Fanny Adams.

Practical jokers had a good time setting off fireworks in gardens and backyards. It is probable that many of the rumours were due to joking statements. One can imagine the peculiar shock of horror in Victorian England when it was reported that a body of Fenians had been discovered drilling on the Kennington Oval Cricket Ground.[30] Incautious Irishmen in bars found themselves being hauled into court accused of taking part in Fenian conspiracies. A certain Michael Finity, who worked at the Imperial Gasworks, when drinking at the Duke of Clarence in St. Pancras Road, London, declared he was a Fenian and would spend his last shilling to blow up every gasworks in England. He added that the first time Queen Victoria went to the House of Commons she would be shot. He was immediately charged with uttering seditious, wicked and villainous words. As in several other cases at the same time the curious situation arose of the prisoner trying to prove he was drunk and the police trying to prove he was sober at the time.[31]

Finity's reference to Queen Victoria visiting the House of Commons might have been made with the feeling she would never go, for the Queen had retired from public life. There was a strong republican feeling in the country and even Gladstone was pessimistic about the future of royalty in England. He wrote to Lord Granville 'The Queen is invisible and the Prince of Wales is not respected'.[32] At the time of the Clerkenwell Explosion the Queen sent a message of sympathy and some hot house grapes to the sufferers and regretted she was unable to visit them.[33] The Prince of Wales came out much better. He visited the scene twice and went to the hospitals to see the wounded.

Although the Fenians do not appear ever to have considered the matter, the police were fearful of an attack on the Queen and elaborate security precautions were taken at the Royal Palaces.[34]

There was almost a police obsession about possible attacks from the sewers and a special order to the police gave instructions for the arrest of anyone seen coming out of a sewer.

The explosion brought national publicity to the Rev. Robert Maguire, vicar of the Anglican church of St. James, Clerkenwell. Maguire was born in Dublin on 3 March 1826. His father was a government Inspector of Taxes. Maguire studied at Trinity College, Dublin, and was ordained in Cork Cathedral in 1850. He quickly achieved distinction as a writer of controversial works and tracts such as 'One Hundred Defects of the Mass' and 'Queries on the Creed of Pope Pius IV'; his pamphlet 'The Early Irish Church Independent of Rome until A.D.1172' was popular and had a large sale. In 1852 Maguire was invited to become Secretary of the Protestant Institute of Islington, a body formed in 1846 to oppose Popery. He accepted the post and was soon in a controversy with the Catholic priest in Islington, Father Oakley, and a Catholic schoolmaster, Mr. Weale.

In 1856 the Rev. Maguire was appointed to St. James Church, Clerkenwell, after a long and lively election; St. James being one the few Church of England parishes where the parishioners had the right to appoint the incumbent. After his appointment he distinguished himself in a controversy with the National Sunday League.

Immediately after the explosion Maguire started the Clerkenwell Explosion Relief Fund and lambasted a hapless cleric from a nearby parish who was foolhardy enough to start a separate fund.

On Sunday 14 December, the Rev. Maguire preached to a packed church. He took for his text Isaiah, Chapter XXVI, verse 16, 'No, Lord, it was in affliction they turned back to you'. He said the explosion 'did not come from God's wrath, or from his vengeance but was done by a father's hand, and a kind father too, who did not willingly chastize one of his children. They were forcibly recalled to the question which, before that time, had commanded the attention of all Europe. Within a stone throw of where they were sitting a thing had happened which was talked of in every country and city of the world.' He went on to say that the perpetrators of the deed did not belong to the Protestant Church and it might be wise for the Government to retrace their steps and think more solemnly of the position God's word and truth must occupy in the Church and State. He trusted the explosion would teach the congregation more wisdom and that they would become better acquainted with the blessings that resulted from an intact Protestant religion and a Protestant government.[35]

A few yards away in Exmouth Street, the Rev. T.E. Thoresby preached in Spa Fields Chapel. He also took for his text a passage from Isaiah and drew an impressive moral and religious lesson from the explosion. After the sermon a collection was taken for the sufferers from the explosion.

The Rev. Thoresby also spoke at a public meeting in Clerkenwell Green two days later. He said the explosion would settle the question of Fenianism for ever. Whatever measures the Government proposed to adopt he thought the country would accept. He added that the conduct of the Queen called forth a warm response among all classes of her subjects, and three cheers were given for her. Mr. Churchwarden Willcocks moved that the meeting express 'true hearted English sympathy for those who had suffered' and added he was sure Clerkenwell would prove loyal to the backbone. The motion was approved unanimously, the national anthem was sung, and three more cheers given for the Queen.[36]

Immediately prior to the explosion the Vestrymen of Clerkenwell had little to discuss except the question of whether or not a mortuary should be erected in Bowling Green Lane. The Vestry felt that the district needed mortuary facilities but the inhabitants of Bowling Green Lane felt there was no such need or, if there was, the mortuary should not be erected on the old burial ground in Bowling Green Lane, immediately facing the prison.[37] The Vestry agreed to receive representatives from Bowling Green Lane at a special meeting on 16 December to discuss the matter. After the explosion no one could deny the need for a mortuary or the appropriateness of Bowling Green Lane for the site. A general meeting of the Vestrymen was held on 19 December and a resolution passed that the Vestry desired 'to record their great abhorrence and detestation with which it views the recent Fenian outrage'. It was agreed that a copy of the resolution be sent to the Secretary of State and that it be advertised in *The Times, Standard, Clerkenwell News* and *Islington Gazette*.

At the meeting a letter from the Home Office was read calling for the swearing in of special constables in Clerkenwell. Four days later Lieutenant Birkin of the Militia Barracks, City Road, was appointed Superintendent of Special Constables in the Clerkenwell District. The Police Station in Old Street was the Specials Headquarters and the Militia Barracks in City Road the Rallying Point.[38] 113 volunteers out of the population of 65,000 were sworn in as special constables. At Clerkenwell Police Court a volunteer asked what were the duties of the special police; he had asked at several police stations but no one seemed to know. Mr. Barker of the Court stated he could not give any information but if the applicant had been sworn in he would have to act, but in what manner he could not tell.[39] The volunteers were stood down on 31 March 1868, when the Secretary of State was able to write that the danger was over.

The relief fund started by Rev. Maguire grew rapidly and a Committee was set up to adminster the fund. A total of £10,073 14s. 2d. was subscribed.[40] The Rothschilds headed the list of subscribers with a donation of £105 closely followed by the Marquis of Northampton, the New River Company, Sir William Martins, and Mr. Pickburn with £100 each. Most of the donations were small and a high number came from Ireland. Mr. Patrick O'Brien, an Irish teacher 'who has for 30 years enjoyed the friendship and hospitality of England' sent £1 while Valencia Island residents sent £4 12s. Strangely enough no donation is recorded from Northern Ireland though the Loyal Orangemen of Portsmouth sent £3 9s. Several donations were the results of penny readings; at St. Johns Gate, Clerkenwell, Henry Marston raised over £8 in this way. In Leominster over £12 was raised by a penny reading and in Widcombe 8s. 6d.[41]

The Committee sent £3 to County Cork for private W.E. Stuart of the 9th Lancers in recognition of help given by him in rescuing some of the wounded from the ruins.[42]

The Committee was pestered with false collectors and had to take legal action about a 'Monster Drawing' run by a group of swindlers.

The Committee considered all claims and awarded various amounts. The register of claims and the register of payments draws a discreet veil on how claims were judged. George Squire, tenant of 55 Rosoman Street, claimed £40 for furniture destroyed, £20 for stock destroyed, £1.4s. for loss of rent, and £150 for repairs, a total of over £200. He settled for £5. His lodger, John Barnes, claimed only £10 for loss of clothes and was awarded £13 17s 6d. James Haynes of 9 Corporation Lane, claimed £3 10s. for his furniture and £1 10s. for his Geneva watch; he got £10. Frederick Yates, a schoolmaster of St. James's Walk successfully claimed £4 for loss of income by children being unable to go to school. John Hooker received over £10 for cuts and bruises received when he fell from a van after the horse bolted. The final report of the Committee showed that the members had given away £9,000. 574 applicants had received a total of 1,386 payments. The Committee had spent the sum of £676 on advertising but the other expenses were low.[43]

The Committee arranged annuities for the eight women seriously injured in the explosion. Twenty years later they were all thriving and all but one married. At least one of the injured lived to be well over ninety and drew a pension for sixty years; 'It was the pension that kept her alive' said Albert Henry Abbott with the utmost sincerity and with unconscious irony.[44] Albert Abbott himself had been injured in the explosion and drew a small pension for well over sixty years. He sold matches in Holborn and occasionally in Corporation Row. He became a well-known figure in London and told the story of the explosion to all who would listen. He died in 1935.

In April, 1869, the Committee presented Rev. Maguire with a testimonial on vellum plus a piece of plate. A similar testimonial was given to the Secretary of the Committee, Mr. Robert Paget, plus a purse filled by public subscription.

In 1888 the Relief Fund was wound up and the balance divided between the Clock and Watchmakers Asylum, the Clerkenwell Visiting Society, the Goldsmiths and Jewellers Annuity Institution, and the Royal Free Hospital. By this time annuities had been arranged for all surviving victims and these were paid by the Providential Clerks Mutual Assurance Society.[45] Thus did the Clerkenwell explosion alienate the sympathy of ordinary Englishmen in the very suburb where English working men and radicals had voiced their support for Irish independence.

## NOTES

1. *Hansard* 19 March 1868 (Lord Campbell).
2. R. Anderson, *Sidelights of the Home Rule Movement*, 1906, p.72.
3. *Western Star* 12 December 1867.
4. D.G. Browne, *The Rise of Scotland Yard*, 1956, p.142.
5. *Clerkenwell News* 26 December 1867.
6. *Fermanagh Mail* 13 January 1868.
7. *Ibid.* 23 December 1867.
8. P.R.O., H.O., O.S.7799/93.
9. *The Cornet* 1 Jan 1868.
10. R. Anderson, *op. cit.*, p.77.
11. P.R.O., H.O., O.S.7799/93/307.
12. R. Anderson *Sidelights of the Home Risk Movement* 1906. p.78.
13. D.G. Browne, *op. cit.*, p.142.
14. D. Ryan, *The Phoenix Flame*, 1937, p.145.
15. *Fermanagh Mail* 20 January 1868.
16. *Ibid.*
17. *Impartial Reporter* 2 January 1868.
18. *The Times* 21 December 1867.
19. *Observer* 15 December 1867.
20. *Banner of Ulster* 17 December 1867.
21. *Impartial Reporter* 7 May 1868.
22. *Banner of Ulster* 26 December 1867.
23. *Fermanagh Mail* 2 January 1868.
24. *Observer* 22 December 1867.
25. W.D. D'Arcy, *The Fenian Movement in the U.S.A.*, 1947, p. 277.
26. *Boston Advertiser* 18 December 1867.
27. *Fermanagh Mail* 26 December 1867.
28. D.G. Browne, *op. cit.*, p.143.
29. *Hansard* 9 March 1868.
30. *Observer* 22 December 1867.
31. *Essex Standard* 25 December 1867.
32. *Political Correspondence of Mr Gladstone and Lord Granville, 1868-1876*, 1952, p.170.
33. *Western Star* 22 December 1867.
34. P.R.O., H.O., O.S.7799/255 and 352.

35. *Clerkenwell News* 17 December 1867.
36. *Ibid.*, 18 December 1867.
37. Clerkenwell Vestry *Minute Book*, 1868.
38. *Letter book* of the Clerkenwell Guardians of the Poor, 1868, p.828.
39. *Clerkenwell News* 23 December 1867.
40. C.E.R.F.C. *Bank Book* 28 April 1869.
41. C.E.R.F.C. *General List of Subscribers*, 1868.
42. C.E.R.F.C. *Minute Book*, 1868.
43. *Ibid.*, 1869.
44. G.A. Aldred, *No Traitor's Gait*, 1955, p.15.
45. C.E.R.F.C. *Minute Book*, 1882.

# Chapter 8

## *The Clerkenwell Trials*

The Clerkenwell Explosion brought intense police activity all over the country. A number of Irishmen and radicals were held for questioning but the leaders of the rescue attempt had disappeared. The chagrin of the police was understandable. They had been given detailed information of the rescue plan and had placed scores of men around the gaol. Despite this the Fenians had made the attempt in broad daylight and escaped. The uniformed police had seized, beaten and arrested a police agent by mistake. The same agent, Jeremiah Allen, had even been accused of the attack by a London Coroner's Court and publicly charged with being a murderer.[1] The two British agents in the Fenian leadership, Beach and Millen, probably supplied information on the planning of the rescue but the police seemed strangely ineffective in their search for the organizers. A reward of £400, plus a free pardon if needed, was offered for information about the Fenians involved.

Among the men arrested in London soon after the explosion was Patrick Mullany, a tailor from Dublin. Mullany had emigrated to England in 1862 and worked in Manchester and Aldershot. He then moved to London and worked for J.B. Johnston of Sackville Street for four years. By 1867 he had his own tailoring business at 20 Sherwood Street, Golden Square, and employed nine men. Mullany had become a member of the Fenian movement in 1865 and attended meetings at the 13 Cantons Public House in Soho. He had been active in the Tailors' Union and in the long strike by tailors in 1867. The deposition of police charges against Mullany can still be seen at the Old Bailey. The document is over 20 feet long and the accusations include 'Combining conspiring confederating consulting and agreeing with evil disposed persons to make and levy war insurrection and rebellion . . . agreeing with certain foreigners and strangers citizens of the U.S.A. and persons resident in America with force to invade Ireland . . . recruiting for the Fenian Brotherhood . . . attending Fenian meetings . . . procuring arms rifles muskets pistols swords bayonets gunpowder bullets slugs percussion caps . . . working for the establishment of a republic in Ireland . . . raising war insurrection and rebellion in England . . . trying to subvert and destroy the constitution.'[2] Sixty-two persons were to be called to give evidence against Mullany; he was implicated in the Manchester and Clerkenwell events and faced a death sentence. He was offered various inducements to give information and on 10 January he gave a guarded and short statement mentioning only those he believed to be safe in France. He denied taking part in the rescue attempt but added 'I am partly sure, that Captain Murphy and Jackson, both from Glasgow, are the two persons who planned the explosion at Clerkenwell . . . Jackson lodged at 8 Pulteney Court . . . he was with Felix Fallon . . . Jackson told me he fired the explosion.' The police asked him if Jackson was also known as Barrett and Mullany cautiously agreed 'it might be so.'[3] Obviously the police had some information about Michael Barrett from another source. Police throughout the British Isles were asked to look for Barrett and an accurate description of him was circulated.

Three days after Mullany had made his statement the Chief Constable of Glasgow reported to the Magistrates that two men had been found firing pistols in Glasgow Green at midnight. The men were James O'Neill and Michael Barrett.[4] The next day the Procurator Fiscal (Scottish public prosecutor) told the Magistrates that the two men had not been 'taken up' but he felt they should be detained for enquiries.[5] At the trial Barrett said he was taken to the Glasgow Police Station and searched, nothing was found on him and he was released after giving his name and address. The police then came to his lodging at 32 Centre Street Glasgow and re-arrested him claiming that they had found a revolver. This charge was dropped when the Clerkenwell charge was made. The circumstances of the arrest remain obscure. No reason has emerged for the firing of a revolver at midnight on 13 January, exactly a month after the Clerkenwell explosion. The shot drew attention to Barrett just after the Glasgow police had received a request from the London police to look for him. The Glasgow police notified the Home Office of the arrests. Detective Inspector Frederick Williamson of Scotland Yard travelled immediately with a warrant and the two men were brought to Bow Street Police Station, London, and charged with complicity in the Clerkenwell Explosion. The prisoners travelled with armed guards on the train. No chances were taken in London and the police van was protected by mounted police armed with revolvers and cutlasses.

The two Scottish constables who made the original arrest were awarded £50 each; the Chief Constable of Glasgow questioned the size of the award and suggested it was 'not what it ought to have been.'[6] James O'Neill faded out of the Clerkenwell case quickly. The strange features of the arrest suggest an elaborate cover for a police agent in Glasgow. Mullany was told that Barrett had been captured and that the other prisoners had made full statements. The police already held his statement that Barrett was responsible for the explosion. Papers kept by the Special Branch for over a century, and recently released to the Public Records Office, show how Mullany was persuaded that his own situation was so dangerous that he should confirm what the police already knew.

On 17 January he made a new statement and later in the day he expanded some of the details. On 19 January he asked how 'he would stand if he gave information'. On 20 January he made a further statement but the police queried some of the names he had mentioned and compared them with statements by Nicholas English and James Vaughan. Mullany was warned that he had concealed many names and that the police already knew more then he had told them. On 22 January he once again made a new and this time longer statement only to be warned that he was still holding back facts and that his help was not essential. He could be charged with capital offences in London and Manchester and his own statements used as confessions of guilt. On 22 January he asked to see senior officials and told them 'Yes, I'll turn informer'. He talked to save his life, all control gone after a month of strain, fear and psychological pressure. Judging from the writing the police scribe was hard put to keep up with the flow of words; the statements fill many pages and are signed 'P. Mullany' in uncertain crude handwriting with many strokes of the pen, like a child copying a difficult word. After each writing session the police came back with more questions and then revised and edited the flow of information. The original papers show the complete collapse of morale.

> I came from Dublin six years ago. I worked in Dawson Street, Dublin and for Shaw, Master Tailor of the 13th Hussars in Manchester . . . I rent the first floor of 2 Sherwood Street from Mr. Hyde, a coffee house keeper in Swallow Street. A sister of my wife's waits on us, she is Julia Welsh. She lives with her daughter at Mrs. O'Shaughnessy's house. Mrs. O'Shaughnessy is the wife of the summoning officer at Marlborough Police Court . . . I attended Fenian meetings at the 13 Cantons Pub . . . I met Ricard Burke at the pub in Castle Street, Leicester Square, also Nicholas English and Michael Barrett.

He told of meetings and raffles to raise funds for arms and of meetings held to introduce members to the officers from America. He had met Thomas Bourke, Augustine Costello, William Halpin,

James Kelly, Godfrey Massey, John McCafferty, and Michael O'Brien, all battle-trained in the American Civil War. Names, aliases and addresses poured forth putting a strain on the spelling ability of the police writer. James Murphy used the name Hastings, Michael Barrett was known as Jackson, Flood was known as Howard, while Nolan was known as Newman. Many further details were added to the information already held by the police. Occasionally London radicals were mentioned. At a meeting in Cavanagh's Bar in Pollen Street, he stated that he had met Burnett, a traveller in cigars and an Englishman. He described a lively meeting when the news of James Kelly's arrest in Manchester had arrived and how Michael Barrett sent a telegram for Burke at the time of the Manchester rescue. He confirmed that James Murphy and Barrett were at the Manchester Conference in the summer of 1867 when all the Head Centres met. He spoke of meetings in Dudley Street at a pub kept by a Frenchman and how Burke had appointed Nicholas English to collect funds for the Fenian movement.

The members of his Fenian group included Timothy Desmond, William Desmond, Nicholas English, Morris Donoghue, Ned Bura, Felix Fallon, Casey, Donegan, James Clancy, Lynch, Edmund O'Donovan, Ryan, Quin, McMahon, Christopher McDonagh, Philip Kennedy, Dr Keenan, Jeremiah Murphy, John O'Donnell, Daniel O'Keefe, Maurice O'Connell, Patton, Sullivan and Jack Taylor. He spoke of a meeting at the house of Dr Keenan, a Northern Ireland man:

> They talked of seizing a ship in the docks and going away with it to land in Ireland, they said Waterford would be good place. Jim Kelly was to command . . . Barrett and Ryan went to Bow Street with the intention of shooting Corydon, the informer. They had loaded revolvers but there was no chance of success. They also watched Scotland Yard . . .'

He added some details of the members.

> Justice went to Ireland for the Rising. He took a lot of ammunition, so did Mrs. Ann Justice. She carried a sword under her crinoline as well as ammunition. Justice is a tailor and worked for Mr. Lucey in St. James Road. Colonel Kelly gave him £15 to buy arms and he went and bought a sewing machine . . . Edmund O'Donovan, who is a very clever fellow who was educated at Trinity College, Dublin, and had £100 a year out of it, used to make Greek Fire (phosphorus bombs) at English's house.

Nicholas English of 8 Pollen Street, Soho, mentioned by Mullany in his statement, was also a tailor who had taken an active part in Irish affairs in London for some years. In 1863 he had been one of the promoters of the '*Irish Liberator*' and held 25 shares in this Fenian newspaper. The editor was Dr. David Bell and the newspaper office was at 6 Southampton Buildings, Chancery Lane. Other shareholders included John Blake, a Mercantile Clerk of 19 Gt. Quebec Street, Montague Square, Thomas Hayes, a Wheelwright of 24 Little Coram Street, and Jeremiah Murphy, a provision dealer of 56 Grays Inn Road, each with forty shares.[8] English was arrested at the same time as Mullany and by the end of January he had been induced to make a statement. His information was not as detailed or as accurate as Mullany's, though he confirmed some details. He included the comments:

> Murphy goes by the name of Moran, he was responsible for the raid on Chester . . . Burke is a Centre for Oldham and was with Kelly in Manchester on the night of his arrest. Burke is not the one at Clerkenwell . . . John Ryan is a Centre in Liverpool and is prosperous . . . the two Bolger brothers are shoemakers, they went to Paris after the Manchester rescue. One returned to Bolton . . . the other is in Paris . . . this is the one who shot Brett . . . Bolger told me he was the one . . . this Bolger is single, he shot Brett. The other is married.

He added that Quin had been at Clerkenwell with a revolver.[9] The John Hayes mentioned by both men was probably another police agent. Dr. Mark Ryan in his autobiography refers to a John Hayes who tried to persuade London Fenians to steal the Coronation Stone from Westminster;[10] he was later exposed as a government agent and a colleague of Thomas Beach (Henri Le Caron).

The large number of Irish tailors active in the Fenian movement was partly due to the long strike of tailors in 1867. Some of the police agents watching militant trade unionists found the latter often had close personal links with Fenian supporters or were members of the I.R.B.

Members of the First International had many links with supporters of Irish independence. Karl Marx had an Irish landlord, Morgan Kavanagh, living in the same house;[11] he had an Irish doctor, and his daughters were active Fenian supporters,[12] quite apart from his personal connection through the I.W.M.A. with the Fenian Amnesty movement described in Chapter 12.

The prosecution decided not to use Nicholas English as a witness. Yet another informer was available and willing to swear as needed. James Vaughan, a tailor of Carnaby Street, had heard of the £400 reward for information and had gone to the police to offer his services. In a long rambling statement he claimed he had been enrolled in the Fenians by Timothy Desmond in 1865. He knew Michael Barrett and had met him in Regent Street, London, three days before the explosion. Barrett then had long Dundreary whiskers and a slight moustache, his chin was clean shaven.

Vaughan stated that on the afternoon of the explosion Timothy

Desmond called at his home in Carnaby Street and told him that he was going to take part in an attack on Clerkenwell Gaol. That evening Nicholas English came to collect money for those taking part in the attack. Nicholas English had told him that Timothy Desmond had been drunk and had no right to be in Clerkenwell at the time of the explosion; it served him right to be arrested. Vaughan claimed that he knew Mullany well and that Mullany had bought him drinks.[13]

Soon after his arrival in London Michael Barrett wrote to his friend Charles McManus of 30 Canal Street, Port Dundas, in Glasgow. The letter was read by the prison authorities and a copy sent to Superintendent McCaul, Head of the Glasgow Police. The letter read as follows:

Millbank Prison, London, 24 January 1868

My Dear Friend,

You will I have no doubt be very much grieved upon hearing of the series of reverses that have befallen me lately, the cause of which I am as ignorant of as yourself; nevertheless, I have got into the meshes of the law, and when once fairly entangled, it is no easy matter to get extricated, of course it is needless for me to enter into details as no doubt you have learned all the particulars through the public press before this, however I wish you to go to Mr. James Mullen and he will bring you to the shoemaker named McNulty in Bridgegate Street. I do not know the number. Mention my name to him and see if he remembers doing a little work for me at the time this crime of which I am charged with being the author was committed; if he does not recollect the name, mention the few following incidents that took place, namely, that I was the party who waited upon him on three different occasions to have my boots bottomed, first on the Thursday, then again on the Friday night when he promised them certainly on Saturday, and upon me going for them on Saturday I kicked up a row on account of him not having done anything to them and that he had to get two men who were in the place to assist him to do them as I could not leave without them and during the time they were working I sent out for the *Evening Post* and read for them an account of the Clerkenwell Explosion which was the first thing they heard of it. Now I think this should bring the matter quite clearly to their remembrance. You will also tell McNulty that if these two men have left him he must find them and also who the other parties are who were in the place at the time. I wish you to go to my lodgings at once, and take anything of mine that there is out of it, and if you can, send me a change of underclothing. There is nothing I need more at present. You should see Mr. Lewis about them. Mr. O'Neill wrote on Tuesday but I do not know who to or whether he got an answer as we do not get speaking. I will write again on Wednesday. I am, sir, as ever, yours.

MICHAEL BARRETT

P.S. You will please send me the red Crimea shirt that you will find in my lodgings and drawers are what I need most. You will also find some collars of which I would like you to send me a few. You may rest assured we are in a miserable enough condition here being without friends or acquaintances to do anything for us. Now please not to neglect what I have told you to do, write at once. All letters are read by the Governor. I would also wish you to send me a pair of stockings. See Mr. Lewis at once. Mr. Mullen will bring you to him he will also bring you to my old lodgings. I hope you at least do not accuse me of being guilty of this charge. Please write by return.[14]

Superintendent Alexander McCaul accompanied by Detective Smith immediately called on Michael McNulty, a boot and shoemaker, of Bridgegate Street, Glasgow. He asked McNulty if he knew O'Neill, Michael Barrett, or Jackson, and received a firm denial from McNulty. The police chief then announced his identity and questioned McNulty. McNulty reluctantly agreed that he had known James O'Neill for about four months. McNulty added that O'Neill had called at his house on Friday, 13 December, when James Lewis, another shoemaker, was also present. O'Neill had called again on 14 December and left a newspaper behind him. He remembered the date because James Lewis had read part of the paper to him, including a report of the Clerkenwell Explosion. McNulty swore he had no men working for him in mid-December, that he did not know Barrett nor had he heard the name before. He had not repaired boots for O'Neill and he did not remember any man coming to his house to get boots buttoned. He swore he had no memory of a man making a fuss because work was unfinished when promised. He was quite sure he had never buttoned any boots for anyone at any time. The questions about buttoning boots were quite irrelevant and due solely to a misspelling by the police writer. In his letter Michael Barrett referred to his boots being bottomed but the copy sent to the Glasgow Police had the word 'buttoned'. This error was to become significant later on. McCaul then read the questions and replies to McNulty who agreed they were correct.[15] Some days later Barrett's original letter was received by Charles McManus; he went directly to McNulty as he knew Mullen had already left Glasgow for America and then McNulty understood the reason for the visit by the police. McManus also took the letter to Peter McCorry, editor of the *Glasgow Free Press* a weekly newspaper that enlivened the Glasgow scene with religious and political controversy. McCorry knew Barrett and offered to give evidence on his behalf.

On Monday 20 April 1868, yet another state trial of Fenians began. Crowded into the dock of the Old Court at the Old Bailey stood Michael Barrett, Timothy Desmond, William Desmond, Nicholas English, Ann Justice and John O'Keefe. They had been held at Newgate Gaol for months, remanded from week to week while the police sought further evidence.

Reporters noted the poor state of the prisoners. Their faces were pallid from long immurement. Their shabby clothes hung limply for Newgate was not noted for cleanliness or washing facilities. Only Barrett stood out; he had not been in gaol as long as the others and his clothes were in better condition. The dark flashing eyes of Ann Justice roved round the Court, taking in the brilliant robes and uniforms.[16] Barrett looked round with interest but the other men seemed cowed by the court.

Facing the prisoners was the cream of the English legal profession. Leading the prosecution was the Attorney General of England, Sir J.B. Karslake, who had led the prosecution in the Manchester trial. He was supported by the Solicitor-General of England, Sir Baliol Brett, and assisted by the experienced leading lawyers, Hardinge-Giffard, Q.C., Poland, Q.C., and Mr. Archibald. For them the resources of the state were available and expense was no problem. The case was to be heard by two judges, Lord Chief Justice Alexander Cockburn and Baron George Bramwell. The charge was murder, the murder of Sarah Anne Hodginson, who had been killed by flying glass when the gunpowder exploded.

In 1868 there were no funds to pay for legal defences for poor prisoners. Appeals in Irish papers had produced just enough to pay young lawyers at the beginning of their careers. These men, very young members of the bar, were willing to undertake the defence for a low fee. For Baker Greene, who defended Michael Barrett, it was his first appearance in a murder trial and he had just ten days to prepare the defence. Montague Williams, who had less then three years experience, defended both Ann Justice and O'Keefe. Twenty-one year old Douglas Straight defended Timothy Desmond, while the equally youthful Warner Sleigh acted for William Desmond and Keogh for Nicholas English.[17] With little experience, with meagre funds to pay expenses for witnesses, and against the legal might of the Government, they won five of the six verdicts.

At the beginning of the trial the jury was shown a model of the House of Detention and the houses in Corporation Lane. A surveyor pointed out the house facing the part of the prison wall shattered in the explosion. Blast had blown in the windows and doors of ten houses in the street. House No. 3a was the nearest to the point of the explosion; it was barely eight yards from the wall, and had suffered most damage.

The first witness was George Richardson. He told how he had found the body of Sarah Hodgkinson on the first floor of No. 3a; he had taken her body into the prison yard and later on to St. Bartholomew's Hospital. House-surgeon Edward McLean reported he had examined the body and found that Sarah Hodgkinson had been hit by flying glass; she had suffered a deep cut on the neck and died partly of haemorrhage and partly from suffocation. The inquest report and findings were then submitted.

After the formal opening evidence was completed the prosecution produced its first key witness, Patrick Mullany. Montague Williams described him as looking miserable 'with hunger in his cheeks and fear in his eyes'. Mullany told the Court he had joined the Fenian movement at the Teetotal Hall in Pollen Street; he knew the leaders James Kelly and Ricard Burke by sight and had been introduced to them. He had met the accused men at various Fenian meetings. A few days after the arrest of Ricard Burke two men had called at his house in Sherwood Street. They were Michael Barrett and James Murphy, both heavily armed, who said they had come from Glasgow to rescue Burke. Barrett had lodged with Felix Fallon, an I.R.B. member, who lived at 8 Pulteney Court. About a week before the explosion Fallon had asked him to store some gunpowder for a rescue attempt. Barrett and Murphy had visited him a number of times; on one of these occasions Mrs Cathleen Barry, Burke's sister, had called and left a letter from Burke. It was written in invisible ink. Murphy had put some green copperas into a cup of warm water and rubbed it on the letter. The message included the lines 'You know my position here; there is a house here called "The Noted Stout House". At that house there is a sewer and a weak part of the wall. If you get a barrel of gunpowder and place it there, you will be able to blow the wall to hell. Get the men to buy it in small quantities and it must be done at the hour of 3.30 or 4 o'clock. If you do not do that you ought to be shot.' A sketch of the prison area was added. Mullany said meetings were held in Holborn and Oxford Street to discuss the letter. Michael Barrett and James Murphy attended these meetings as well as William Desmond, Nicholas English and Felix Fallon. Collections were made to raise money for the purchase of the gunpowder. On 11 December he attended a meeting in William Desmond's house at 10 Cross Street Holborn. Eighteen were present, including Michael Barrett, William Desmond, Nicholas English and James Murphy. It was agreed that the rescue attempt be made the following day, Thursday, 12 December, at 3.30 p.m. This attempt was made but James Murphy was unable to ignite the fuse. Michael Barrett then said he would do it the following day. Mullany claimed he had met Barrett on the evening of the explosion and saw that Barrett had shaved off his whiskers and changed his clothes. Barret had told him he had fired the explosion and that Murphy had helped him.[18] Warders from Clerkenwell Gaol gave evidence of Ricard Burke's actions on 12 and 13 December and described events in the gaol before and after the explosion.

On the second day of the trial, Sleigh and Keogh cross-examined Mullany. They drew from Mullany the admission that he could read very little and could not have read the letter he quoted in his evidence. Mullany said he knew nothing of the reward for information but he knew the English Crown always paid people for their services; he had got drunk on Friday, 13th December and was not quite sober until he was arrested on the 19th. He agreed he had contributed towards the cost of the gunpowder. He had not turned up for the rescue attempt because he was too busy and anyway it was not proper for a married man to go. He had turned informer for the sake of his family and because he was sure English was going to inform. He was now the property of the English Crown. This remark brought a smile to Barrett's face. Mullany was then asked if he knew James Vaughan and replied he had never seen him at Fenian meetings and had no recollection of ever meeting him before the hearings at Bow Street Police Station.

The next witness for the prosecution was James Vaughan. He swore he had been enrolled in the I.R.B. by Timothy Desmond in 1865. He swore he knew Michael Barrett and had seen him in London, three days before the explosion. Vaughan repeated his statement that on the afternoon of the explosion Timothy Desmond had called at his house in Carnaby Street. Desmond had been drinking and said his wife had left him and that he had just seen his son off to sea. He told Vaughan he was going to take part in an attack on Clerkenwell Gaol that afternoon. He asked for Vaughan's prayer's, kissed him and shook hands before leaving.

Despite Mullany's denial of knowing him, Vaughan claimed he had known Mullany for some time and that Mullany had brought him drinks. He said he had easily identified Barrett in Millbank Gaol in January though Barrett then had no whiskers but did have three or four weeks growth of beard.

Vaughan was closely cross-examined by the defence and made damaging admissions. He admitted he had deserted from the British Army, that he was receiving payment from the police, being an inmate of the work house, and that he was a sufferer from delirium tremens. He agreed he had received treatment for mental trouble. After claiming to be a Roman Catholic he said he knew a Fr. O'Connor who was a Fenian supporter and ran raffles for the purchase of rifles for the Fenian movement. He agreed he had gone to the police after reading about the £400 reward and that he hoped to get a reward if the prisoners were convicted.

The next witnesses were from Messrs. Curtis and Harvey, gunpowder manufacturers of Lombard Street. They told how 200 lb. of gunpowder was ordered and delivered to a Mr. George Smith at 8 Pulteney Court on Friday, 6 December. Payment of £3 7s. 6d. was made in cash. No. 8 Pulteney Court was a greengrocers shop with living quarters. A number of rooms were let to lodgers by the proprietor, Mrs Martin.

Then came nineteen year old Martha Kensley, a waistcoat-maker, who lived with her parents on the first floor of 8 Pulteney Court. She had seen Michael Barrett there eight or nine times, the first time was about two months before the explosion and the last time on 9 December. She had particularly noted him because he was going out with Mrs. Martin. She had been shown Barrett's photograph by the police and recognized him as the man she had seen in Pulteney Court. At an identification parade in King Street Police Station, Westminster, she had failed to recognize Barrett. She had gone to see the prisoners at Bow Street Station and later went to Millbank Prison. She had seen Barrett twice before she had identified him. She added that Mrs. Martin had threatened to kill her and had been arrested.

Martha's brother then testified that he had seen Michael Barrett at Mrs. Martin's shop. He had first seen Barrett about five or six weeks before the explosion; he remembered him because Barrett 'had a very peculiar way with his eyes of noticing you as you passed out'. He did not know if Barrett lodged in Pulteney Court, but he had seen him in the parlour with Mrs. Martin. He said he had not discussed Barrett's appearance with his sister before he was taken to an identity parade in Millbank Prison, neither had he been shown a photo of Barrett.

The prosecution called witnesses who testified to seeing the prisoners at the scene of the explosion; their evidence was challenged by the defence lawyers who pointed out the weakness of the conflicting testimony. Several of those giving evidence had, at earlier court hearings, sworn that Jeremiah Allen, the police agent, had caused the explosion. There was a good deal of evidence that the identity parades had been conducted in a partial manner and that witnesses had been shown photographs of the prisoners before being asked to identify them. The odour of perjury at the trial was uncomfortably strong.

As soon as the case for the prosecution was completed, Montague Williams rose and pointed out that no evidence had been given to connect Ann Justice with the explosion that had caused the death of Sarah Hodgkinson. She had taken some food to Joseph Casey on 13 December and spoken to him in the presence of warders; she must have known that the exercise time for the prisoners had been changed that day and that an attack on the prison wall around 3.30 p.m. would be useless. Both judges agreed that the evidence against

Ann Justice was slight, at most it amounted to her speaking to William Desmond and the police agent, Jeremiah Allen. She had been loitering near the prison area but there was nothing to connect her directly with the explosion. The Attorney-General rose and said that in view of the judges' remarks he wished to withdraw the case against Ann Justice. This remarkable breakdown in the prosecution case against Ann Justice was followed by a strange scene which drew particular attention to Michael Barrett. Ann Justice was told she was discharged from the case and that she could leave the Court. She was sitting next to Michael Barrett, she turned to him, took his hand and kissed him. She then shook hands with the other prisoners and left the Court tears streaming down her face.[19]

The case against John O'Keefe was the next to collapse. The evidence against him was slight and nearly all of it was provided by the informer, James Vaughan. The Attorney General rose to say that he had gone through the evidence against O'Keefe and though he thought it was bona fide, he felt it was not such as he ought to rely upon to ask the jury to convict. The judges agreed that the evidence of complicity and identification was much too weak for a conviction. The jury agreed and John O'Keefe was removed from the dock.

Mr. Straight then strongly defended Timothy Desmond. Hammering home the fact that the only evidence against him came from the informer James Vaughan. At the time of the explosion Timothy Desmond had been at the opposite side of the prison and in a drunken state. The evidence against him was no stronger than that against Ann Justice.

Mr. Keogh spoke for Nicholas English, stressing the fact that of the many witnesses produced not one swore to having seen English at the explosion scene. After the collapse of the case against Ann Justice and John O'Keefe the case against the Desmond brothers and English began to look very weak. The evidence against Michael Barrett was not strong; he had been identified very uncertainly by witnesses whose evidence was contradictory. The chief witness against him was Mullany, who had named him even before his arrest. But Mullany had declared that Michael Barrett and James Murphy had come specially from Glasgow to rescue Ricard Burke, thus flatly contradicting the witnesses who claimed they had known Barrett in London for some weeks before the explosion. But Barrett's defence did not rest on insufficient evidence or misidentification, there was the letter from Barrett to his friend Charles McManus. If the details in the letter were correct Barrett was in Glasgow at the time of the explosion. Only Barrett offered an alibi and produced witnesses to support it.

Michael Barrett made no secret of his nationalism and his support for the Fenian Movement. He was an Ulsterman, born in Drumnagreshial in the parish of Drumkeeran, County Fermanagh. At the time of the trial he was twenty-six years old. He made a good impression on all who met him. The *Times* reporter noted his bright, resolute eyes, short crisp beard, thick hair, muscular body, and his look of determination and frank courage.[20] Montague Williams described Barrett as 'a square-built fellow, scarcely five foot eight in height, and dressed something like a well-to-do farmer'. He also noted a frank, open expression and added 'a less murderous countenance than Barrett's indeed, I do not remember to have seen. Good humour was latent in every feature'.[21] The *Daily Telegraph* reported Barrett 'was evidently a man of high intelligence'.[22] The background of Michael Barrett has remained a mystery and he has been termed the unknown Fenian.[23] The surname is unusual in County Fermanagh. An Edward Barrett of Fermanagh was named as a United Irishman by an informer in 1797[24] and another Barrett played a part in the rising of 1798.[25] Michael Barrett was a Catholic but his name cannot be traced in the poorly kept Catholic records for the area. The Drumkeeran Protestant records include a Michael Barrett attending the local charity school in 1797[26] and the baptism of a number of Barretts in the Drunkeeran Church. The former Barrett home still stands in Drumnagreshial and the farm is owned by a relative. In his speech and letters Michael Barrett showed evidence of a good education; his speech in the dock, made without notes, included biblical quotations and lasted forty minutes. Fermanagh was the scene of agrarian and political unrest in the early nineteenth century and suffered in the great famine of 1845-8. In the decade 1841-51 the county lost a quarter of its people. The short lived Irish Parliament had given the vote to forty shilling freeholders in 1793 thus enfranchising a number of Catholics. In 1829 the British Government disenfranchised the forty shilling freeholders and raised the county qualification to £10 a year; this was five times the qualification in England and an effective piece of political gerrymandering. There was an immediate increase in secret organizations with working class Catholic and Protestant members. Two members of the Barrett family lost their votes when the qualifications were changed. Michael Barrett appears to have been the only son of Edward Barrett of Drumnagreshial. The small farm of twenty-eight acres, with two families on it, was probably too small to provide a living; by the age of twenty-one Michael Barrett had emigrated. He worked in Glasgow and became a member of the Fenian Movement.

Barrett's alibi was supported by Peter McCorry, editor of the *Glasgow Free Press* newspaper, and by a number of members of the

Glasgow Irish community. They swore that Michael Barrett had been with them at a meeting on 12 December to commemorate the Manchester executions. A statement that Barrett was in Glasgow on 12, 13 and 14 December was made by the shoemaker Michael McNulty and supported by two other shoemakers, John Peak and John Walsh. They swore that the facts set out in Barrett's letter from Millbank Prison were correct. They also said that Barrett's friend, Mullan, had emigrated to America. McNulty was closely question-ed at the trial as to why he had denied all knowledge of Barrett to Superintendent McCaul. McNulty stated he had been asked if he had 'buttoned' boots for Barrett; he did not button boots for anyone and had said so immediately; he claimed McCaul had 'humbugged' him by asking questions about buttoning, a specialized job he never tackled. The three shoemakers were not shaken by a long cross examination by the Attorney-General. Yet another set of witnesses were called by J.B. Greene. The first of these was Arthur Burgoyne, who claimed he had known Michael Barrett for some months and had seen him almost daily in Glasgow in December. Next came Charles McManus. He took the Bible in his hand, repeated the oath, then raised the book reverently above his head at arm's length before kissing it. He swore that Michael Barrett was with him in Glasgow on Friday, 13 December. The Attorney-General failed to shake his evidence and much of the cross examining of this witness and the others concerned their opinion of Fenianism and their views on Ireland and the British Government.

The stiffest cross-examination was that of Peter McCorry, the newspaper editor. He was an ex-schoolteacher and occasionally wrote under the pen-name of Shandy McSherry; he had been the centre of religious and political storms in Glasgow for some time. The *Glasgow Free Press* had long supported the activities of the Brotherhood of St. Patrick and at the same time had waged a bitter battle against some of the Scottish clergy. At that time over 90% of the Catholics in Glasgow were Irish immigrants and the *Glasgow Free Press* represented their views. The three main com-plaints of the immigrants were that the Scottish clergy discouraged the political aspirations of the Irish immigrants; that they gave no account to the congregations of the spending of the Church collections; and that the Scottish Bishops pursued a policy of nepotism in appointments which was unfair to Irish-born priests. There was some truth in the three complaints and the Scottish priests reacted bitterly to the criticism. In 1864 twenty-two Irish priests met in Glasgow and drew up a series of resolutions express-ing dissatisfaction with the rule of the Scottish Bishop and calling for reform. The resolutions were moderate in tone and demand but a century ahead of their time. The resolutions were sent to the Vatican and received much publicity in the *Glasgow Free Press*. In October, 1867, Archbishop Manning was appointed by the Holy See to enquire into the political and religious dissensions of the faithful in the Western District of Scotland.[27] Archbishop Manning's views were well known and his saying 'Show me a lapsed Catholic and I will show you a Fenian' was often quoted. He reported in favour of the Scottish bishops. On Sunday, 9 February 1868, the *Glasgow Free Press* was denounced from the altars of all Catholic churches in Scotland. Priests were forbidden under pain of suspension to take any part in the production or circulation of the paper. All Catholics were warned that it was a grievous fault to read or support the paper. The last issue of the paper appeared on 15 February but it was resurrected a week later as the *Irish Catholic Banner*.[28]

The cross-examination of McCorry dwelt at length on his editorship of the paper, the nationalist policy supported by the paper, and the political and religious battles of the editor. McCorry stated on oath that Barrett had been with him at various meetings in connection with the Manchester Martyrs demonstrations; in particular he remembered Barrett being at a meeting in the Bell Hotel, Glasgow, on 12 December and staying until after midnight.

The Attorney-General summed up by attacking Barrett's alibi. He stressed that the evidence of two witnesses showed that Barrett had been in London for some weeks before 13 December. He commented on the improbability that the missing Mullen, a shoemaker, would introduce Barrett to another shoemaker to get some urgent repairs done. He attacked the evidence of Peter McCorry as coming from the editor of a paper 'in which the most detestable and seditious writing habitually appeared'. He said it was strange that Barrett had made no mention of the meeting at the Bell Hotel in his letter to McManus. He asked why Barrett did not produce the men with whom or for whom he worked, or men with whom he had lodged, to confirm his story. The Attorney-General pointed out that two witnesses, a young lad named Morris and Mrs. Koppel, claimed they had seen Barrett from day to day in London and on the evening of the explosion; he felt they could not be mistaken.

Lord Chief Justice Cockburn then summed up the case for the jury. He said the main evidence of an alleged conspiracy to release Richard Burke rested upon the word of James Mullany, an accomplice in the explosion. Juries for many years had been recommended by judges not to convict upon the evidence of a man who came forward to save his own life at the expense of others, unless the evidence was corroborated. However, it was not necessary for the evidence of an informer to be confirmed in every detail. He hoped that those engaged in treasonable practices would note that their greatest danger arose from those with whom they associated and who would betray them. Mullany's story of a letter in invisible ink must have been received by the jury with doubt and suspicion. However, he must point out that when Burke was arrested the police had found on him a small glass bulb, hermetically sealed, containing chloride of gold. It had been shown also that Mrs Barry had attempted to smuggle to Burke a quantity of green copperas.[29] The inference from this was that Burke had used green copperas and chloride of gold to write secretly to friends, thus confirming Mullany's story. Cockburn went on to draw attention to a warder's evidence that on 12 December when a ball was thrown over the prison wall, Burke immediately fell out of the ring of prisoners, leaned against the wall and appeared to be doing up his boot. He did this very slowly and had to be forced back into the line of prisoners. It was certain that Burke knew the rescue attempt was to be made and his actions confirmed the statement by Mullany as to the rescue plan. Cockburn dealt briefly with the evidence against the Desmond brothers and Nicholas English and went on to say that the alibi of Michael Barrett was one of the most remarkable he had ever known. The jury would have to decide on the credibility of the witnesses for the prosecution; on the other hand the defence alibi was so remarkable and peculiar that it required vigilant attention before it could be adopted. The witnesses for the defence had only appeared at the time of the trial. If Barrett had declared immediately on arrest that he was in Glasgow on and before 13 December the police would have searched for witnesses for him. But Barrett had not said one word to that effect when he was arrested and the Judge thought this was unnatural. The evidence of the defence witnesses seemed at first sight satisfactory and conclusive. The statement of the three shoemakers might be true though the whole affair of the boot repairs might have taken place a week later. The evidence of Barrett's attendance at the Glasgow meetings in December was strong but he felt that evidence of those who had lodged with Barrett was needed. Barrett must have had a home of some sort. Someone must have known where he slept, employers or fellow workmen could surely have come forward to speak for him.

The jury retired to consider their verdict. The dingy, over-crowded court buzzed with conversation; the corridors of the building were blocked with people, while outside an immense crowd gathered to hear the trial result. After two and a half hours the jury returned. The foreman was pale and did not look at the prisoners, a sure sign that one or more of the prisoners had been convicted. The judges took their places, the prisoners stood in the dock. Amid absolute silence the Clerk of the Arraigns called the names of the jury and asked if a verdict had been agreed upon. In a low voice the foreman answered 'Yes' and the Clerk went through the list of prisoners though not in alphabetical order.

> Clerk: How say you, gentlemen of the jury, is William Desmond guilty or not guilty of the wilful murder of Sarah Hodgkinson?
> Foreman: Not guilty.
> Clerk: Is Timothy Desmond guilty or not guilty?
> Foreman: Not guilty.
> Clerk: Is Nicholas English guilty or not guilty?
> Foreman: Not guilty.
> Clerk: Is Michael Barrett guilty or not guilty?
> Foreman: Guilty. [He spoke softly and there was a murmur from the spectators as some asked their neighbours what had been said.]
> Clerk: You say that William Desmond, Timothy Desmond, and Nicholas English are not guilty and that Michael Barrett is guilty and that is the verdict of you all?
> Foreman: It is.[30]

The three acquitted prisoners were removed from the dock leaving Michael Barrett alone. The Clerk turned to him and asked if he had anything to say why sentence of death should not be passed on him. In 1868 prisoners were not allowed to give evidence in such trials but were allowed to speak just before sentence was passed. Barrett held the dock firmly with both hands, looked at the Judges and declared he had something to say. Speaking without notes he made a speech which brought tears to many eyes[31] and made a deep impression even on those hostile in every way to Irish republicanism. Speaking slowly and quietly, except when mentioning Mullady and Vaughan, he said:

> I have a great deal to say. Nevertheless, I do not intend to occupy much of your Lordship's time, being fully conscious that any words of mine would in no way alter your Lordship's mind in this matter. Still, I cannot allow this opportunity to pass, as it is likely to be the only one I shall have on this side of the grave, of endeavouring to place myself as I should like to stand before my fellow men. In doing so I may be compelled to expose the means that have been resorted to for the purpose of securing my conviction. I am not, however, going to adopt a whining tone or to ask for mercy; but yet I address your Lordship as a humble individual whose career has been mercilessly assailed and I wish to defend it, conscious as I am that I have never wilfully, maliciously or intentionally injured a human being that I am aware of . . . no, not even in character. True, I stand charged with one of the most repulsive of crimes . . . that of murder, yet when I come to examine the terribly conflicting character of the evidence I find there are not two of the witnesses who do not directly contradict each other. Those who profess to have been eye witnesses of

the deed all agree that the man who fired the barrel was of gentlemanly appearance . . . a tall man, five foot ten or more in height. Considering the impossibility of mistaking such a person for a man of my humble appearance and who is only five foot six. After taking all these things into consideration, and after the incontestable testimony that I was not in London at that time, I express my firm conviction that there is not an unprejudiced man . . . if it were possible for such a one to find his way into this place, that will not be convinced of my innocence. No, it is my most conscientious conviction that the jury cannot in their hearts believe me to be a murderer. I would now endeavour, with your permission, and as far as my humble abilities will allow me, to review a little of the evidence that has been brought against me. But, it would be presumptious, and almost impertinent, in me to deal with the matter after the manner in which my talented Counsel has analyzed that evidence. In consequence, however, of some remarks of the Attorney-General and your Lordship I am compelled to advert to that evidence. I will first speak of my arrest in Glasgow and the way in which I was subsequently smuggled to London. I was taken to the police court there and searched, and yet nothing was found which they could twist into a charge against me. I was set at liberty, and before I was liberated I gave them my name and address, which no man would have done in such a position if he was apprehensive of being taken on a charge of murder. They afterwards came to my lodgings and re-arrested me, urging as their reason the finding of a pistol, and I must confess my regret that the witness was not called by the Crown, for in that case I should have proved that the pistol which he alleged I fired three shots from on a Glasgow Green was perfectly useless. This I heard from a person who was present at the police court. No one could use that pistol. I was brought up two days for examination without once being permitted to open my mouth, and I was ordered off to gaol for nine or ten days with a view of allowing time for further enquiries into the case. They found everything I told them was correct, but they also found what suited their purpose exactly, namely, that I was just recovering from a lengthened illness, and had exhausted my means, and once they got me out of Scotland I was completely in their power. I was hurried off to London, where they knew I was alone and in their power. Their nervous haste, indeed, has subjected me to the most flagrant injustice. I do not allude to the high authorities in Glasgow, but I do to the mean, petty, truckling creatures who hang about police courts, and who would not hesitate to have recourse to the most vile and heinous practices to benefit themselves, or even to gain a smile of approval from their superiors. They will now congratulate themselves on the success of their schemes. I will next speak of that boy Wheeler. When I was first confronted with him in London, after a careful and lengthened examination, and after going to a considerable distance, he was seized by a police-officer, or rather a wretch bearing the uniform of one, and brought back in front of me and held there by the shoulder until he was compelled to admit that he knew me. I cannot find words to express my utter contempt and detestation for a wretch who could so intimidate a child for the purpose of swearing away a fellow-creature's life. The boy's timidity in the witness box must have been apparent to all who saw him. However repulsive the act may have been, it may have been in harmony with the principles of a man who has been familiar with the dens of

London thieves, and with the treachery, trickery and deceit so often found in the official costume of Scotland Yard. I would now speak of the man Bird . . . or rather that miserable Bird. He first identified O'Neill, and here comes in the treatment of officials. After he had done so and gone away he returned and I was called out, and in the hearing of Bird asked my name and where I was born; in the presence of the Chief Warder. Upon that Inspector Thompson at once took up his cue, and, coming back to the cell, said he preferred me. No doubt he did, and was desperate at the idea of losing his portion of the bribe. I will now turn to the highly respectable witnesses from Pulteney Court. As to the evidence of the woman Kemsley, I think it is rather too inconsistent to bear part in depriving a human being of life. She swore she saw me for two months at that woman's house, and on several particular occasions, on one of which she said I was going to take a walk of pleasure with the woman of the house on a Sunday evening, and was carrying a carpet bag. It is, I think, a very inconsistent and improbable story that I should be carrying a carpet bag at such a time. Here standing and looking into the grave I most solemnly declare that at the time those people swore I was at that place I was in Scotland; and the statements of the others are equally false.

Judge: Is there anything else you wish to say?

Barrett: I would next speak of the boy Morris. His contradictions were so apparent as to the time at which he said he saw me that I think no one would admit that his evidence had any importance and I may pass it by. I will now come to that prince of perverts, Mullany, and his satellites. I will first speak of the boy Morris. He swore on the evening of the explosion that I came to his master's place with my face and neck black with gunpowder. Well, I think, even such a ridiculous assumption requires no comment, and nobody but a puny minded tailor's boy would be guilty of such a fabrication. He was brought here to corroborate his master, Mr. Mullany, and see how far he does it. He swears I spent ten minutes in Mullany's house that evening. Mullany swears he never saw me there. This is what Her Majesty's Attorney-General calls corrobative evidence. Let me see how far the woman Koppel corroborates Mullany. Mullany says I had a full beard all round my face. The woman says I had not. The Attorney-General calls that corroborative evidence. Let us see how Koppel and Morris corroborate each other. The boy swore Mullany sat on his board on the evening of the explosion until eight o'clock and the woman swore that soon after six o'clock she met him in the street drunk. This is what the Attorney-General calls corroborative evidence, and if you, gentlemen of the jury, believe him, you will get few to believe you or the Attorney-General. If one fact more than another could be urged to show the utter groundlessness of these people's statements, it is that Mrs. Mullany has been unable to identify me as the man Jackson; and if she could have done so the Crown would most willingly have brought her here as a witness against me. While dealing with these facts I will just mention one single incident, for which the Attorney-General for all his ingenuity was unable to account. We are told by the informer Mullany that I and Captain Murphy came from Scotland with the avowed intention, and no other, of rescuing Burke from prison. Morris and Koppel, on the other hand, swore that I had been in the habit of visiting Mullany's six weeks before the explosion. On returning to the depositions, I find the warder of the House of Detention states on oath that Burke was only three weeks in prison at the time of the explosion. This is what the evidence of the witnesses is worth when you come to test it by independent facts, and that is what the Attorney-General calls corroborative evidence to send a human being to the scaffold. Now referring to that fiend of iniquity, Mullany, I will pass him over with as few words as possible, as though by the very mention of his name I should inhale a most deadly poison. Him I shall allow to remain in his wretchedness and misery. In the words of Holy Writ: 'When your fear cometh as a desolation, and your destruction cometh as a whirlwind; when distress and anquish cometh upon you. Trouble and anquish will make him afraid; they shall prevail against him, as a King ready to the battle. Men shall clasp their hands at him, and shall hiss him out of his place.' His indeed is a life that no one will envy, and everyone even the most abandoned, will despise him. The very parties who now smile upon him and have recourse to him will spurn him. A thousand times more welcome is death to a criminal convicted of the highest crime than life and so-called liberty at the sacrifice of everything that tends to elevate the human being and renders him worthy of the name of man. With reference to the explosion, I will say just a few words. It is useless for me to enter into protestations of innocence, being fully aware that no declarations of mine will have the slightest tendency to prevent your Lordship from following the course you have determined to pursue. But this I can and will most solemnly declare; there is no one who more deeply commiserates with the sufferers from that explosion and no one who more earnestly deplores the fatal consequences than I do. No, I am not one to rejoice over misery, or find pleasure in the suffering of my fellow creatures, the statement of Mullany to the contrary notwithstanding. Him, even him, I can forgive, and pray that his sufferings may not be so great as he deserves. I would wish to correct a statement that has been made here that I was the author of the explosion. There never was a greater mistake than to give me credit for such an undertaking as that explosion. It was utterly absurd to suppose so, being as I am, a total stranger to acts of daring, and without any experience which would in any way fit me for engaging in such an enterprise, and if it be attributed to the Fenian organization, then it becomes ridiculously absurd. According to Sir Richard Mayne, and the *Pall Mall Gazette*, there are ten thousand armed Fenians in London, and that they should have to send to Glasgow to do this work, and there to select a person of no higher condition and no greater abilities than the humble person who now addresses your Lordship is a stretch of imagination which the disordered minds of the affrighted officials could alone be capable of entertaining. It was said why did I not bring up my master and my lodging house-keeper. I gave the police at Glasgow my late master's name, with whom I had been working for months. The police went and found the place but they carefully avoided to publish. I could have established my innocence. It was urged why did I not bring them to the police court. My solicitor applied for the means to bring them from Glasgow and he was denied. How to account for the conduct of the Governor of Millbank I am at a loss to know. He suppressed a letter I had written to a friend, and sent it to that most respectable gentleman, that notorious detective McCaul of Glasgow, who, with the true ingenuity of a detective, went to McNulty, and so misrepresented the facts to him as to throw him off his guard. I am far from denying, nor will the force of circumstances, compel me to deny my love of my native land. I love my country, and if it is murderous to love Ireland dearer than I love my life, then it is true I am a murderer. If my life were ten times dearer than it is, and if I could by any means redress the wrongs of that persecuted land by the sacrifice of my life I would willingly and gladly do so. As your Lordship has said, I will now turn my attention to that other land where the injustice of selfish mortals cannot follow me, where man has no longer the power to persecute his fellowmen, and where might no longer triumphs over right.[32]

When Barrett was finished Cockburn passed sentence of death adding that there was no hope of reprieve and that Barrett should prepare himself for death. The judge's summing up and comments became a classic example for English law for nearly a century and were quoted in many murder trials until the passing of the Homicide Act of 1957.[33] The rules applied to Irish prisoners in British courts did not admit political motives but allowed the charge of treason or treason-felony. The Clerkenwell Explosion was the first explosion of an Irish bomb in England and the trial led to a number of important rulings. In brief, an act committed for political purposes but known to be dangerous would be treated as premeditated murder if any life was lost. If two or more persons took part in such an act leading to a death all the persons involved were liable to a death sentence and not only the person who did the actual killing intentionally or un-intentially.[34] Cockburn accepted that the Fenians did not aim to kill anyone but he pointed out that the death of Sarah Hodgkinson could have been forseen. A forseen outcome was enough for the law, even if the possible outcome was not wanted. There was logically room for the Fenians to hope that no one would be killed by the explosion but they had the indirect intention as they had taken a reckless chance with full knowledge of the possible consequences. Strangely enough the case is often referred to in law books as 'Desmond's Case' and occasionally as Regina V. Justice, 1868.[35]

Barrett was taken from the dock to the condemned cell at Newgate. The court was hastily prepared for another trial for on the very next day Ricard Burke was to be tried for offences against Queen Victoria and for 'certain overt acts'.

On Tuesday, 28 April 1868, Ricard Burke stood in the dock of the Central Criminal Court of the Old Bailey. He stood where Michael Barrett had made his long speech just twenty-four hours before. At the side of Burke stood Joseph Casey and Henry Mulleda. Casey had been arrested at the same time as Burke but Mulleda had been held without trial for over a year. He had been taken prisoner near Drogheda in March 1867, during the abortive rising.[36] He had been

Burke's assistant in Birmingham and his place had been taken by Joseph Casey.

The original indictment against the three prisoners is still kept at the Old Bailey. The sheet is in neat writing but is rather unwieldy being over thirty feet in length. The main charge was that the prisoners 'did feloniously wickedly and unlawfully compass devise and intend to depose' Queen Victoria from 'the style honour and royal name of the Imperial Crown of the United Kingdom and that they did manifest such intention by certain overt acts' in England and Ireland. Included in the charges were the names of many Fenians who had worked with Ricard Burke. They ranged from the founders of the organization, John O'Mahony and James Stephens, to Michael O'Brien, who had been publicly executed in Manchester five months before. Professional soldiers and revolutionaries like Gustave Cluseret and Octave Fariola were mentioned; they had hoped to take part in a rising in Ireland. Their names were linked with Cesare Orsini and Victor Vilquain and thus with the First International. Both Kelly and Burke had recognized the importance of Radical support in England and had been in contact with English Republicans such as Bradlaugh, Cremer and Odger. One of the Fenian proclamations of 1867 called on the working men of England to recognize that the struggle in Ireland was essentially their struggle as well. The point was immediately accepted by Engels and Marx but both men doubted if the English working class could overcome its chauvinistic and subservient attitude. Marx believed it was 'the direct and absolute interest of the English working class to help overthrow British rule in Ireland and that the English ruling class were invulnerable in England as long as it retained its power over Ireland. Marx had to admit he found it difficult if not impossible to communicate this view to the English workers.

The trial of Ricard Burke was to be a political masterpiece. A demonstration of the power and influence of the British Secret Service and police. At the same time it was to destroy the credibility of the Fenian Movement without arousing sympathy for the prisoners; it was to expose the venality and unreliability of leading members of the movement. The identity of some agents and informers was to be kept secret but broad hints given that the Government had much more information available and the power to use it if republicans continued to support the Movement.

The Manchester trial had been badly managed. Its injustice had aroused world wide criticism and brought sympathy and support to the Fenians involved. The executions had brought Ireland to the point of revolt. The Clerkenwell trial with its obvious perjury had been unsatisfactory for the Government and only one of the six prisoners had been convicted. The trial of Ricard Burke was a third chance for the Government to appear omnipotent, merciful but just. In the Clerkenwell trial Burke had been named as the originator of the explosion and identified as the leader of the Fenian Movement in England. He was not being tried on a capital charge so the case lacked the drama and volatile emotion of a fight for life. But if found guilty he could be sentenced to penal servitude, to suffer conditions that many Irish political prisoners were to find as fatal as the death sentence but with the agony prolonged.

Two judges, Alexander Cockburn and John Bramwell, tried the case. The prosecution team was the same as for the Clerkenwell trial and was led by the Attorney-General and the Solicitor-General. The defence was stronger however as the American Government had instructed its Ambassador in England to obtain legal assistance for Burke. The ambassador had obtained the services of the leading radical lawyer of the day, Ernest Jones. Jones had much experience of such trials, he was unwell and near the end of his life, but he fought the case with the same energy he had shown in defending Feargus O'Connor at the time of the Chartist trials twenty years before. His own views on Ireland were well known. As early as 1848 he had written 'There are times and circumstances when not to fight is treason. The Irish understand this well . . . as an English Chartist it is my duty to aid them by every means.' In 1855 he had helped form the International Committee to work for Polish, Finnish and Irish political freedom. In the following year he addressed himself to the men of Ireland 'Your foes are our foes, your hopes are our hopes, your battle is our battle . . . Ireland for the Irish . . . if we unite we are invincible.'[37]

Ernest Jones for the defence attacked even before the trial opened; he asked for a jury *de mediate linguae*. This little used right in British law allowed an alien to ask for a jury to contain a number of his own countrymen. The Attorney-General ridiculed the request and claimed that as Burke was born in Ireland he owed allegiance to Britain. Ernest Jones produced an American passport belonging to Burke and called an American lawyer to show that Burke was an American citizen and a former officer in the American Army. The British claim that American citizens of Irish birth were still British was a contentious matter for the American government; the claim was soon to be withdrawn as part of the Alabama Settlement. The two judges decided not to accept the evidence of American citizenship but the point was taken and charges of treason were not pressed.

The prosecution case was long, detailed and confusing. The variety of names used by Burke and Mulleda, added to some highly independent spelling by police and secret agents was one source of confusion. Ricard Burke was charged under the name of George Berry; in evidence his first name was given as Ricard, Richard, Rickard, Ricardo or George; his second name varied from Barry, Berry, Bowrie, Brown or Burke to Lawrence, Wallace and Winslow. For good measure he was occasionally confused with Thomas Bourke, a Tipperary Fenian, who had been sentenced to death by hanging, drawing and quartering a few months before.[38] Henry Mulleda was charged under the name of Shaw but was reported as being known as Mulleda, Mullidy, Mullaney, Mulledi or even Mullarky. The permutation of possible names must have bewildered the jury.

The prosecution case was presented by using four informers; John Joseph Corydon, who had turned informer in Liverpool; John Devany, who had identified Burke to the London police; Godfrey Massey, who had turned informer after being betrayed by Corydon; and Patrick Mullany, whose evidence was so vital in Michael Barrett's case.

Red-headed, jaunty John Corydon had been paymaster of the American officers and his defection to the British police was probably the heaviest single blow suffered by the Fenian Movement in England. He had joined the Fenians in 1862 when he was serving in the Irish Brigade of the American Federal Army. At the end of the Civil War he was sent to Ireland and was active in preparations for the rising; he was trusted by the leaders and given important tasks. Like so many Fenians he became disillusioned and discouraged by James Stephen's delay in naming the day for the rising; the erratic supply of funds from American Fenians meant his meagre pay of £1 a week was not always forthcoming. He had an expensive weakness for certain Liverpool ladies and this eventually led to his being arrested in unflattering circumstances in a Liverpool brothel;[39] in this unhappy state he needed little persuasion to change from being an ill-paid Fenian to a well-paid police spy. He gave detailed reports on Fenian plans for diversionary attacks in England. The British authorities learnt of the proposed raid on Chester, the names and location of the American officers, and the date and time of the rising.

Corydon had known Burke in the United States as early as 1862 and had worked with him in England and Ireland; he also knew Mulleda well. Corydon's position in the Fenian Movement had brought him into contact with the smuggling of arms from England to Ireland; he was able to give a detailed account of how arms were bought openly in England, ostensibly for South America, then sent to Ireland marked as American drapery. The crates were addressed to well-known firms and were collected from the docks by Fenian agents. Some arms were stolen from British military depots or brought in by deserters from the Army or County Militias. Corydon's evidence was factual, correct and difficult to shake.

The cross-examination by Ernest Jones ranged over an astonishing variety of subjects, some of them connected with the trial. He asked Corydon about his religion and got the reply 'I am half and half, between Protestant and Catholic. My father was a Protestant and my mother a Roman Catholic. I am a Christian.' Corydon agreed he had given evidence in so many Fenian trials that he had lost count of them; he admitted that juries had acquitted a number of men he had accused of being Fenians. Corydon's personal reputation had already been blackened in previous trials; he had been castigated as being the illegimate child of a Liverpool prostitute after admitting he lived in a brothel with a notorious trollop of the day.

Ernest Jones spent a long time on drawing from Corydon details of payments he had received and hoped to receive. Corydon first claimed he had not received any rewards from the police and that he had given information because he felt he had been swindled by James Stephens; he had been sent on dangerous missions by the Fenian Movement but had received very little pay from America. After some verbal sparring he agreed he had been given board and lodgings by the police, then that he had money for expenses, possibly as much as £250 but not as much as £500. Finally, he agreed 'I expect to be well rewarded for my services . . . I expect some thousands of pounds.' Actually, Corydon was receiving £5 a week plus board and lodging from the London police. He added 'I expect to get as much as will keep me for life.'

The next informer was also an experienced witness at state trials. Ulsterman John Devany had not held high rank in the Fenians but he had known Ricard Burke in America and Britain and was responsible for his arrest. He was closely questioned by Ernest Jones about how much he had earned for giving information and how much he hoped to get. He could not remember how much he had received, agreeing that it was more than £200 in 1867 and nearly as much in the Spring of 1868. He had been to Paris on holiday but added 'I have not thought yet about how much or how little my reward will be.' He agreed he was often in Corydon's company but denied they were sleeping together. A lot of time was spent on Devany's relationship with John Kellyer of New York, the latter claimed that Devany had robbed him and tried to murder him by pushing him into a sewer.

After Devany came Godfrey Massey, who had been in charge of Fenian forces in Ireland pending the arrival of General Gustave

Cluseret. His defection was an astonishing success for the British Secret Service. Like Corydon, Massey had been easily persuaded to accept a substantial reward in return for information. He accepted the money in the hope of starting a new life with ample funds.

In his evidence Massey told how he and Burke had attended the enthusiastic meetings of Fenians in New York; how the demobbed American officers had volunteered their services for a rising in Ireland. He spoke of the meeting with foreign military officers in London and how General Cluseret had been named as Commander; it had been agreed that Cluseret would not take over as military commander until the rising was well under way. Irish-American officers under the general direction of Massey were to start the rising. Massey ended by giving detailed evidence of Burke's work in getting arms and ammunition to Ireland.

The attack on Massey began with his illegitimate birth in Ireland and ended with questions on how much he expected to make from the trial. Massey had been brought up under the name of Philip Condon and the story of his birth had been made public in other trials. His real name was the same as that of an Anglo-Irish military hero of the Crimean War, popularly known as Redan Massey. Godfrey Massey denied on oath that he had passed himself off as Redan Massey, though he had served with the British Army in the Crimea; he also denied deserting from the British Army and he denied reports from New Orleans that his military service in the Confederate Army could be considered as military fiction. Massey denied receiving any payment from the Fenian Movement and claimed he had paid all his own expenses until deciding to change sides. He said 'Since I have turned informer, I have been living on the money that the authorities have supplied me with.' He added he was entirely in the hands of the British Government; he would refuse money offered as a reward for information but would accept British aid while he was so helpless. Massey was feeling the effect of his constant exposure to public scorn. The constant guard on him was irksome but vital because of his fear of being shot; a fear that confidential police reports confirmed as being well founded.[40] He wrote to the British Authorities asking how he was to be disposed of'; he was offered an annuity but rejected this and demanded a lump sum for his services. He got £6 a week for expenses and a number of holidays at Government expense and with a personal bodyguard. His relations in Ireland who feared for their safety were moved to the colonies at Government expense.

Patrick Mullany's role in the trial was minor. He confirmed that Burke used the names of Brown and Winslow and he gave details of Burke's attendance at various meetings.

Much of the trial was taken up with evidence from Birmingham gun dealers. The chief witness from this group being George Kynoch of the famous armaments firm. Kynoch had been doing good business with Burke and appeared to have been remarkably unsuspicious about the possibility of his products being used against British soldiers. In the three weeks between 23 December 1865 and 13 January 1866 he had sold to Burke for cash, two million military percussion caps, a quarter of a million revolver caps, five hundred rifles and bayonets, bullet moulds and implements, and fifty revolvers. He remembered Mulleda and Casey working for Burke in Birmingham but under cross-examination he agreed he had identified Casey as Mulleda and that he could not identify either man with certainty. Kynoch had become quite friendly with Burke, he had presented him with a gilt engraved pistol, and they had exchanged a number of letters. In one of these Burke had referred to German soldiers and modern weapons; he ended with the words 'wait till they keep it up for four long years; won't there be a fine field in Germany then for the sale of crape?' In another letter Burke referred to Liverpool as 'a dull, dirty, disgusting town, a modern Gomorrah, with the din of a thousand Babels'.

Railwaymen from the London and North-Western Railway Company gave evidence of dealing with crates sent by Burke to Liverpool. They said he used the name of Lawrence. They were unwilling to identify Burke, Casey or Mulleda with certainty. A similar uncertainty afflicted most of the Irish witnesses. An Englishman, Henry Fisher, who claimed he was certain he could identify Mulleda was cross-examined by the defence. Fisher reluctantly agreed he had lost his job with the railway company after complaints about his heavy drinking and general unreliability; he agreed even more reluctantly that he had got money under false pretenses by pretending to his fellow workers that his child had died and he had no money for the funeral; he was even forced to admit he had abandoned his children to the workhouse. It must have been an embarrassing afternoon for him and his credibility as a witness was damaged.

Finally police officers gave evidence linking Burke and Mulleda with Fenian activities in England and Ireland. The result of the trial was never in doubt and it came as a surprise at the end of the prosecution case when the Attorney-General announced that the case against Casey was to be dropped; he was discharged as not guilty and left the court. The jury quickly found Burke and Mulleda guilty. Judge Baron Bramwell announced a sentence of fourteen years penal servitude for Richard Burke and seven years penal servitude for Mulleda. Neither man spoke before the sentences were announced.

## NOTES

1.   West Middlesex Coroner's Court Register, 1867.
2.   Indictment at Old Bailey.
3.   Mullany statement (unclassified) at New Scotland Yard.
4.   Glasgow Chief Constable's Letter Book, 1868.
5.   *Ibid.*
6.   *Ibid.*
7.   Mullany statement (unclassified) at New Scotland Yard.
8.   Clogher Record, 1967. p.276.
9.   English statement (unclassified) at New Scotland Yard.
10.  M. Ryan, *Fenian Memories*, 1946, p.127.
11.  Census Return, 1851.
12.  Y. Kapp, *Eleanor Marx*, 1972, p.85.
13.  *C.C.C. Sessions Papers*, Vol. LXVII, 1868, p.497.
14.  Ibid, p.530.
15.  Ibid, p.540.
16.  *The Irish Times* 25 April 1868.
17.  M. Williams, *Leaves of a Life*, Vol. 1, p.182, 1890.
18.  Mullany statement (unclassified) at New Scotland Yard.
19.  M. Williams, *op. cit.*, p. 191, 1890.
20.  *The Times* 21 April 1868.
21.  M. Williams *op. cit.*, p. 103, 1890.
22.  *Daily Telegraph* 1968.
23.  *The Irish Times* 7 June 1968.
24.  Enniskillen Summer Assizes Charge Book, June 1797.
25.  T. Pakenham, *The Year of Liberty*, 1969, p.317.
26.  Drumkeeran Charity School Roll Book, 1797.
27.  J.E. Handley, *The Irish in Modern Scotland*, 1947, p.85.
28.  *Ibid*, p.88.
29.  Annual Register, 1868,
30.  C.C.C. Sessions Papers, Vol. LXVII, 1868, p.486-552.
31.  B.O'Donnell, *The Old Bailey and its Trials*, 1950, p.145.
32.  M. Williams *op. cit.*, p.196—203, 1890.
33.  H.L.A. Hart, *Punishment and Responsibility*, 1968, p.256.
34.  L. Fairfield, *Trial of Peter Barnes and Others*, 1953, pp.119 & 256.
35.  R. Cross and P.A. Jones, *Introduction to Criminal Law*, 1964, p.135.
36.  J. Devoy *Recollections* p.232. See also CSO Registered Papers 1867/22488.
37.  *Northern Star* 26 February 1848. See also J. Saville *Ernest Jones* p.27 and p.216.
38.  L. O'Broin *Fenian Fever* p.174.
39.  D Ryan *The Phoenix Flame* p.146.
40.  C.S.O. Papers 1867/14459.

# Chapter 9

## *The Last Public Execution*

The Government's pleasure in the handling and result of the trial of Ricard Burke was diminished by growing protests about the death sentence pronounced on Michael Barrett. The protests would have been stronger if it had been known at the time that Lord Chief Justice Cockburn was unconvinced of the justice of the result; another Government official who was unconvinced was John Mallon, Superintendent of the Dublin police, who wrote that Barrett did not cause the explosion though he was involved in the rescue attempt. According to Mallon another Fenian with an unusual name beginning with 'Q' was responsible.[1] Mallon felt that the death sentence on Barrett was a political execution.

There were many requests for a reprieve or a re-trial. On the Continent the press condemned the manner and result of the trial and even in Britain the national papers expressed their dissatisfaction. The *Daily Telegraph* editorial claimed that the trial was unsatisfactory and added 'while the police charged six persons with the crime, they have afforded sufficient proof to convict only one. The case against O'Keefe and Ann Justice utterly broke down, and, when sifted, that of Desmonds and English seems to be far from completed. The police have manifestly failed . . .'[2] In Parliament John Bright called for a re-trial and several Members expressed their disbelief in the justice of the trial. The Government agreed to make further enquiries and to postpone Barrett's execution.

There was strong pressure on the Government to carry out the execution. Queen Victoria in a letter to the Home Secretary said she was grieved 'to see the failure of the evidence against all but one of the Clerkenwell criminals . . . it seems dreadful for these people to escape . . . one begins to wish that these Fenians should be lynch-lawed and on the spot. What is to be done about Barrett?'[3]

In Parliament Conservative Members called for firm action and the immediate execution of Barrett. They were led by C.N.Newdegate, an eccentric M.P. who for twenty-five years had pursued a vendetta against the Catholic and Jewish minorities in England.[4] Feeling in the House of Commons was exacerbated by an Irish Member who asked if the Government intended to ask the Queen to abdicate in favour of her son, Edward. The Speaker refused to accept the question on the grounds that the question was not couched in respectful or parliamentary language. The general feeling in Parliament was strongly anti-Irish and the consensus of opinion was that even if Barrett was not guilty of causing the Clerkenwell Explosion he was a self-confessed nationalist, a Catholic and a Fenian and should therefore be executed. Two shootings at this time harmed effects to gain a reprieve for Barrett. In Canada, Thomas D'Arcy McGee was assassinated and in Australia, the Duke of Edinburgh was shot and wounded; in both cases the attacker, alleged to be a Fenian, was given a hasty trial and executed. Thomas McGee, poet, writer and politician, was born in County Louth Ireland. He had taken part in the 1848 rising and had escaped to America with a price on his head. He founded *The Nation* newspaper in New York and *The American Celt* in Boston before emigrating to Canada. His political career in Canada was meteoric and he became a Cabinet Minister and one of the founders of the Canadian Confederation. Gradually he changed his views on the Fenian movement and he denounced the Fenian raids on Canada. The Duke of Edinburgh, a son of Queen Victoria, was on a tour of the world in 1867-8; the tour had attracted little publicity except when it was reported that the Duke had asked 'to see a lewd hula-hula dance'.[5] The Duke's wound was not dangerous and he recovered quickly. The Australian legislatures took the opportunity to rush through some strong anti-republican laws; a person failing to join a loyal toast or expressing sympathy for Fenians, or suggesting the peaceful separation of Australia from British rule, became liable to a sentence of two years hard labour.[6]

The Home Office sent representatives to Glasgow to test the alibi put forward by Barrett. Details of their search were not made public, but press and public opinion hardened to the view that Barrett should be hanged. Editors took the stand that the evidence of the informers and witnesses was good enough in the circumstances; the circumstances being that, on Michael Barrett's own showing, he was involved in the Fenian movement. A few papers described the trial and death sentence as judicial murder but most saw the outcome of the trial as an act of justice. The Glasgow investigation produced little new evidence. Most of Barrett's friends had left for America; one girl came forward to say he was with her—until

Five leading members of the IRB. A photo taken in 1871. From left to right:– John Devoy, Charles O'Connell, Harry Mulleda, Jeremiah O'Donovan Rossa and John McClure. (Author's collection)

Robert Anderson (1841-1918). Dublin born author and lawyer. Special adviser to the Home Office on Fenianism. Organised secret service activities against Fenians. (Author's collection)

midnight on Thursday, 12 December, but later she changed her story.[7]

In Parliament John Bright and John Stuart Mill asked for clemency for Barrett. The Home Secretary, Gathorne Hardy, said that the Lord Chief Justices Cockburn and Baron Bramwell had reconsidered the case and taken into account additional evidence in the hands of the Government. John Bright pointed out that a decision was being made based on evidence not tested in open court. In fact, Alexander Cockburn had expressed the opinion that the court decision was not sound in law; he had been persuaded by Robert Anderson of the Secret Service that the sentence should stand.[8] The Home Secretary was under much pressure at the time from Queen Victoria and he was relieved to be able to order a second postponement of the execution; the official reason being the need for more time to consider the evidence. In his diary, Gathorne Hardy noted that the Queen had become anxious about appearing in London to open St Thomas' Hospital; she had asked 'that the public should not be allowed too close to any part of the route to be taken'. He added to his note 'the delay of Barrett's execution may be useful as there will be nothing to raise revengeful feelings'. The Home Secretary had studied the report of the trial and wrote 'I am morally convinced that Barrett has been rightly convicted'.[9]

Barrett himself seems to have had little hope of a reprieve. The British press noted that no member of his family called to see him. In Fermanagh his mother, a widow with two young children, had walked six miles through heavy snow to beg the local M.P. to help efforts to gain a reprieve; the Unionist Member, Captain M.E. Archdale, had scornfully rejected her plea and told her that her son and all other Fenians should be hanged, the sooner the better. A century later the bitter rejection was still remembered and quoted in Fermanagh.

On 25 May Michael Barrett was told the Home Secretary had rejected all pleas for mercy and that the execution would take place on the following day. Contrary to custom Barrett was not to be allowed to make a speech on the scaffold; the Government did not wish to have a repetition of the remarkable speech in the Old Bailey. The warders commented that Barrett was calm and dignified during his four weeks in the condemned cell; he spent much of the time with Fr. Hussey, a Catholic priest from Moorfields Church. The warders also noted that Barrett never claimed to be in Glasgow on 13 December but only that he was convicted on insufficient evidence and that he had never committed murder.[10]

On the eve of the execution the sheriffs and under-sheriffs of London arrived. Outside armed police and troops began taking up their positions. William Calcraft arrived to do his grim work for a fee of twenty guineas. He was an old man, fond of brandy, with a reputation for being a chronic bungler.[11] It was his practice to climb on the back of his victim to kill him if the length of rope had been miscalculated. One newspaper reported Calcraft to be a good and tenderhearted man, an habitual frequenter of the Church of England, modest, unassuming, white-haired and venerable in appearance. Other papers described him as hard-hearted, cruel, low living, a crouching fawning wretch.[12] He was public executioner for England for forty years.

It was well known that the execution was to be the last public execution in England and a large crowd was expected. By 11 p.m. nearly two thousand were present outside the gaol and the local bars did a roaring trade. There were a few songs as patriotic onlookers sang 'Rule Britannia', 'Champagne Charlie' and 'Oh my, I've got to die'. Contrary to expectation the crowd did not grow much during the night. Spectators took their places in the Magpie and Stump public house and in other houses facing the gaol. Prices for a room with a view of the execution went as high as £10. One shopkeeper declared he had not fallen so low as to let his windows to see a fellow creature strangled and he turned down all offers and requests.[13] Spectators had to be present by 5 a.m. or the reserved seats were not guaranteed.

At 7.30 a.m. the bell of St. Sepulchre's began to toll slowly. There was a cry from the crowd 'hats off', but otherwise there was little noise or confusion. A few men were drunk, singing and shouting, but there was little sign of the levity and vulgarity that usually marked executions in England. It was noted that a number of Irishmen and girls were in the crowd, silent and tense. A solitary street preacher was listened to quietly.

Michael Barrett was called at 6.30 and received Communion from Fr. Hussey at 7 a.m. As the bell of St. Sepulchre's started to toll, Calcraft entered the condemned cell and began to pinion Barrett. There was no struggle and the priest began the prayers for the dying. Barrett was led through a long corridor. The walls were scratched with initials marking the graves of executed prisoners.[14] He walked firmly and answered the prayers of Fr. Hussey in a cool voice. His face was pale. Observers reported his demeanour as being remarkably firm without a trace of bravado.[15] He was dressed in the same suit of Donegal tweed he had worn at the time of his arrest and trial. Barrett walked up the steps to the scaffold. As he came into view there was a cheer from the crowd, plus a few boos and hisses. Barrett ignored the scene and seemed attentive only to the voice of the priest beside him. When Calcraft came into view there was a burst of boos and hisses from the crowd. Near the foot of the scaffold stood William Desmond and by his side was a heavily veiled young woman;[16] she was crying. Calcraft quickly placed a hood over Barrett's head and put the noose round his neck. Barrett spoke to Calcraft through the hood and asked for the rope to be adjusted.

The bolt was drawn and the drop fell with a loud boom. Barrett's body plunged down and he died without a struggle. A great cry came from the crowd. Not an exclamation or a scream, but with elements of both. The body hung for an hour and the immense crowd waited in a slowly shifting mass. When nine o'clock struck there were calls of 'Come on, body snatcher' and 'Take away the man you've killed'. Calcraft appeared and cut down the body amid a storm of yells and execrations seldom heard from such a crowd.[17] There was nothing more to be seen and the crowd dispersed quickly.

At the time of the execution the Home Secretary was in church. He walked back to his house and had a long discussion with Alexander Cockburn. He confided to his diary 'Cockburn finally gave his opinion that there were no grounds to mistrust the verdict . . . the examination of the pocketbook by an expert was really conclusive as to the writing in it. Poor man! His suffering are now over as I have just heard from Sir Richard Mayne. I cannot doubt his guilt from the direct testimony'. Barrett's friends kept up their efforts until the last moment and Gathorne Hardy recorded 'McCorry whom I believe to be without truth or scruple has kept telegraphing that he had more evidence and threatened me with responsibility. God grant that I may have exercised it wisely and truly. I have done my best.'[18] The Home Secretary received a number of letters, some signed, accusing him of the murder of Barrett. Among those who wrote was William Smith, Vicar of Overbury, near Shrewsbury. Sombre thoughts did not last long for Gathorne Hardy for he had an invitation to the jollifications at the Marlborough Wedding breakfast; the next day was Derby Day, Parliament took a holiday and the weather was perfect.

That evening a death mask of Michael Barrett was made for the prison museum. The face was calm and composed with no sign of the violent death.[19] The body was taken to the corridor outside the condemned cell and buried in the presence of the Governor and various officials.

In 1870 a Mr. S.J. O'Halloran of 38 Union Street, Lambeth, wrote to Prime Minister Gladstone and asked for permission to have the bodies of executed Fenians removed to 'the land they loved not wisely but too well'. O'Halloran added 'the majority of my countrymen, while they deeply deplore such crimes as the deceased have been found guilty of, yet they believe in the innocence of the victims named.' (Allen, Barrett, Larkin and O'Brien.) He pointed out that the American Government had returned the body of Lincoln's assassin, while even the body of the mass murderer, Haupmann, had been returned by the French Government. He appealed to Gladstone to show a spirit of generosity and forgiveness by allowing the bodies to be taken back to Ireland for burial. 'By such an act of clemency on your part you will merit the fervent prayers of the Irish people.'[21] Gladstone replied with stiff formality that the application had been referred to the Irish Government, the legal synonym for the British authorities in Ireland. Dublin Castle passed the request to the Home Office and so the body of Michael Barrett remained in the company of those who lie in prison graves; the after death punishment of the Government lasting until the more humane days of Harold Wilson.

In 1902 Newgate Prison was pulled down and the site cleared. Barrett's body was moved to the City of London Cemetery in Manor Park, Ilford. The remains of all prisoners buried in the long corridor were disinterred and reburied in fifty cases in six adjoining graves.[22] Plot 340 is a grass covered expanse, there is nothing to mark graves 42928-42933. In one of these graves rests Michael Barrett.

**NOTES**

1.  F.M. Bussey, *Irish Conspiracies* Recollections of John Mallon, 1910, p. 156.
2.  *Daily Telegraph* 28 April 1868.
3.  Queen Victoria to Gathorne Hardy (Lord Cranbrook) 1 May 1868.
4.  D.N.B.
5.  *Irishman* 5 February 1870 (quoting *Melbourne Daily Telegraph*).
6.  *Banner of Ulster* 26 May 1868.
7.  *Irish Catholic Banner* 16 May 1868.
8.  R. Anderson, *The Lighter Side of My Official Life*, 1910, p.16.
9.  Lord Cranbrook's Private Diary 11 May 1868.
10. Annual Register, 1868, p.65.
11. A. Glynn, *High Upon the Gallows Tree*, 1967, p.119.
12. D.N.B.
13. *Banner of Ulster* 26 May 1868.
14. B. Holmes, *London Burial Places*, 1896, p.320.
15. *Essex Standard*, 29 May 1868.
16. *Irishman* 6 June 1868.
17. C. Duff, *A Handbook of Hanging*, 1961, p.155.
18. Lord Cranbrook's Private Diary 26 May 1868.
19. R. Harris (Ed.) *Reminiscences of Sir Henry Hawkins*, 1904, Vol. 1, p.166.
20. *Irishman* 6 June 1868.
21. H.O., O.S.//99/412.
22. Ilford (City of London) Cemetery Register; 1902-1903.

# Chapter 10

## *The Aftermath*

Burke and Mulleda were removed from Newgate and began a painful tour of Chatham, Millbank, Portland and Woking prisons. Conditions in English prisons in 1868 were harsh to the point of being sadistic. Absolute silence was enforced, the food was poor and insufficient, the discipline harsh. The Irish political prisoners were treated more harshly than the ordinary British criminals and Ricard Burke, having been openly blamed for the Clerkenwell Explosion suffered more than others. In two years seven Fenians died in gaol, four committed suicide, and four went completely mad. An official British enquiry into gaol conditions found that one Fenian prisoner Jeremiah O'Donovan Rossa had spent 123 days on a bread and water punishment diet, 231 days on a penal class diet in a darkened cell, 28 days in a completely dark cell, and 34 days with his hands manacled behind his back, after this he was occasionally punished for singing.[1] The report added 'the signal failure of all repressive measures in this case, furnishes a most forcible illustration of the necessity of separating prisoners of this class from ordinary criminals. Such conspicious and successful defiance of discipline is in itself a scandal of prison life and a most dangerous example to the other convicts.'[2]

The treatment of Burke and other American citizens led to the American Ambassador asking for some relief for them; in the American Senate questions were asked about the suffering of ex-American officers in British gaols.[3] In London the International Working Men's Association wrote to the Home Secretary urging the mitigation of the severe treatment of Irish prisoners.[4] By December, 1869, Burke's physical and mental condition had reached breaking point. He was removed to Woking Prison Hospital and received the last sacraments. A report that he had been poisoned was widely circulated. Karl Marx interrupted a meeting of the First International to announce that a report of Burke's death had been received.[5]

The work of the Amnesty League saved his life. When he was released in 1872 he went to the County Cork and was nursed back to health. He went to America where he made a complete recovery and took a leading part in Irish-American affairs. He campaigned on behalf of presidential candidates and made a number of lecture tours. He supervised the building of the Laredo-Mexico City railway and after this was appointed Assistant City Engineer of Chicago.[6] At the age of forty-five he met and eloped with a young American girl from Fort Wayne;[7] the marriage was a happy one. Two children were born but the death of his only son at an early age was a great blow to Burke.

Ricard Burke introduced Charles Stewart Parnell to the American House of Representatives during the historic visit of 1880.[8] In 1915 he went to Ireland and spoke with Padraig Pearse at the funeral of O'Donovan Rossa, thus making a direct link between the men of the 1867 rising and the leader of the 1916 rising.[9] Burke died in Chicago in 1922 and was buried in Mount Olivet Cemetery. His funeral was an impressive ceremony; the requiem mass was attended by Bishop Thomas O'Reilly and six priests. Military, political and civic leaders followed the coffin which was draped in the American and Irish flags; among the pall-bearers were John Devoy and Edward Dunne, former Governor of Illinois. The funeral oration was by Fr. Frank McCabe, former President of St. Paul University, Chicago. He took the text 'I have fought the good fight; I have kept the faith'.[10]

Henry Mulleda went to America on his release in 1871. He played a big part in the efforts to unite the various Fenian groups in the United States. His experiences in gaol proved too much for his physique and he died in 1876, possibly by suicide,[11] at the age of thirty-six.

Joseph Casey, who had escaped a prison sentence, went with three brothers to Paris. One of his brothers was killed in the Franco-Prussian War of 1870-71 and another died of wounds soon afterwards. Casey worked for the New York *Herald* and took part in Irish republican activities in Paris. He married and had a family.[12] Today he is remembered more for his links with James Joyce than with the Fenians. James Joyce had learnt about the Fenians in his Dublin days; his father had been a drinking companion of Captain Weldon who had piloted the ship that took James Stephens to safety after his 1865 escape.[13] James Stephens and John O'Leary had been living in Dublin when Joyce was there. In Paris James Joyce was pleased to look up Joseph Casey and to listen to stories of the Fenians in England. The events of Clerkenwell are traced in the 'Proteus' section of *Ulysses* and Casey has been identified as Kevin Egan.[14]

James Murphy, the organizer of the Clerkenwell Rescue attempt, escaped to France and spent some time in Paris. He returned to America and gave a full report of his work to a Fenian convention in 1868. He spent the rest of his days in the United States, working first as Superintendent of national cemeteries and later as a New York tax collector.[15] He played an active part in Irish-American political activities. He died in New York in 1891.

In 1872 the Glasgow police reported to the Home Office that Felix Fallon, who had given shelter to Michael Barrett in London, had been found and identified. He was living at 132 Barrack Street, Glasgow, under the name of James Carrol; he was reported to have been injured in the Clerkenwell Explosion. It was decided that no action be taken against him owing to the difficulty of tracing witnesses.[16]

Peter McCorry emigrated to America when the *Irish Catholic Banner* failed in Glasgow. He succeeded John O'Mahony as editor of the *Irish People*. Later on he became editor of the *Catholic Herald* in Boston and New York.[17]

Colonel Kelly lived until 1908 holding a position in the New York Custom House. He is buried in Woodlawn cemetery New York. A plaque in honour of Colonel Kelly was recently unveiled in Tuam and the three men executed in Manchester are commemorated by annual ceremonies in Manchester and in many parts of Ireland. The memory of Michael Barrett however, has faded even in his native Fermanagh.[18] For a time the term 'Mick Barretts' was used as a perjorative for nationalists, this was shortened to 'Micks' and was the origin of the term 'Mick' bestowed on all Irishmen and oddly enough on members of the Irish Guards Regiment serving in the British Army.

In contrast to the Manchester Martyrs there is no memorial to Michael Barrett though there have been calls to erect one in Fermanagh and in Dublin. His name is included on the National Monuments in Cork and Dublin and an annual memorial service was held in Cork until recent years. The first Republican Club in Irvinestown, Co. Fermanagh, was known as the Michael Barrett Club. The Sinn Fein Club in Irvinestown was also named after Michael Barrett.[19] In 1968 an exhibition to mark the centenary of the last public execution was held in the London Museum; it attracted a large attendance. References to Michael Barrett appeared in the national papers.

Michael Barrett's grim prophecy about the future of Patrick Mullany came true. Mullany got £100 from the British Government and free travel to Australia. He led a short and miserable life there and died a violent death. A Melbourne paper reported

His existence here was a miserable prolongation of the life he had saved by his infamous treachery . . . . Despite frequent moves and changes of name. 'sooner or later, his infamy was exposed, and retribution followed him. He had led the life of a hunted dingo in this colony, and in the painful death there must have been the bitter accumulation of all the sufferings of his life since he purchased it with Barrett's blood.'[20]

Two little-known memorial tablets commemorate the Clerkenwell Explosion. One is set in the former prison wall and marks the section damaged in the attack; the wall is now part of Hugh Myddelton School. A number of cells still exist under the school. The second memorial is in the parish church of St. James, Clerkenwell. It was unveiled by Prime Minister Benjamin Disraeli in 1868. The plaque gives the names of the six persons killed by the explosion and buried in Finchley: Minnie Abbott, William Clutton, Humphrey Evans, Martha Evans, Sarah Hodgkinson and Martha Thompson.

The Clerkenwell Gaol was largely rebuilt and became the Hugh Myddelton Schools. The schools were opened by King Edward VII, then Prince of Wales, on 13 December 1893, the anniversary of the Clerkenwell Explosion. Guy Alfred, the youngest boy in the school made a presentation to the Prince; this was possibly a traumatic experience for young Guy as later in life he became a republican.[21] The area seems to have an attraction for explosives, being hit by a zeppelin bomb in World War I and by a 1000 lb. bomb in the World War II.[22]

But a postscript was written in 1973 when a car bomb exploded by the Old Bailey; it was on the spot where Michael Barrett had died over a century before. Perhaps the spot was chosen by republicans as appropriate for that reason but more probably it was seen as a symbol of British rule and law in Northern Ireland. History has a curious way of coming full circle.

## NOTES

1.  J. O'Donovan Rossa, *My Years in English Jails*, 1874.
2.  Devon Report, 1870: report of Dr. R.D. Lyons.
3.  W. D'Arcy, *The Fenian Movement in the United States*, 1947, p.341.
4.  *Documents of the First International*, Vol. III, p.190, n.d.
5.  *Documents of the First International*, Vol. III, p.200, n.d.
6.  *Devoy's Post Bag*, 1948, Vol. 1, p.36.
7.  J. Devoy, *Recollections*, 1929, p.361.
8.  *Irish Independent* 5 October 1956.
9.  *Ibid.*
10. *Gaelic American* 27 May 1922.
11. *Devoy's Post Bag*, 1948, Vol. 1, p.13.

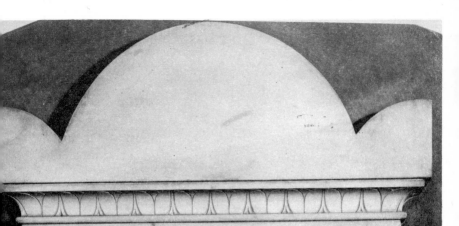

## IN MEMORY OF

THE VICTIMS OF THE TERRIBLE OUTRAGE WHICH OCCURRED IN THIS PARISH

ON FRIDAY, DECEMBER 13TH 1867.

PERPETRATED BY CERTAIN MISGUIDED AND WICKED PERSONS, WHO, BEING MEMBERS OF THE SO-CALLED

### FENIAN CONSPIRACY

AND, SEEKING TO RELEASE ONE OF THEIR CONFEDERATES FROM THE ADJOINING HOUSE OF DETENTION,

PLACED A BARREL OF POWDER AGAINST THE NORTHERN WALL OF THE PRISON,

AND, FIRING THE SAME SUDDENLY RENDERED THE IMMEDIATE LOCALITY A MASS OF RUINS

THREE PERSONS WERE KILLED AT THE MOMENT OF THE EXPLOSION:—

| WILLIAM CLUTTON. | AGED 47 YEARS. |
| SARAH HODGKINSON. | „ 30 „ |
| MINNIE JULIA ABBOTT. | „ 7 „ |

THREE OTHERS DIED IN THE HOSPITAL, WITHIN A FEW DAYS:—

| HUMPHREY EVANS. | AGED 67 YEARS. |
| MARTHA EVANS, | „ 65 „ |
| MARTHA ELIZABETH THOMPSON. | „ 11 „ |

THESE SIX PERSONS WERE BURIED IN ONE GRAVE IN THE CEMETERY AT FINCHLEY.

NINE OTHER DEATHS OCCURRED FROM THE EFFECTS OF THE EXPLOSION

MORE THAN FORTY PERSONS WERE REMOVED TO THE HOSPITALS MOST OF THEM DISABLED AND INJURED FOR LIFE

SIX HUNDRED FAMILIES SUFFERED LOSS OR PRIVATION BY DAMAGE DONE TO WORK, HOME, FURNITURE, &c.

A RELIEF FUND WAS SPEEDILY RAISED

UNDER THE AUSPICES OF A LOCAL COMMITTEE WHICH REACHED THE MUNIFICENT SUM OF £10.075

EXPENDED IN TEMPORARY ASSISTANCE, AND IN MAKING PROVISION FOR THOSE PERMANENTLY DISABLED

THE DAMAGE TO HOUSE PROPERTY WAS MET BY A VOTE OF £7.500 FROM THE EXCHEQUER

KINDLY PROMOTED BY THE RIGHT HON. BENJAMIN DISRAELI, M.P. FIRST LORD OF THE TREASURY

AND THE RIGHT HON. C. WARD HUNT M.P. CHANCELLOR OF THE EXCHEQUER.

AS AN EXPRESSION OF SYMPATHY WITH THE SUFFERERS, TO PERPETUATE THE MEMORY OF THE EVENT, AND IN GRATEFUL RECORD

OF THE LIBERALITY AND KINDNESS OF THOSE WHO VISITED AND RELIEVED THE AFFLICTED

### THIS TABLET IS ERECTED.

| FREDK. WM. WILLCOCKS. | } CHURCHWARDENS | ROBERT MACUIRE, M.A. |
| RICHARD NUNN. | TREASURERS OF RELIEF FUND. | VICAR OF CLERKENWELL. |
| ROBERT PAGET, VESTRY CLERK. | | CHAIRMAN OF RELIEF COMMITTEE. |
| HON. SEC. | | |

The memorial plaque in the Church of St. James, Clerkenwell. (Author's collection)

ALLEN, LARKIN AND O'BRIEN
TIM DALY.
LAURENCE KELLY.
GENERAL THOMAS F. BOURKE
JAMES STEPHENS.
COLONEL JOHN O'MAHONY.
COLONEL JOHN O'NEILL.
CAPTAIN MACKEY.
COLOUR SERGEANT McCARTHY.
SERGEANT DARROW
BRYAN DILLON.
JOHN LYNCH.
CHARLES U. O'CONNELL.
EDWARD KELLY.
EDWARD DUFFEY.
THOMAS D. REILLY.
THOMAS CLARKE LUBY.
CHARLES J. KICKHAM.
DANIEL FITZPATRICK.
PATRICK AND JOHN O'CALLAGHAN
DAVID BARRY.

COLONEL RICKARD BOURKE
MICHAEL BARRETT.
J. J. GEARY.
JOHN BOYLE O'REILLY.
JOHN J. COUGHLIN.
P. F. BARRY.
DENIS D. MULCAHY.
EDMOND O'LOUGHLIN.
MARK ADAMS.
JOHN O'CONNOR.
JAMES MOUNTAIN.
DOMINICK O'MAHONY.
PATRICK O'HERLIHY.
WILLIAM HASSETT.
JACK DONOHUE.
DRUM MAJOR BUTLER.
GENERAL HALPIN.
COLONEL NAGLE.
CATHERINE, MARCHIONESS OF QUEENSBERRY
THE DEVOTED FRIEND OF THE MANCHESTER MARTYRS
GOD SAVE IRELAND.

CHARLES GUILFOYLE DORANCE
JEREMIAH O'DONOVAN ROSSA.

CHARLES O'CONNELL.
MICHAEL EGAR.
VICE CHAIRMAN MONUMENT COMMITTEE
DENIS O'CALLAGHAN ALD HON TREASURER
JOHN J. CROWLEY CHAIRMAN.

MAURICE SCANNELL.
P. N. FITZGERALD.

TIMOTHY O'CALLAGHAN
RICHARD BARRETT.
RICHARD CRONIN ALD.
MICHAEL POWER.
THOMAS WALSH.

JAMES HOURICAN.
PATRICK DYNAN.
JOHN McCARTHY.
PHILIP M'O'KEEFFE.
JOHN O'LEARY.

The National Monument in Cork includes the names of William Allen,
Michael Barrett, Michael Larkin and Michael O'Brien who were executed
in public in England, 1867-8. Ricard O'Sullivan Burke of Cork is
commemorated but strangely his name at the top of the plinth includes two
spelling mistakes. (Courtesy of *Cork Examiner*)

12. H. Gorman, *James Joyce*, 1941, p.102.
13. J. Ryan (Ed.), *A Bash in the Tunnel*, 1970, p.128.
14. M. Brown, *The Politics of Irish Literature*, 1972, p.224.
15. J. Denieffe, *A Personal Narrative of the I.R.B.*, 1906, p.109.
16. Papers relating to P. Mullany. Unclassified at New Scotland Yard.
17. W. D'Arcy, *The Fenian Movement in the United States*, 1947, p. 374.
18. *Irish Independent* 27 May 1962.
19. *Irish Independent* 7 June 1962.
20. *ADVOCATE* (Melbourne) 29 September 1879.
21. G.A. Aldred, *No Traitor's Gait*, 1955.
22. P. Quinlivan, *History of Hugh Myddelton North School*, 1955, p. 12.

# Chapter 11

## *The Amnesty Movement*

One of the most significant aspects of the Fenian period in England was the combination of groups which pleaded for amnesty for the Fenian prisoners. The Manchester episode had led to the intercession of various strands of radical opinion on behalf of the condemned men. After the failure of the Fenian Movement to achieve a successful uprising, the legacy of imprisoned Fenians became the focal point for sympathizers with the Irish cause.

The Manchester executions followed in the wake of a spontaneous agitation at the emotional level. This was almost a rehearsal for the movement which developed in the Autumn of 1869 for the release of the prisoners detained and transported.

The *Reynolds Newspaper*[1] served as a channel for much of the news and correspondence concerning the Movement. The minutes of the I.W.M.A.[2] reveal the distinctive part played by that organization in the Movement. But amongst the bodies which took part in the famous Hyde Park Amnesty demonstrations on 24 October 1869 were the St. Patrick's Brotherhood, the United Labourers, the International Democratic Association, the Clerkenwell and Holborn branches of the Reform League, the Workingman's Political League and various Irish Temperance and Friendly Societies.

Writing to *Reynolds Newspaper* from the Central Committee room at 35 Brooke Street, Holborn, on that day, Joseph Patrick McDonnell, the honorary secretary announced that:

> united masses of English, Irish, French, Italian and other nationalities in London will give their final verdict in favour of unconditional amnesty...
>
> The enlightened masses of the capital of the British Empire shall tomorrow in respectful but resolute terms send forth the cry which shall be heard in every town and hamlet of the United Kingdom — Give back to Ireland her suffering children.

The note of internationalism in the notice to 'People of All Nations' in the letter quoted and the I.W.M.A. was a remarkable demonstration of the refusal of radicals a hundred years ago to compromise with chauvinist and religious sentiment that had manifested themselves during the Murphy riots. Few demonstrations of the Left today make their appeal on such an international scale, and this perhaps represents the first self-conscious stirring of a sense of international identity on the part of radicals, socialists and 'freedom fighters' from the new emerging nations of Europe.

Elaborate police precautions were taken for the demonstrations while the Chairman of the English Amnesty Committee, Josiah Merriman, settled his programme with assembly points at a large number of centres in London with processions four deep converging upon Trafalgar Square. (It is curious that over a century later such freedom of demonstration was made unlawful in Trafalgar Square).[3]

At Trafalgar Square the marchers were to join the 'great procession of ladies' under the control of the Ladies National Committee. Trades, Leagues and various associations were to carry banners and a curious feature was the wearing of rosettes, 'denoting by their colour' the nationality of the wearers.

Horsemen bearing flags rode before the procession, headed by the Central Committee and their 'leading friends.' A brass band followed with the Ladies Committee behind. The organizers were as anxious as the police to maintain order.

> The Committee earnestly entreat that every person who may take part in this demonstration will consider that upon the strict maintenance of decorum and respectability of conduct . . . Any attempt at disorder, or the slightest unseemliness of conduct on the part of any man, shall be viewed as the act of an enemy.

Curiously on the same day, 24 October 1869, came the news of John Boyle O'Reilly's escape from Western Australia on an American whaler.[4] The United States was to provide a haven for Irishmen which Britain had provided for political prisoners from Europe in the past.

Indeed the dual standards adopted *vis-a-vis* the Irish were heightened in a full column in the *Reynolds Newspaper* written by an anonymous contributor calling himself Gracchus, contrasting the advice given by Britain to Louis Napoleon to adopt liberal and conciliatory policies, 'when and while retaining political captives'.[5] 'In spite of the arguments of *The Times* and its fellow flunkeys of the Press that the incarcerated Fenians are not political prisoners, because they are engaged in a hopeless and wicked crusade against English government,' the letter represented the widespread feeling that they were indeed political prisoners.

The 'sanctimonious hypocrisy' of the upper classes by papers which justified the flogging of pregnant women in Jamaica but objected to North Americans imprisoning slave owning ladies in New Orleans was similarly castigated in a letter containing sentiments clearly identifiable with views expressed in similar terms throughout this period. Their source might well have been the same:

> We affect to find pre-eminent virtues in all other insurrectionists, save and except these, who trouble our own quietude. For them no name is too vile, no treatment too bad . . . O'Donovan Rossa and his noble minded high spirited fellow prisoners, are as pure patriots as Garibaldi and Kossuth.

Blame was placed fairly and squarely upon the aristocracy, and Mr. Gladstone was asked to grant an amnesty on the anniversary of the Prince of Wales' natal day. 'But I suspect Mr. Gladstone has the courage of a louse, not of the lion.'

The language is a compound of the sophisticated and the naive and reflects both the international vision and the unconsciously reformist attitudes of Englishmen who sympathized with the Fenians. Yet, in this, it is precisely representative of the British Left during the first seventy years of the nineteenth century in a society which had not known civil war or regicide for more than two centuries and where such treatment as aroused protest was usually meted out to the Irish and other colonials rather than to the comparatively privileged British working class.

If the letter was an individual viewpoint, the collective opposition to the continual imprisonment of the Fenians was manifested in what Joseph Patrick McDonnell claimed as the most imposing demonstration ever witnessed in London.[6] It was, of course, belittled and denigrated in the London press and the orderly marchers were even termed a 'mob'. McDonnell's claim that 'hundreds of thousands of brave men and fair women of all nationalities' assembled to demand the release of all political prisoners was no doubt an exaggeration, but an estimate of 100,000 covering 27 acres was given in another letter. The correspondent takes pride in orderliness, sobriety and good dress, rather indicative of the Methodist and Nonconformist tradition associated with the early Socialist Movement in Britain. Nevertheless the letter finished with an apocalyptic vision that 'perhaps before the dawn of another Summer's morning the papers will be filled with fearful accounts of the terrible bloodshed, when England will be stained with the blood of its own country,' but this appears to be less of a forecast than a warning to those in the Government who failed to respond to reason. It was in any event an illjudged assessment of the temper of the Englishmen, however true of Ireland.

Gladstone was not to be moved at that time. In his words 'to rise or to incite to insurrection against the Government of this country and against its public order, is ever to be regarded as a great crime; to permit it would be no less great.'

Predictably, *The Times* of 25 October 1869 stood firmly behind Mr. Gladstone's intransigence and its description of 'The Fenian Demonstration' was a mixture of scorn and illwill in direct contrast to the columns of *Reynolds Newspaper*, while the documents of the I.W.M.A. at the other extreme of the political spectrum destroyed the illusion that there was at any time one monolithic view within the Amnesty Movement and the Fenians. The same divisions which manifested themselves in 1867 over the Manchester Martyrs now came again into the open after the failure of the Movement. It was nevertheless the acid test of attitudes towards the Irish question.

The case for the view that English opinion was overwhelmingly anti-Irish has been put by Dr. Norman McCord. He admits that[7] '*The Times* was not an infallible guide to opinion' and adds that it 'clearly was believed to exercise considerable influence, a belief which in itself played some part in moulding opinion.' This one-sided assessment is of the 'predominant element' in the U.K. and this was a view as erroneous as that which suggested that the Hyde Park or earlier Clerkenwell demonstrations were representative of public opinion as a whole. But such manifestations are an indication every bit as valid as *The Times* in demonstrating public feeling which at any one time is composed of strongly divergent elements. The Fenian Amnesty Movement can no more be ignored than those who sympathize with the Irish Civil Rights Movement a century later. What is more the Amnesty Movement was to be vindicated and met with a measure of success.

Dr. McCord's conclusion that 'certainly it would be wrong to suppose that Fenianism evoked widespread sympathy among the working classes of Britain'[8] (although he acknowledges the role of Odger and elements in the Reform League), seems to be based almost exclusively upon those who were predictably hostile and one highly selective quotation from Marx. It is almost as if one were to test the strength of the British Labour Party upon the circulation of *Tribune* or attendance at ward meetings with the inevitable conclusion that perhaps less than one per cent of the British public were in sympathy with it. McCord confuses trends and overt manifestations for the totality of feeling and isolates negative anti-Irish feeling as if to prove a preconceived disposition on the part of English public opinion to be congenitally and hysterically anti-Irish. To rely on *The Times* and Marx, when Marx, himself, stated that 'Gladstone has to contend with the opposition of *The Times*, demonstrates the danger of such polarized selectivity.

*The Times'* approach to the Hyde Park meeting was indicative of its general attitude to the Irish question, but to put it in perspective it should be placed side by side with the *Reynolds Newspaper*.

It saw fit to devote five out of six columns to the demonstration and Ireland,[9] hardly an indication of the lack of interest among the groups participating as *The Times* and Dr. McCord would appear to wish us to believe. For even *The Times* correspondent stated that:

> There was a large amount of popular feeling engaged, but other motives operated than a genuine desire to open the prison doors. Some joined in . . . to display their hostility to the British Government and found in the punishment of the prisoners a convenient grievance to stir up the passions of the ignorant masses.[10]

The report conceded that the demonstration interrupted for an hour or two the traffic of some of the leading thoroughfares in the West End, and for a portion of the day put some thousands of roughs in possession of Trafalgar Square and Hyde Park. The processions and meetings were systematically denigrated. Fringe meetings and the speech of Josiah Merriman, Chairman of the English Amnesty Committee were reported, among them one by a member of the Reform League in terms almost identical with the anonymous letter in *Reynolds Newspaper*[11]. A 'remarkable address, proceeding from a person of fluent speech, comfortably attired, and to all appearances sane.'[12] Messrs. Osborne, Cohen, Johnson, Bligh, McSweeney and others were on the platform presided over by Mr. Hennessy, and there is little doubt that the Reform League was held by *The Times* to be an embarrassment to the Fenians and not inspired by the same forces as some of their opponents suggested.[13]

Certainly the official meeting received messages from Mr. Downing, M.P., Mr. H. Mathews, M.P., Sergeant Parry, Mr. Baxter Langley, Mr. Edmond Beales and other apparently respectable persons, and the official resolution moved by Leeds Councillor Clapham followed a very moderate speech imploring Mr. Gladstone not to alienate the sympathies of the Irish Nation.

> That this meeting considers the political condition of Ireland and renders it expedient that the whole of the political prisoners should be liberated: that their further detention is liable to engender prejudice and ill-feeling against the Government and people of England.

A memorial only for amnesty of the prisoners was addressed to Queen Victoria, while 'Justice for Ireland' and 'Free the Captives' were two of the banners which summed up the sentiment of the meeting and processions.

The role of the International Council of the I.W.M.A.[14] was

highlighted in *Reynolds Newspaper* in 1869 when it reported that on
the previous Tuesday Karl Marx opened a discussion 'on the attitude
of the British Government on the Irish Question'. Interestingly he
pointed out[15] that 'Mr. Bright had declared that if no radical change
was made, Ireland would always be ripe for revolution.' During the
election Gladstone had justified the Fenians and declared that every
other nation would have revolted under similar circumstances.

On assuming power, Gladstone failed to live up to the hopes of
the Amnesty Movement and meanwhile Mr. Moore, M.P., asked in
the House of Commons for an enquiry into the treatment of
prisoners which he alleged was infamous. An enquiry was refused,
notwithstanding the growth of the Amnesty Movement in Ireland
commencing with a meeting of 30,000 in Limerick and culminating
in a gigantic demonstration of 300,000 in Dublin on the 10 October.

The comparison with Louis Napoleon was again used in that
'Napoleon had not made renunciation of republican principles a
condition of his amnesty' whereas Gladstone wanted to degrade the
prisoners morally. Marx accused Gladstone of insulting the Irish
nation while imposing degrading conditions. By contrast he 'cheered
on the American Slaveholders rebellion' while preaching to the Irish
people the doctrine of passive obedience. Seconded by a Mr. Harris,
the meeting supported this position and expressed its admiration of
the Irish Amnesty Movement.

Nevertheless, by 20 December 1870 some prisoners had been
released although the supporters of Amnesty charged Gladstone
with breach of faith, alleging that he had promised an unconditional
pardon as soon as the state of the country permitted him to grant it.
The exercise of Royal clemency pleased all sections of the press, but
the prisoners were not to be allowed to return to Ireland.

*The Irishman* commented that he had given 'exile not amnesty'.
The *Flag of Ireland* pointed out that neither soldiers nor the men
convicted for the rescue of Colonel Kelly of Manchester were
included. The Irish papers joined together in proposing a fund for
the needs of liberated prisoners. The amnesty applied to those
convicted of treason and treason felony, so Christmas Day
1870 was a day of liberty for many an Irish rebel.

Meanwhile *The Times* published panegyrics on the benefits of
British Rule in Ireland, and on the day the partial amnesty was
announced spoke ironically of 'poor downtrodden Ireland'.

The Amnesty Association stated that the prisoners had no official
word of their release and 'living death to exile was not a very
comforting change'. However, it was a change for the better, since
Charles O'Connell, John McClure, and John Devoy, whose
recollections became the invaluable source material for a period

spanning half a century and more, together with O'Donovan Rossa and others were to go to New York while William Halpin reserved his decision.

On 14 January 1871, Mr. James O'Connor in a letter to the Amnesty Association stated that he had been officially informed that Fenian prisoners confined in Portland Prison had all refused a conditional amnesty.

Those who arrived in the United States were however described by *The Times*[16] as 'the lions of New York — political parties are competing for the honour of their patronage. Gifts of money are offered them on all sides. A purse of one thousand dollars was given to them on their arrival, and a sum of fifty thousand dollars is to be raised for the purpose of enabling them to accomplish what is the grand aim of existence in American philosophy and start in business.' The British representatives in the U.S.A. were incensed enough to ask for an explanation of this heroes' welcome.

By August the Irish were preparing for the biggest demonstration of support for the remaining Fenian prisoners. Mr. P.J. Smythe, M.P., complained bitterly of the police intervention in a legal and peaceful demonstration as a result of which 'peaceable citizens were maimed and trampled upon by the men claimed to be conservateurs of order, and the protectors of life and property.'[17]

The massive meeting was to be held in Phoenix Park on 6 August 1871, but the authorities posted notices banning the meeting from the Park. Mr. Smythe, Mr. A.M. Sullivan and John Nolan, Secretary of the Amnesty Association, appeared near the monument where onlookers — men, women and children — were gathering. The police officer attempting to prevent the meeting was knocked down and beaten, and the crowd swept speakers and reporters from the base of the monument and repulsed reserves of police so enabling the meeting to take place with Mr. Smythe in the Chair, stating 'I want the whole thing to go on quietly. I take all the responsibility upon myself because I mean to test the legality of the proclamation that has been used.'

Then the police charged with batons drawn. They struggled with those defending the meeting and were roughly driven from the scene. Swinging their batons, a hundred policemen faced a dispersed and now stone-throwing mob. Supporters and speakers went down before the blows of the police, Mr. Sullivan, editor of the *Nation*, being severely struck. A *Freeman's Journal* reporter was knocked down and his leg severely injured, and one Mr. Smythe M.P. was among those who felt the edge of the batons. Several men were struck about the head and their faces streamed with blood. The crowds flew in all directions as women screamed and men shouted.

One policeman was flung down the slope at one side of the monument and was kicked and beaten before assistance arrived.

A band marched onto the scene playing 'The Fenian Men' but were routed by a police charge. Stones flew and more police poured onto the scene together with a small body of mounted police and even the esteemed Marquis of Hamilton, M.P., came to see what had happened. *Saunders News Letter* commented with satisfaction:

> We cannot record the exact number of broken heads which were occasioned by this most ill-timed and culpable attempt to break through the law and hold a mob meeting. The police did their duty with vigour and effort, and it is to be hoped that the course which they took will have the effect of putting a little respect for the law into the hearts of those whose habitual contempt for it is one of the miseries under which the country suffers.

Nevertheless, it viewed with regret

> that two gentlemen of the press were absolutely knocked down by constables who were ignorant that they were there in the discharge of their duty as well as themselves . . . We are further bound to record a very brutal knock-down of a woman by a policeman near King's Bridge.

Two policemen received serious injuries while one hospital treated sixty injured demonstrators. A man named Kelly had been batoned and sabred and several policeman were named as having been injured by stones and blows. Windows were smashed on Dublin's quays as the police chased the crowds into the City itself. Harley Carey who fought with the Irish Brigade in France was cut badly about the head in several places by blows from policemen's batons, and no preparations had been made to face the police attack. There is little doubt that Phoenix Park was the scene of as vicious a clash as ever occurred without the use of guns. Even ten of the bandsmen were treated in hospital and their instruments deliberately thrown about and damaged by the police. Curiously, only four arrests were made. In a sense this savage confrontation was the culmination of the Amnesty Movement's widespread agitation.

*The Times* Dublin correspondent estimated the crowd at the foot of the steps to have been between 4,000 and 5,000 at the beginning of the incident. In spite of the papers indignation at the treatment received by the police as the crowd tried to make its way up the monument steps, it bears out the wild scenes of flailing batons and flying shingle:

> while the meeting was at its height a band was heard approaching and the mob hastened to meet it. The police rushed forward to the gates and attacking the musicians who were unprepared for such a reception,

smashed their instruments, flung them into the air and beat the players very roughly. They spared no one when their blood was up, and several women are stated to have received rough usage at their hands.

And Mr. Smythe could well comment wryly that this should happen

at a moment when the crowds of Republicans of London are allowed to assemble in the public parks of that City to express sympathy with the Communists of Paris and to assail the Crown, the constitution and the law. At present the Socialist and the infidel may freely address assemblages in the London Parks . . . the people of Dublin have been assaulted in the public park of the Irish metropolis.

To the Irish middle class nationalist, the green flag was a good deal more respectable than the red, whatever tenuous links through O'Mahony, Stephens and later Rossa, were forged between Fenians and Marxists. The passage is highly significant. However, the Irish are a stubborn people, not easily resisting a challenge and preparations were quickly made to 'complete the proceedings of the interrupted meeting and assert and establish the right of the public to hold meetings in the Park for legal and constitutional purposes.'

The *Irishman* advised Dublin Castle to 'order its constables to keep their hands from bludgeons and their feet from evil kicking' or 'better still withdraw them from the scene altogether.'

The prime object was to free the soldiers and those involved in the Manchester affair who still remained incarcerated. The Clerkenwell prisoners had been released and in all logic fellow Fenians in Manchester or those who happened to be in the forces could not be deemed worse than any other group.

The *Flag of Ireland* commented 'that under no Government, in Europe would the right of public meeting have been interfered with as it was in the Phoenix Park, and the people meet tomorrow to celebrate their own triumph.'

On the advice of Isaac Butt, lawyer and leading Irish parliamentarian, court action was taken to challenge the action of the police. It was declared to be illegal. It was in this atmosphere that a second demonstration was held at the foot of the Wellington Monument. Mr. Smythe harked back to Manchester once again before the crowd assembled on 3 September, four years after the executions:

Let a statement of these men's cases be tried before the Commander of the Forces in Ireland, and they would abide by its result. The Manchester men (tremendous cheering) went forth in the open day on the public road to give honourable battle for the rescue of their chief. No base, no sordid motive activated them (cheers). On the contrary, they obeyed the noblest impulses that could inspire the human breast . . . the Manchester rescue was a deed of heroism (loud cheers).

As the audience returned home further clashes with the police turned into a pitched battle raging for over four hours with the free use of batons and stones as on the previous occasion. About twenty arrests were made while fifty-two policemen were injured and a public house was wrecked; rather an anti-climax after the earlier clash.

However, while the promoters claimed an attendance of 100,000, the *Daily Express* put the figure at 1,500, though the latter estimate conflicts somewhat with a *Times* comment that the 'the sequel surpassed the scene of rioting and disturbance witnessed on the 6th August. The result was that 30 more Irishmen were sent to gaol for the maximum period of six months imprisonment with hard labour.'

Although this was the high water mark it was not yet the culmination of the Fenian protests which went on in a desultory fashion. Indeed a study of the Minutes of the I.W.M.A. over these years provides a fascinating insight into the far left's view of British politics and the divisions in emphasis and objects between such personalities as Marx and Odger, while Marx's own correspondence sheds light on his revolutionary aims and those of his collaborator Friedrich Engels. [18]

The Fenians first became a serious topic of discussion on 18 November 1867 when the Manchester prisoners were under sentence of death. Mr. Dupont had stated that:

> The Council would be wanting in its duty if it remained indifferent to the Irish Cause. What is Fenianism? Is it a sect or a party whose principles are opposed to ours? Certainly not. Fenianism is the vindication by an oppressed people of its right to social and political existence. The Fenian declaration leaves no room for doubt in this respect. They affirm the republican form of government, liberty of conscience, no state religion, the produce of labour to the labourer, and the provision of the soil to the people. What people could abjure such principles?

These latter remarks were to set the tone for the I.W.M.A.'s approval:

> Is it well for the English to talk of legality and justice to those who on the slightest suspicion of Fenianism are arrested and incarcerated and subjected to physical and mental tortures? [19]

Mr. Morgan's view that it was rather unfortunate that the Irish had chosen the name Fenian, which many Englishmen considered synonymous with all that is bad, preferring the name of Republican. This is a curious commentary on the failure of even the most sympathetic Briton to understand the yearning for national identity and roots in a specifically Irish Republic.

It has been reported that on 5 November the Reform League had passed a resolution in favour of Fenianism. Odger and Lucroft, the two prominent trade unionists had in fact clashed with the other members of the League and Marx wrote on 2 November to Engels that 'you will see what a row "our people" kicked up in the Reform League. I sought in every way to provoke this manifestation of the English workers in support of Fenianism.'

The Manchester Martyrs provided the catalyst for action by the I.W.M.A. which was to continue until the zenith of the Fenian Amnesty Movement as Ireland began to loom more large in the eyes of its leaders by reason both of its apparent revolutionary potential and a genuine regard for the right to national sovereignty, which early Internationalists found entirely consistent with their ideals.

Nationalism and liberalism went hand in hand in nations like Italy before the degeneration of some nationalist movements into the chauvinism with which nationalism is too easily identified by many socialists today.

After the frenzied agitation against the Manchester executions, it was not for another two years when the Hyde Park demonstration took place that the I.W.M.A. again became involved in defence of imprisoned Fenians.

On 26 October 1869 John Weston suggested a vote of thanks to Mr. Merriman for a speech he had made in Hyde Park. Mr. Jung preferred a resolution in favour of the release of the prisoners and was supported by Mr. Morris, while Mr. Lucraft in the Chair tactfully agreed that 'it was an opportune moment to do something.' Marx felt that whatever passed would be suppressed by the London press and the main feature at the demonstration had been ignored ... 'it was that at least a part of the English working class had lost their prejudice against the Irish. This might be put in writing and addressed to somebody, not the government.' Mr. Hales opposed the vote of thanks on the grounds that Mr. Merriman had resigned his post at the Reform League when the Council had passed a vote in favour of Fenianism. He supported the idea of Mr. Jung's resolution and this was unanimously adopted.

The Council again met on 16 November when Marx opened what must have been a lengthy debate on the attitude of the British Government to the Irish question, reported in part in *Reynolds Newspaper*. He castigated Gladstone and pointed to American pressure in securing the release of the two Americans sentenced to ten years each, while Martin Carey, an Irish journalist sentenced in 1865 to five years penal servitude was in the lunatic asylum.

The first note of dissent came at the Council meeting of 20

November when Odger objected to the bills calling the Hyde Park meeting for containing a 'demand' for the unconditional release of prisoners. More cautious and practical in tactics and inclination he explained that he was as much in favour of their release as anyone, but it was impolitic to proceed in that way as it prejudiced the case. Jung's rejoiner was that 'our purpose is not to release the prisoners but to express our opinion on the conduct of the government'. It was the age old battle between those wanting genuine reform and those using a cause to further wider revolutionary objects. This is not to question Jung's sincerity, for his view was that 'everything in this country is carried by pressure from without'.

Robert Applegarth accepted that Odger 'simply raises the question whether it is right to use strong language' and concluded that 'they have been too long in prison. It is no use to apply soft language, the time has come to demand.'

Applegarth was a blunt man who preferred to call a spade a spade, but the argument went further when Thomas Mottershead admitted the right of insurrection but regretted that some Englishmen had applauded Marx's statement since Ireland could not be independent. It lay between England and France and if Britain relinquished its hold it would be only asking the French to walk in. A century later it seems a strange view but some democrats feared the power of Louis Napoleon just as later they feared the Kaiser and abandoned their international viewpoint.

Mottershead made a spirited defence of Gladstone *vis à vis* Napoleon, but to Marx, a liberal from a Tory background was a greater danger than an open dictator. The theme is not new and is evergreen.

Odger objected to too wholesale a condemnation of Gladstone's policy, while Mottershead was bitter because the 'Irish had thrown stones at the English for being in favour of Garibaldi', to which Lucraft replied that 'Whatever the Irish were the English had made them'.

Jung objected to Mottershead's narrow view. 'Odger says we owe a certain amount of liberty to Garibaldi, we owe much more to the Fenians. The Clerkenwell affair was certainly a shocking affair, but Garibaldi caused much bloodshed and would have caused more if the blowing up of the barracks at Rome had not been prevented. The police were as much to blame in the Clerkenwell affair as anywhere.' Marx tactfully agreed with Odger while at the same time stating that it was more important to make a concession to the Irish people than to Gladstone.

On 17 December 1869 Marx wrote to Engels that 'our Irish resolution was sent out to all trades unions in alliance with us. Only one of them — a small branch of the carriers — protested against it as being political and beyond the Council's competence. To explain things we are sending a deputation to them.'

Ireland was to these revolutionaries the vulnerable underbelly of British and therefore European capitalism. They were of course wrong in the event, despite the fact that Ireland has always proved to be a running sore. This helps to explain the enormous interest in Irish affairs displayed by Karl Marx and his associates in the reformist climate of an otherwise stable, mid-Victorian England.

Bradlaugh, Cremer and Odger supported the Fenian Movement up to a degree on an entirely different basis[20] They assured the Fenians that if only they were satisfied that the Fenian principles were merely democratic and not anti-English, they would promise their full support and advocate an alliance between their respective organizations. They would consult with Beales, President of the Reform League. However, nothing had come of these contacts since Colonel Kelly and no doubt other Fenians, attached little importance to English support. Perhaps one sees here the seeds of the Sinn Fein ideal of self reliance in the achievement of Irish Independence, notwithstanding the frequent attempts to obtain military support from Britain's enemies. Nevertheless, it was to friends like the I.W.M.A. and the Reform League that the Amnesty Movement turned for support over the detention and treatment of the Fenian Prisoners.

Apart from the detention of Fenian prisoners and the movement for their release, the other issue which disturbed the complacency of the British Government was their ill-treatment. Some were the subjects of deliberate brutality inflicted over long periods. The sufferings of Michael Davit and Jeremiah O'Donovan Rossa are the best known and well documented,[21] and it is not the purpose of this chapter to catalogue the prisoners or the treatment they'received. Suffice it to say that even by the generally barbaric standards in prisons and penal colonies, some of the Fenians evoked a particularly hostile response from their captors while others, by reason of their abilities and difference from common criminals, became comparatively privileged.

Much of the attention was focused on O'Donovan Rossa and a Commission was in fact set up to report on his treatment. It bears the most striking resemblance to the Compton Report on the treatment of I.R.A. suspects a century later, albeit within a rather different context. Verbal gymnastics and euphemisms intended to play down the unpalatable truth have apparently changed little over the hundred intervening years.

The foreign press was the source of the complaints eventually published in *The Times*. One sided as its editorial comments may have been, the freedom of the press in Britain was an important reality. *La Marseillaise* devoted a special number exclusively to contributions from political prisoners. A letter conveyed with difficulty to Rossa's friends was to find its way into *The Times*, [22] thus bringing the issue out into the open. Rossa accused his gaolers of having placed him in a position that compelled him to rest on his knees and elbows in order to take his food, of half starving him and depriving him of light while giving him only chains and a Bible.

The authorities, he wrote, 'stripped me naked once a day during several months to examine my arms, legs and all parts of my body.' He related that 'one day I resisted and then came five officers who assaulted me with blows and tore off my clothing.' He was, he claimed, forced to bathe in the water that had already been used by half a dozen English prisoners. He had spent forty-eight hours in the dark cell on bread and water for reading a book. His fellow prisoner Edward Duffy was allowed to die without a visit from him. John Lynch had complained that the cold was 'killing him'. Their flannels had been removed on arrival at the prison and Rossa accused them of assassinating Lynch through ill treatment and neglect.

If the sufferings of Rossa and Davitt have become well known, the fate of lesser known prisoners was frequently deportation to penal colonies or long incarceration followed by exile. The passage to Australia or Dartmoor was the common experience of felons and Fenians, but the latter were frequently singled out for humiliation. It was in these circumstances that the treatment of Fenian prisoners became the subject of a Commission of Enquiry, the results of which were published in January 1871. Its findings were remarkably complacent in view of the subsequent evidence. It reported that:

> After a patient and minute investigation we do not find any ground for the belief that the treason felony prisoners in English prisons have, as a class, been subjected to any exceptionally severe treatment, or have suffered any hardships beyond those incidental to the condition of a prisoner sentenced to penal servitude. It appears, on the contrary, from the evidence of the prison officers, confirmed in certain cases by the evidence of the prisoners themselves, that the prison authorities have sanctioned from time to time, certain relaxations of convict discipline in their favour. They have for the most part been formed into separate working parties, and have seldom been associated in labour with other convicts except by way of punishment; they have generally been placed in cells of a superior class, the ordinary restrictions on writing and receiving letters have been often relaxed on their behalf; their diet is slightly better; and their enforced labour is lighter, than in the case of other prisoners under similar sentences. At both Woking and Chatham we learnt that this is the case and at Portland we saw all the prisoners of this class placed on the public works under a separate shed, apart from the other prisoners, under the charge of a warder, and, as we were

informed, allowed to remain there without doing any work at all. It is perhaps inevitable that men in the position of treason-felony prisoners should resent the degrading through ordinary incidents of convict discipline with peculiar impatience, and the more so if they have received a good education and filled respectable positions in life. The treason felony convicts here have, in fact, never ceased to protest against being classed with criminals, as moral degradation, and every privilege however trifling, which they have succeeded in obtaining, has but confirmed their belief in the justice of this demand.

The Report concluded that a detached portion of some convict prisons should be set aside for the Fenian prisoners. It mirrored the fact that it frequently needs articulate political detainees to expose the barbarity of the penal system. The furthest it went into criticism was to state vaguely that 'There are certain incidents of treatment which we have commented on with disapprobation in the remarks upon the cases of individual prisoners.' Rossa as one such individual described[23] the privations of cold and hunger, the heavy labour, censorship of his writings, bread and water punishment, his four months of solitary confinement and thirty-five days in irons.

Meanwhile his wife, Mary Jane O'Donovan Rossa (1846-1916) campaigned on his behalf together with the Fenian Amnesty Movement. As a consequence he was released in January 1871 on condition that he went into exile. Davitt did not fare so well and bore his years in gaol with a remarkable fortitude, resilience and lack of bitterness before launching his New Departure. His fifteen year sentence was at last cut in 1877 after mounting pressure won over Mr. Gladstone and the Liberals to the granting of an amnesty to the Fenians and ultimately forcing Disraeli's Government to act.

The Movement was by no means ended by the liberation of Rossa whose persistence in refusing censorship and smuggling out details of his conditions made him an unwanted nuisance to the authorities. On 3 November 1872 a combined meeting of Irish Home Rulers, English Republicans, Radicals and Internationalists held yet another demonstration in Hyde Park to 'demand the release of the Fenian Prisoners.' These 'dirty and noisy specimens'[24] marched into Hyde Park headed by bands and banners.

Mr. Chaddock presided over their meeting while George Odger was a prominent figure on the platform. Odger pleaded for Irish freedom "England has tried for 700 years to govern Ireland and there is no such black history as that rule. Was it not time to let the Irish govern themselves?" It is significant that this meeting was as concerned about the treatment of the Fenian prisoners as about their detention. In particular it deplored 'the practice of degrading political prisoners to the class of felons, enforcing upon them the horrors of the silent system and otherwise subjecting them to a cruel and vindictive regime, repugnant to every human instinct and disgraceful to our vaunted civilization.'

Other speakers included a Mr. Ryan and a Mr. Walks. The demonstration was significant but not particularly eventful. However, it succeeded in provoking yet another of those self-righteous editorials which were the stock-in-trade of *The Times* during the Fenian period. It denigrated the 'Noisy friends of the Fenians' while commenting that 'it is so far satisfactory to have it thus established beyond dispute that the mass of our working people have no great sympathy with the follies of Fenianism.'[25]

This was in contrast to the earlier tremendous rioting in Dublin in August of the previous year. Indeed, by 1872 the heat had largely gone out of the movement. For many, transported to Australia or confined to prison, the ordeal was to continue with only the spectacular escapes to encourage the dispersed remnants of the movement. It was from those remnants gradually freed and meeting up mainly in the United States that the tradition was to be handed down to new generations. Unhappily, most of them failed to see the significance and possibilities of the Amnesty Movement and some learned little from the Clerkenwell explosion. What was drama and tragedy in the years between 1867 and 1873 was to be repeated as black comedy and even blacker tragedy a century later when the tradition was to reassert itself in Northern Ireland.

## NOTES

1. See in particular the following issues of the *Reynolds Newspaper* for 1869: 24 and 31 October; 14 and 21 November; 5 and 12 December. And for 1870: 2 January; 6, 20 and 27 February; 6, 20 and 27 March; 3 April; 8 May; 5 and 12 June; 24 and 31 July; 7 August; 2 November; 4, 18 and 25 December.
2. Minutes of the First International 1867.
3. In 1972 Trafalgar Square was denied to demonstrators concerned with the internment of prisoners without trial in Northern Ireland.
4. For a full account see W.J. Lauberstein, *The Emerald Whaler.*
5. *Reynolds Newspaper* 24 October 1869.
6. *Ibid.*, 31 October 1869.
7. See M. Harmon's essay in *Fenians and Fenianism.*
8. *Ibid.*
9. *The Times* 25 October 1869.
10. *Ibid.*
11. *Ibid.*, 31 October 1869.
12. *Ibid.*, 25 October 1869.

13. *Ibid.*
14. A fuller account is contained in the Minutes of the First International.
15. *Reynolds Newspaper* 24 November 1869.
16. *The Times* 12 February 1871.
17. *Reynolds Newspaper* 31 August 1870.
18. See *Marx and Engels on Ireland.*
19. *Minutes of the First International.*
20. Liam O'Broin, *Fenian Fever.*
21. See Sheehy Skeffington, *Life of Michael Davitt* and O'Donovan Rossa, *My Years in English Gaols.*
22. *The Times* 10 March 1870.
23. O'Donovan Rossa, *op. cit.*
24. *The Times* 4 September 1872.
25. *Ibid.*

# Chapter 12

## *The Fenians: An Assessment*

As the dust settled on Clerkenwell, and the tide of Fenianism receded, it was to give way to an era of land agitation and Parliamentary struggle. The seeds planted by the United Irishmen had burst forth only to be trampled underfoot for another half century. However, it was the living thread of the Fenian tradition which led to the events of Easter 1916. The happenings in England during those turbulent years in the late sixties have left their mark on subsequent history and even upon contemporary events. Some of the lessons have been learned but the debacle at Clerkenwell seems to have taught nothing to those who in 1972 and 1973 were to bomb Aldershot, Guildford, the Old Bailey and Birmingham.

Particularly significant however in the context of Irish history, was the composition of the Fenian movement and its sympathizers in the industrial cities of England. Apart from the Irish-American officers and the small group of Irish intellectuals around Stephens, it brought the broad mass of Irishmen into political action within a radical national movement with distinct social undertones. The nature of that movement has been much disputed and is more complex than the theorists and historians often admit.

However, not for nothing did the Lord Lieutenant of Ireland, Lord Wodehouse, appointed by the Liberal Government of 1865, observe:

> The whole mass of the peasantry are sullenly or actively disloyal, so are the small tradesmen, the artisans and the railway and telegraph clerks, porters, engineers.

The movement mirrored in a less developed country, the more self conscious working class organizations in Britain. In those, Irish immigrants with a militant tradition played a more than average part, not least in the Chartist Movement which had thrown up such leaders as Bronterre O'Brien and Feargus O'Connor. James Connolly observed the same phenomenon of nascent working class development:

> Coincident with the inception of Fenianism, 1858 commenced in Ireland a determined labour agitation which culminated in a vigorous movement amongst the baker journeymen against night labour and in favour of a reduction of the working hours. Great meetings were held all over the country during the years 1858-60 in which the rights of labour were most vehemently asserted, [and concluded] . . . where the movement was the strongest, Fenianism developed the most.

Connolly's analysis of the relationship between the revolutionary movement and the class movement was neither wholly wrong nor wholly right, but it was sufficiently true to lead to accusations of communism and accounts to a high degree for the hostility of much of the clergy to the Fenian Movement. But it would be wrong to claim it as a movement with a social and political programme of a recognizably socialist character. There were personal links between Stephens, O'Mahony and Rossa and the continental revolutionary circles in Paris and with the First International.

Primarily, Fenianism was a national movement springing from deep social discontents, the famine, the landholding system, the disadvantages of Catholics and above all the longstanding resentment of the alien nation at whose hands these humiliations had been suffered.

The very organization of the movement made political education and mass politics difficult. This aspect of the movement has been much criticized in retrospect as an inhibiting factor in political development. However, the movement spread beyond these rigid limits, not least in the British Army, to become the first substantial embodiment of the national spirit of revolt since the United Irishmen made their bid for liberty in 1798.

> There was nothing in the content of the Fenian programme to mark it out as the expression of a social movement. The special interest of the oppressed classes of Irish Society were never mentioned in it. But the radicalism of the Fenians although confined to the political sphere cut them off from the respectable classes of Irish Society.[3]

Interestingly, Robert Anderson regarded the Land League as Fenianism under another name and although this view represents the over-simplification of a policeman, it does reveal the common denominator which made the national movement the obvious banner around which the forces of a largely economic discontent were to gather.

If Ireland had been an independent nation the process of social differentiation, which was such a distinctive feature of this era, would have almost certainly led to an open struggle for political power between movements representative of the conflicting social interests, but in Colonial Ireland this issue was interwoven with the problem of national self assertion against English rule. To the Fenians and their opponents alike, nationalism and hostility towards England was the acid test of political sincerity; social interests they regarded as secondary matters which were unimportant except in so far as they affected the main issue, the attitude of the group or individual in the anti-English struggle. They did not know and probably would not have cared to understand, that the attitude was in the last resort determined by social interests and reflexes, and their inability to grasp this intricate but decisive connection enveloped the Fenians in an ideological fog which most of them found quite impenetrable. Internal dissensions, quarrels expulsions and the more or less permanent impotence of the movement as such were the inevitable consequences of their failure.[4]

However, this is perhaps to underestimate the underlying demand for democracy, the unequivocal opposition to landlordism and the non-sectarian tradition of the Young Irelanders and United Irishmen from whose inspiration they sprang. If their methods were conspiratorial, their actions were sometimes more akin to those of anarchists and nihilists in their action theories.[5] The tradition of the ribbonmen and moonlighters was caught up in the wider revolt of the Fenians. Nowhere did this manifest itself more than in the Chester Castle, Manchester and Clerkenwell episodes when they were separated from their mass of support in Ireland.

Indeed the idea that Fenianism was divorced from social issues was fiercely attacked in later years by James Connolly:

> . . . deliberately unscrupulous and superficial historians have concealed the fact that the Fenians, like the Young Irelanders and like the men of '98 before them, were intent upon freeing the people from economic slavery as well as the nation from political bondage.[6]

Certainly, Thomas Luby attacked the social order of his day and stood for 'An Irish Republic in which the people of Ireland would own the wealth of Ireland adn administer it for the benefit of the entire community, and not for the selfish interess of a section or class.[7]

This is the direct antithesis of the view that recognizes only the romantic nationalism rooted in the mythology which gave Fenianism its name and Padraig Pearse much of his inspiration, in almost symbolic union of the two strands, when he fought side by side with Connolly in 1916. Thus Liam O'Flaherty wrote:

> The Fenians were idealists, whose main interest was to die for their country without any reward. The Fenian is the artist in Irish politics. He is an inspiration, an ornament, a hero. He is generally hated when he is alive and a monument is raised to him when he is dead.[8]

The message is cynical and more appropriate to the term Fenian as used to describe those in the Fenian tradition at times other than the period with which we are concerned.

Nevertheless the Fenian ideal is rather nebulous and like every other national movement it embraced much diverse characters as the Socialist land reformer Davitt and the American adventurer McCafferty, whose careers we have described to illustrate this curious combination of personalities and ideas.[9]

There was no single unified object other than the common antipathy to English rule. 'Pagan' O'Leary could share a common platform with pious believers. Cardinals could curse and priests bless the Fenians. These are some of the paradoxes of a movement which carried within it many streams in a particular national and pre-industrial society separated by water and history from the rest of Europe, but no less aware of the economic disparities which they suffered compounded by alien rule. In England itself, the new Irish proletariat was both militant and drawn from the restricted bounds of Fenianism towards the political left. Many were inhibited from joining the freethinking and Marxist segment only by reason of their religious background. Similarly the American Democratic Party, the Australian Labour Party and not least the British Labour Movement have as a consequence been greatly influenced by the descendants of the radical dissidents who sympathized with the aims of the Fenian Movement. In Ireland itself the tradition is more obvious and explicit, spanned by the outstanding personalities and life histories of Stephens, Devoy and Tom Clarke.

Desmond Ryan[10] saw in these characters the founders; the man who three times in his lifetime brought it within sight of victory; and the strong enduring man who signed the 1916 proclamation (and his death warrant). There is an obvious continuity before the tradition was to be claimed by diverse elements in the wake of partition and civil war.

> Fenianism was conceived in the defeat of an insurrection, amid the horrors of famine and born in the betrayal of all Ireland's constitutional and social movement . . . Its inspiration came in its origins from Tone, the United Irishmen, Davis and the men of forty eight, from the republicanism of Cave Hill and the white, green and orange tricolour of Thomas Francis Meagher of Waterford.

Devoy was the chronicler of Fenianism. He was a reflector and an agitator rather than a theorist, but his pact with Parnell and Davitt took Fenianism out of the shadows of conspiracy into the sphere of political and economic campaigns as opposed to the clumsy and senseless dynamiting of McCafferty. There may well be a parallel between the activities of the Social Democratic Labour Party in modern Ulster using the political process, and the bombing campaigns of the Provisional I.R.A. One derived from the failure in 1867 and the other from the grievances which matured a century later. Yet Clarke, the dynamite campaigner, went on to join Pearse and Connolly in the Dublin Post Office, bringing in another of the strands of which the fabric of Fenianism is woven. These traditions have undoubtedly had their influence on current thought and action, so that Fenianism takes on a new historical significance if one is to unravel the web of republican politics in modern Ulster, albeit in the context of an independent but mutilated Irish Republic anxious to avoid confrontation and an England equally anxious to disengage from conflict.

The curious juxtaposition of Marxism and Fenianism reveals much of the nature of the movements which have been discussed from conflicting angles in recent general studies of their relationship.[11] The period of Fenianism was also a period of working class revival in England. But it was the treatment of the Fenians that created sympathy for them. Thus the execution of the Manchester Martyrs and the release of Kelly and Deasy brought this response from Engels:

> All the Fenians lacked was martyrs. These they have been presented with . . . Through the execution of these men, the liberation of Kelly and Deasy has been made an act of heroism which will be sung over the cradle of every Irish child . . . The Irish women will take care of that. The only instance of an execution for a similar act is . . . that of John Brown after Harper's Ferry.[12]

The amnesty movement was the closest that the two movements came to any sharing of objectives, other than within a small spectrum of the radical left. The *Irish People*, with its emphasis on the Irish land for the Irish people, represented an important strand of agrarian socialism but was still removed from the urban basis of the early working class movement that grew from the Industrial Revolution. Anti-clericalism was a point in common with left freethinkers and Marxists and Charles Kickham (although himself a Catholic) told the Priests 'that Bishops and Priests may be bad politicians and worse Irishmen.'[13] Both Marxists and Fenians regarded the issue of Catholic emancipation which had created a genuine mass movement of agitation, as diversionary, in benefiting the upper and middle class Catholics and seducing them from the national movement.[14] Radical town workers as well as peasants or tenant farmers were the backbone of the Fenian Movement but their allegiance while influenced by their social position, was on the basis of national feeling rather than consciousness of their class.

It may well be emphasized by protagonists of the view that

Socialism and Fenianism were closely linked ideologically that James Stephens, Michael Doheny and John O'Mahony were members of Socialist societies in Paris during the fifties and that John O'Leary[15] described O'Mahoney as 'an advanced democrat: and that the Fenians would become a socialist movement. Rossa was accused by the Crown Prosecutor at his trial of 'inciting the lower orders to believe that they might expect a redistribution of property.' Enemies of Fenianism were not slow to accuse them of being reds wrapped in green and of harbouring socialist and atheistic tendencies. The taint of Communism was no more than one influence among much stronger traditions deep in the national consciousness of the Irish.

Interestingly there was little support from the Irish Trade Unions of the time for Fenianism. They preferred to concentrate their effort on economic nationalism to protect Irish industry.[16] Nevertheless there was, even in that dire action, some overlap personified above all by Frank Roney, an active member of the Friendly Society of Ironfounders. Roney, after imprisonment emigrated to the U.S.A. and, died at Long Beach in 1925. He had been an outstanding trade union leader in San Francisco.[17] Interestingly, John Connell who wrote the words of 'The Red Flag' was a Fenian. The legacy of this tradition is now embodied in the names of Larkin and Connolly. Although Joseph Patrick MacDonnell reported regularly to the I.W.M.A. until 1872, the objective fact was that this was only one stream of a movement which was essentially Irish, rooted in national sentiment and republicanism rather than in a conscious socialist doctrine, notwithstanding that it fed upon social ills and seemed to be directed at their solution.

Indeed Fenianism embodied many strands of thought. It transcended class and creed in the search for the self-reliant national movement which eventually gave way to Sinn Fein. It relied on expatriates in England to do much of its work and called upon English sympathizers only in the movements of amnesty and clemency. Above all it was the tradition that linked the United Irishmen of 1798, the Young Irelanders of 1848 and their descendants in the twentieth century struggle which led to the emergence of a free state.

It was a tradition, however, that had little compunction in employing physical force for political ends and as such has given justification to numerous groups which claim, frequently in bitter opposition to one another, to be the heirs of the Fenian tradition. It was conspiratorial and as such has superficial similarities with today's I.R.A. However, it was a genuine mass movement and few members would have approved of indiscriminate bomb attacks.

Manchester was an accidental killing inevitable in an independence struggle and Clerkenwell was an example of bungling and misfortune. Chester Castle had specific strategic ends. Terror for its own sake was no part of its strategy. It did however give birth not only to the dominant influence of the Land League and Parnell's Parliamentary Party but also to the Dynamiters and the Invincibles. This dichotomy persists and it seems that terror is the product of failure, while a disciplined movement is the fruit of success and wide scale support.

The social, agrarian and class conflicts which existed within the context of English rule were certainly reflected. However, Fenianism subordinated everything to the primary object of removing the latter and in this sense left an indelible mark on Irish thinking. Though means of struggle in Ireland have been curiously radical by British standards, socialist movements as such have taken less root in Ireland than in any other European country.

Fenianism drew upon romantic nationalism in the myths and legends of the Fianna but this aspect was not highly developed. Nevertheless it re-established the ideal of nationhood, a nationhood in which Marx took little interest except in so far as it seemed to hold potential in revolutionizing the British working class. It was to be followed by the Gaelic League which sought to resurrect a distinctly Gaelic culture and it was no accident that John O'Mahony drew from this source the Movement's very name. Nevertheless, in a sense, the movement was unconsciously Marxist. As Professor T.W. Moody has acknowledged:

> Unlike previous revolutionary movements Fenianism made its contacts almost entirely among the poorer classes — small farmers and labourers, soldiers, schoolmasters, clerks, shop assistants and urban workers generally . . . they wrote off the landed aristocracy as a whole, were suspicious of the well-to-do middle class and pinned their faith to the common man.[17]

That class composition was not necessarily reflected in ideology — 'The well spring of nationality is in the heart of the people,' wrote O'Leary,[18] while Professor Moody in contrast to Connolly's view, has concluded that 'a crucial fact about the largely working class movement was that its thinking was simply nationalist; it had no specific social programme for the Irish Republic of its dreams . . . from the Marxist standpoint it was incredibly naive.'[19]

Emigrant nationalism meant that the expatriate Irish in England as well as in the U.S.A. added a significant new dimension which still has its counterpart in the Northern Ireland problem today. This foreshadowed the movements of expatriate Algerians in France or Jews in Western Europe and the U.S.A., who organized support for a national movement elsewhere and, in the former case, the parallel is heightened by the physical force movement within the metropolitan country which claimed that Algeria was part of France. Another analogy might be the Austro-Hungarian Empire in the nineteenth century, but what is important is that such movements, while nationalist in character, picked up a great deal of socialist or social revolutionary ideas which fused with nationalism at the height of their struggles. The average Fenian in industrial England like his Algerian counterpart in metropolitan France was functioning within a more developed society with the class divisions of the industrial era and was therefore inevitably more class conscious and broader in his vision than the poorer compatriot in a relatively undeveloped and less sophisticated society at home.

Fenianism embraced ordinary men and women, often with the overt hostility of the Church hierarchy leaving them undeterred notwithstanding their personal piety. It revived half forgotten legends in seeking roots that had not been erased by forced assimilation to the rest of Britain over the centuries and it was the essential link from '98, through the Young Irelanders who bequeathed the tricolour flag, down to the Dublin Post Office over which it flew and now flies with the legitimacy of nationhood.

Unhappily, the new dimension added in England was frequently led by those with little understanding of any potential sympathy on a class basis, many of them hailing from the U.S.A. and they were often counter-productive in consequence. Violence and martyrdom are not part of the British heritage in the way they have been in countries given to revolutionary struggle. Hence, Mazzini, who hardly understood Irish Nationalism, not only pleaded for the commutation of Thomas Bourke's sentence but said that 'Bourke will be the Robert Emmet of 1867'. . . 'feelings of revenge will rekindle the energy of the discouraged Fenians. The dream will become through martyrdom, a sort of religion.'[20]

Engels had felt the same about the executions of Allen, Larkin and O'Brien with much more justification, for that action was as divisive and significant for Anglo-Irish relations in the nineteenth century as the executions after the Easter Rising were for the twentieth. For him it was 'the definite deed of separation between England and Ireland.' Significantly, even Engels was talking in national rather than class terms.

Louis Blanc, then correspondent for *The Times* referred to the Manchester martyrs as 'obscure names belonging to oblivion . . . Ireland will remember them eternally thanks to yesterdays executions

Thus the Fenians in their failure lit the 'Phoenix flame' again. It

Friedrich Engels (1820-1895). Author and socialist philosopher. Close associate of Karl Marx. Wrote *The Condition of the Working Class in England*. Lived with Lydia and Mary Burns in Manchester. Had close links with Fenians but was sceptical of IRB activities. (Courtesy of Marx Memorial Library)

THE ORDER OF THE DAY; OR, UNIONS AND FENIANS.

The Trades Unions and the Fenians were regularly linked and attacked by
*Punch*. A typical cartoon of the time. (*Punch* 12 October 1867, from
Author's collection)

was significantly the Manchester executions which fired the sensitive and fertile imagination of Parnell and brought him into politics. It was through Fenianism that Davitt found his way into the making of Irish history, but less tangible was the trauma in the Irish subconscious which turned failure and martyrdom into inspiration:

> But that spirit is not dead but merely sleepest, if there be men still in Ireland and more, boys growing into men, willing to strive and sacrifice if need be, liberty or life for Ireland, to Fenianism more than ought else is that spirit and feeling due.[21]

The same sense of continuity was the theme of Padraig Pearse's now classic panegyric at the grave of the veteran Fenian O'Donovan Rossa:

> The seeds sown by the young men of '65 and '67 are coming to their miraculous ripening today. Life springs from death; and from the graves of patriot men and women spring living nations. . . . They (the British Government) think they have pacified Ireland. They think they have purchased half of us and intimidated the other half. They think they have forseen everything, think they have provided against everything; but the fools, the fools, the fools! They have left us our Fenian dead, and while Ireland holds these graves Ireland unfree shall never be at peace.[22]

At peace or not, the Fenian Movement must have a special fascination for those concerned with analyzing the nature and interrelationship of class and national struggles and not least for those wrestling with the complexities of the Irish question as it is being fought out in Ulster today. However, there is one particularly unusual feature of the Fenian Movement in that it turned westward to the United States and to expatriate Irishmen there and to England for much of its support, finance and inspiration. That also has obvious parallels in relation to say the F.L.N. in Algeria or in post-1948 Zionism. But it was perhaps unique in that so little of its ideology came direct from Europe, notwithstanding the influences at work on Stephens and O'Mahony. By the same token many Europeans shared the English lack of understanding of the force of Irish nationalism and ultimately of separatism. Marx and Mazzini shared a scepticism about Irish national claims, even if men like Charles Bradlaugh did not.

However Fenians were later connected with national movements as far away as Finland and Poland, espousing the same separatist and national ideas. By the same token it awoke the latent sense of separate national identity within Irishmen and a realization of their potential force.

Marx saw the struggle primarily in class terms, but class was overlaid by the form of the struggle and antagonism between the two nations. Ireland was to be the spark for a more important flame of revolution in England. Self-government, agrarian revolution and protective tariffs against England were the methods he advocated.[23] Engels, with warm feelings towards the Irish people and their countryside joined Marx in condemning 'terrorist' activities, including the Clerkenwell explosion, not least on the basis that it was counter-productive. Engels summed up Fenianism as 'in the first place violent and in the second place anti-English . . . unheard of in English conditions and really amazing.'[24]

Indeed the sheer daring and bravado of such exploits and failures as Chester, Manchester, Clerkenwell, the Catalpa escape from Australia, the border attacks into Canada or the spectacular demonstrations of the Amnesty Movement must still astonish. Engles repudiated 'Bakunistic, braggart, aimless propaganda through action' and no doubt would repeat those words in respect of the 'action' policies of the Provisional I.R.A. The current daring feats of physical courage for almost nihilistic ends is one that runs through several hundred years of Irish history born in the rural terror that produced the Peep O'Day Boys or the Defenders and well understood by Michael Davitt when he tried to channel this fervour into a coherent political movement.[25]

Thus, while Marx and his supporters could see through the national façade to the underlying economic tensions they underestimated the sheer omnipotence of national fervour in the Irish context. The same duality of thought in Connolly's citizen army led him to do battle as part of the nationalist movement rather than as the liberator of Ireland's workers. The two ends of the spectrum are expressed by Marx and Connolly or Moody and Mansergh in their oft quoted works. They tend to oversimplify in order to prove something. The truth is diverse, paradoxical and infinitely complex by reason of the unusual social development of Ireland which Strauss's analysis helps one to understand. The paradox is as evident in the religious sphere as it is in the politico-economic field.

> In their often inarticulate non-philosophical way the Fenians had insisted on separating the state which they sought to overthrow from the Church to which the majority of them belonged. And this, as much as their gospel of physical force or their republicanism was to be an essential part of the Fenian heritage.[26]

Counter-productive as their violence may have been the actions of the Fenians concentrated many English minds on the Irish problem. They significantly affected Gladstone in converting him to Home Rule in a period during which the Irish Question was to become central to constitutional British politics and the basis of today's problem was to be laid in the playing of the Orange Card to stop Home Rule.

The Fenian Movement also succeeded in tapping the latent forces among English reformers from the working men of Clerkenwell to intellectual giants such as John Stuart Mill and Charles Bradlaugh. It brought together the early Marxists and gradualists of a more traditional stream in defence of the basic rights of liberty and nationality in Ireland and in some part redeemed England's inglorious record in respect of its Western neighbour. This minority was willing to march side by side with Irish sympathizers in a way that has happened from the time of the Chartist Movement in which the Irish played so notable a part, down to the present.

However, when all the violence and protest had died down it may well be argued that what followed in its wake was even more important. The 'New Departure' of the Land League might well be regarded as Fenianism in disguise by British policemen such as Anderson but it was of a very different character in concentrating upon social evils. In linking up with Parnell's Parliamentary Party it went even further and it was only when constitutional methods were to be repeatedly frustrated that the submerged violence again came to the surface leading to the uprising exactly half a century after its apparent failure as a movement.

In so much as it pioneered a particular form of romantic nationalist violence it resembled such later movements as the F.L.N., E.O.K.A. or the Irgun, but unlike them it was a national rather than a section of a national movement. Contemporary movements such as Fremlino or even the Tupamaros have something of the Fenian tradition in their aims and methods. It is not only that all national movements have an obvious similarity and many in the nineteenth century saw the remarkable parallel with Hungary, but that this was the first armed revolt to carry its battle into the heart of enemy territory and eventually to set a precedent for the nations of the world's largest Empire.

Thus when Lord Mayo wrote to the Home Secretary to protest that his warnings over Kelly and Deasy had not been heeded he commented:

> There is now much more Fenian activity on your side of the channel than here, and I think you should at once place Williamson at the head of the Fenian police department and insist on the police at Liverpool, Manchester and the large towns in the north of England giving much more attention to the Fenians than they have hitherto done.[27]

Only the F.L.N. in this century can claim to have carried the battle over to the enemy's territory in that way and then only to a limited degree. England had become the centre of the Fenian conspiracy by 1867 in the wake of the failure to mobilize with any degree of success in Ireland itself. When Yeats was to write that 'A terrible beauty is born', he was writing rather of the rebirth of what had stirred the most violent and contradictory of emotions in England and Ireland a half century earlier. For in the daring rescue at Manchester and the futile deaths at Clerkenwell, England had seen Fenianism at first hand. The Fenianism described by its most romantic and poetic martyr Padraig Pearse as 'the noblest and most terrible manifestation of this unconquered nation.'

Above all the Fenians acted as a catalyst to England where the issue of Home Rule was to dominate fifty years of political struggle and to the Irish, whether in England or the U.S.A., Scotland or Australia and above all in Ireland, who resurrected Fenianism and made the greater part of the country a nation once again and who have never disguised their wish to see their ideal of uniting Protestant, Catholic and dissenter under the common name of Irishmen.

## NOTES

1. Liam O'Broin, *Fenian Fever* p. 28.
2. J. Connolly, *Labour in Ireland*, pp. 159, 161 *et seq.*
3. See E. Strauss, *Irish Nationalism and British Democracy.*
4. R. Anderson, *The Fenian Conspiracy.*
5. Strauss, *op. cit.*
6. Connolly, *op. cit.*
7. *The Irish People.*
8. L. O'Flaherty, *The Life of Tim Healy*, p. 40.
9. *The Life of Tim Healy*, chapter 4.
10. Desmond Ryan in *The Shaping of Modern Ireland*, ed. C.C. O'Brien.
11. See T. Jackson, *Ireland Her Own*, P. Berresford Ellis, *A History of the Irish Working Class* and contrast N. Mansergh, *The Irish Question.*
12. P. Berresford Ellis, *op. cit.*
13. *The Irish People.*
14. See Marx and Engels on Ireland and *The Irish People.*
15. J. O'Leary, *Recollections Fenians and Fenianism.*
16. A. Boyd, *The rise of the Irish Trade Unions 1729-1970.* ch. 9, p. 89.
17. T.W. Moody, *The Fenian Movement*, p. 106.
18. O'Leary, *op. cit.*
19. Moody, *op. cit.* p. 207.
20. N. Mansergh, *op. cit.*, p. 77.
21. O'Leary, *op cit.*, vol. II, pp. 242-3.
22. P. Pearse, *Political Writings and Speeches*, pp. 136-7.
23. See N. Mansergh, *op. cit.*, ch. 3, for a full analysis.
24. Gustav Meyer, *Friedrich Engels: a biography.*
25. Michael Davitt, *The Fall of Feudalism in Ireland* for a full account.
26. David Macartney, *The Church and Fenianism.*
27. Mayo Papers Ms 11188: 24 September 1867.

# BIBLIOGRAPHY

# BIBLIOGRAPHY

**Original Sources** in order of importance
*A Manuscript*

*State Paper Office, Dublin:*
  Police Reports 1857-70
  Fenian Papers 'F' Series 1866-74
*National Library, Dublin:*
  Larcom and Luby papers
*Public Record Office, London:*
  Home Office Papers (H.O.42, 43 and 45 series)
*Public Record Office, Belfast:*
  Drumkeeran Charity School Roll Book
  Enniskillen Summer Assizes Charge Book 1797
  Diary of James Stephens 1859
*Islington Central Reference Library:*
  Bank Book of the Clerkenwell Explosion Relief Fund Committee
  1867-70
  Clerkenwell Vestry Minute Book 1867-68
  Clerkenwell Guardians of the Poor Letter Book
  General Register of Subscriptions CERF Committee
  Letter Book of the CERFC 1867-92
  Minute Book of the CERFC
  Register of Claims CERFC
  Register of Weekly Payments by CERFC 1869-81
*Manchester Central Library:*
  Papers relating to Manchester Martyrs
*Middlesex County Record Office:*
  Minutes of the Committee of Justices to the Clerkenwell House of
  Detention 1867-68
  Regulations for Clerkenwell Gaol 1860

Reports to Court Quarter Sessions (Clerkenwell) 1867-8
West Middlesex Coroner's Court Register 1867-8
*East Suffolk Record Office, Ipswich:*
Cranbrook Diary and MSS
*Bishopsgate Institute, London:*
Papers of the Reform League
*New Scotland Yard, London:*
Statements by J. Mullany and N. English (uncatalogued)
*City of London Record Office:*
Ilford Cemetery Register 1902-3
*City Archives Office, Glasgow:*
Letter Book of Chief Constable 1868
Minute Book of Magistrates Committee 1868
*Army Museum, Camberley:*
South Cork Militia Order Book 1855
*Library of Congress, Washington:*
Diary of Benjamin Moran 1867
*St. Patrick's Church Registry, Manchester:*
Letter of William Allen
*Old Bailey, London:*
Indictments of J. Mullany and R. O'S. Burke 1868.


## B: Printed

Very useful to anyone studying the Fenian movement is *Devoy's Postbag* edited by William O'Brien and Desmond Ryan. During his long and adventurous life John Devoy preserved nearly half a million words and his correspondence illustrates the history of the Irish Revolutionary movement between the eighteen-sixties and the nineteen-twenties.

*Documents of the First International*, four volumes, 1864-70, (Ed.) L. Belyakova. (Moscow 1963-68).
*The Political Correspondence of Mr. Gladstone and Lord Granville, 1868-76*, ed. A. Ramm, 1952.
*Letters of Queen Victoria*, ed. G.E. Buckle, 1926 (covers 1862-69).
*Register of Burials, St. James, Clerkenwell*, Harleian Soc., Vol. 17, 1891.
*Selected Correspondence of Karl Marx and F. Engels*, 1956.
*Karl Marx Letters to Dr. Kugelmann*, 1954.
*Karl Marx/F. Engels Gesamtausgabe*, vol. 111 ed. D. Rjazanov.
*Life and Letters of Cavour*, ed. A.J. White, 1925.
*The Diaries of John Bright*, ed. R.J.A. Welling, 1930.

*Karl Marx and Frederick Engels on Ireland*, (Ed.) R. Dixon (Moscow 1971)

*Handbook of Manchester*, B. Love, 1848.

*Manchester Martyrs Committee Pamphlet — Seamus Barrett* (1857-1943).

*Census Reports:*  1861(2846)  HC(1861)
            (3221)  HC(1863)
       1871(C381)  HC(1871)
           (872)  HC(1873)

*Devon Commission Report Parliamentary Papers 7653/4/5.*

*Hansard Parliamentary Debates, 1865-1872.*

*C.C.C. Sessions Papers, 1867-1868.*


*C: Newspapers and Magazines*


*Advocate* (Melbourne) 1879

*Bamer of Ulster*, 1867

*Beehive*, 1867-71.

*Birmingham Daily Post*, 1867.

*Blackwood Magazine*, 1848-1910.

*Boston Advertiser*, 1867.

*Bristol Daily Post*, 1868.

*Clerkenwell News*, 1867-68.

*Clogher Record.*

*Connaught Patriot*, 1864.

*Cork Examiner*, 1962.

*The Comet* (Guernsey), 1868.

*Daily Graphic*, 1892.

*Daily Telegraph*, 1867-92.

*Donegal Democrat.*

*Dublin University Magazine*, 1867-68.

*Durham Chronicle*, 1867-68.

*Enniskillen Advertiser*, 1864-76.

*Essex Standard*, 1867-68.

*Fermanagh Herald.*

*Fermanagh Mail*, 1867-68.

*Fermanagh News.*

*Flag of Ireland.*

*Fraser's Magazine*, 1871-72.

*Freemans Journal*, 1867-71.

*Gaelic American.*

*Glasgow Free Press*, 1861-68.

*Glasgow Herald*, 1867-68.

*Illustrated London News*, 1865-68.
*Impartial Reporter*, 1867-68.
*Irish Catholic Banner*, 1868.
*Irish Catholic Chronicler People and News of the Week.*
*Irish Independant.*
*Irish Liberator* (London), 1863-64.
*Irish News* (London), 1867.
*Irish People* (Dublin).
*Irish Press.*
*Irish Times.*
*Irish Vindicator* (London)
*Irish Workers Voice*, 1953.
*Irishman*, 1866-71.
*Islington Gazette*, 1956.
*Leeds Mercury*, 1864.
*Liverpool Journal.*
*Liverpool Mercury.*
*Manchester City News*, 1899, 1918 and 1928.
*Manchester Guardian.*
*Manchester Examiner.*
*Manchester Evening Chronicle.*
*Manchester Evening News.*
*Nation*, 1867-68.
*New York Herald*, 1867.
*New York Times.*
*Northern Star*, 1848.
*Norwich Mercury*, 1867-68.
*Observer*, 1867-8.
*Pall Mall Gazette*, 1866.
*Porcupine*, 1867.
*Punch*, 1866-70.
*Reynolds Newspaper*, 1867-72.
*Southern Star.*
*Stage*, 1867-68.
*Standard*, 1867-68.
*Star*, 1867.
*Tablet*, 1878.
*Tailor and Cutter*, 1866-68.
*The Times*, 1864-70.
*Tuam Observer*, 1867.
*Western Star, 1867.*

*D: General book bibliography*
Unless otherwise stated the place of publication is London.

J. Abels *The Parnell Tragedy* 1966.
G.A. Aldred *No Traitor's Gait* (Glasgow 1955)
H.C. Allen *Great Britain and the United States* 1954.
R. Anderson *A Great Conspiracy* 1910.
    "         *Sidelights on the Home Rule Movement* 1906.
    "         *The Lighter Side of my Official Life* 1910.
M. Arnold *Irish Essays* 1882.
W.L. Arnstein *The Bradlaugh Case* (Oxford 1965)
P.H. Bagenal *The American-Irish and their Influence on Irish Politics* 1882.
W. Bageshot *The English Constitution* 1867.
T.A. Bailey *A Diplomatic History of the American People* (New York 1950)
T.B. Beach (Le Caron) *Twentyfive years in the Secret Service* 1892.
G.A. Beck (Ed.) *The English Catholics* 1950.
J.C. Beckett *The Making of Modern Ireland* 1966.
P.M.H. Bell *Disestablishment in Ireland and Wales* 1969.
S.F. Bemis *A Diplomatic History of the United States* 1937.
G.F.H. Berkeley *The Irish Battalion in the Papal Army of 1860* (Dublin 1929)
P. Berresford Ellis *History of the Irish Working Class* 1972.
W. Bixley *The Guilty and the Innocent* 1957.
R.D.C. Black *Economic Thought and the Irish Question* (Cambridge 1960)
R.N. Blake *Disraeli* 1966.
W.S. Blunt *The Land War in Ireland* 1912.
M. Bourke *John O'Leary* (Tralee 1967)
A. Boyd *Holy War in Belfast* (Tralee 1969)
J. Boyle *Leaders and Workers* (Cork 1966)
G. Broeker *Rural Disorder and Police Reform in Ireland* 1970.
A. Briggs *Victorian People 1851-67* (Harmondsworth 1965 reprint of 1954 issue)
    "    (Ed.) *Chartist Studies* 1962 re-issue
M. Brown *The Politics of Irish Literature* 1972.
T.N. Brown *Irish-American Nationalism, 1870-90* (Philadelphia 1966)
D.G. Browne *The Rise of Scotland Yard* 1956.
T. Burke *The Streets of London* 1943.
E. Burns *Handbook of Marxism* 1935.
F.M. Bussey *Irish Conspiracies (Recollections of John Mallon)* 1910
T. Cavanagh *Scotland Yard Past and Present* 1893.
G.B. Cobb *Critical Years at the Yard* 1956.

G.D.H. Cole *British Working Class Politics 1832-1914* 1941.
    "            *The Common People* 1956.
H.J. Collins and C. Abrahamsky *Karl Marx and the British Labour Movement* 1965.
J. Connelly *Labour in Irish History* (Dublin 1910)
    "        *Socialism and Nationalism* (Ed. D. Ryan) (Dublin 1948)
J. Corbett *The Birmingham Trades Council 1868-1966* 1966.
T. Corfe *The Phoenix Park Murders* 1968.
P.J. Cornish (Ed.) *History of Irish Catholicism* Vols 3 and 4 (Dublin 1967)
D. Corkery *The Fortunes of the Irish Language* (Dublin 1954)
M. Cowling *Disraeli, Gladstone and Revolution* 1967.
A. Crew *London Prisons of Today and Yesterday* 1933.
F.L. Crilly *The Fenian Movement* 1908.
T.A. Critchley *A History of the Police in England 1900-1966* 1967.
    "          *The Conquest of Violence* 1970.
S. Cronin *The Revolutionaries* (Dublin 1971)
R. Cross and P.A. Jones *Introduction to Criminal Law* 1964.
T. Cullen *The Empress Brown* 1969.
E. Curtis *A History of Ireland* 1950.
L.P. Curtis *Anglo-Saxons and Celts* (Bridgeport, Cam. 1968)
W.D. D'Arcy *The Fenian Movement in America 1885-1886* (Washington 1947)
R.P. Davis *Irish Issues in New Zealand Politics* (Dunedin 1974)
M. Davitt *The Fall of Feudalism in Ireland* 1904.
    "       *Leaves from a Prison Diary* 1885.
W. Dawson *A Mid-London Parish* 1885.
J. Denieffe *A Personal Narrative of the Irish Revolutionary Brotherhood* (Shannon 1967 reprint of New York 1906 issue)
J. Denvir *The Irish in Britain* 1892.
    "      *Life Story of an old Rebel* (Shannon 1972 reprint of Dublin 1910 issue)
J. Devoy *Recollections of an Irish Rebel* (Shannon 1969 reprint of 1929 New York issue)
A.V. Dicey *Lectures on Law and Public Opinion in England in the 19th Century* 1905.
G. Dickson *Revolt in the North* (Dublin 1960).
M. Dillon *Early Irish Literature* 1948.
G. Dilnot *Scotland Yard* 1929.
R. Dixon (Ed.) *Marx and Engels on Ireland* (Moscow 1971)
C. Duff *A Handbook of Hanging* 1961.
C.G. Duffy *The League of North and South* 1886.
R. Ellman *James Joyce* 1958.
    "      (Ed.) *Selected Letters of James Joyce* 1975.

L. Fairfield *Trial of Peter Jones and Others*.

G. FitzGibbon *Ireland in 1868* (Dublin 1868)

R. Fox *Marx, Engels and Lenin on the Irish Revolution* 1932.

J.A. Froude *The English in Ireland* 6 vols 1872-74.
     " *Thomas Carlyle: His Life in London 1834-81* 1882.

R.C. Gammage *History of the Chartist Movement* (Whitstable 1976).

A.E. Garthorne-Hardy *Garthorne-Hardy, a Memoir* 1910.

A.G. Gardner *Sir William Harcourt* 1923.

S. Gilbert (Ed.) *Letters of James Joyce* 1957.

F.E. Gillespie *Labour and Politics in England 1850-67* (Durham 1927)

W.E. Gladstone *Gleanings of Past Years 1843-78* 1879.

A. Glynn *High Upon the Gallows Tree* (Tralee 1967)

H. Gorman *James Joyce* 1941.

A. Gregory *Gods and Fighting Men* 1970.

A. Griffiths *Chronicles of Newgate* 1884.
     " *Mysteries of Police and Crime* 1901.

T.W. Grimshaw *Facts and Figures about Ireland 1841-90* (Dublin 1893)

D. Gwynn *Young Ireland and 1848* (Cork 1949).

J.L. Hammond *Gladstone and the Irish Nation* 1938

H.J. Hanham *Elections and Party Management* 1959.

J.E. Handley *The Irish in Scotland* (Cork 1945)
     " *The Irish in Modern Scotland* (Cork 1947)

M. Harmon *Fenians and Fenianism* (Dublin 1968)

R. Harris (ed.) *Reminiscences of Sir Henry Hawkins*, 1904.

R. Harrison *Before the Socialists* 1965.

H.L.A. Hart *Punishment and Responsibility* 1968.

L.M. Hayes *Reminiscences of Manchester from the Year 1850* 1958.

R. Herd *Seven Editors* 1955.

J.M. Hernon *Celts, Catholics and Copperheads* (Columbus, Ohio 1968)

R. Hibbery *King Mob* 1958.

F. Hitchman *The Public Life of the Earl of Beaconsfield* 1879

E. Hoagland (Ed.) *One Thousand Years of Irish Poetry* (New York 1947)

B. Holmes *London Burial Grounds* 1896.

W.E. Houghton *The Victorian Frame of Mind* 1956.

H. House *The Dickens World* 1942.

G. Howard *Guardians of the Queen's Peace* 1953.

R. Howe *The Story of Scotland Yard* 1965.

B. Huchinson *The Struggle for the Border* (Toronto 1955)

J. Irving *The Annals of Our Times* 1880.

J.A.Jackson *The Irish in Britain* 1972.

T.A. Jackson *Clerkenwell Green* 1938
     " *Ireland Her Own* 1947.

W.E. Jackson *London's Fire Brigades* 1966.

M. Jenkins *Frederick Engels in Manchester* (Manchester 1951)

R. Jenkins *Sir Charles Dilke* 1958.

E.H. Stuart Jones *The Last Invasion of Britain* (Cardiff 1950)

P. Jones *The Irish Brigade* (Washington 1969)

J. Joyce *Ulysses* 1937.

P.C. Joyce *A Concise History of Ireland* 1927.

E. Kapp *Eleanor Marx* 1972.

R. Kee *The Green Flag* 1972.

S.O. Kelly *The Bold Fenian Men* 1967.

A. Kenealy *Memoirs of E.V. Kenealy* 1908.

W.J. Lauberstein *The Emerald Whaler*.

W.L.M. Lee *The History of the Police in England* 1910.

S. Leslie *The Irish Tangle* 1946.

P. Livingstone *The Fermanagh Story* (Enniskillen 1969)

G. Lockyer-Lampson *The State of Ireland in the 19th Century* 1907.

F.S.L. Lyons *Ireland Since the Famine* 1971.

E.R. Lytton *England and the Englsh* 1874.

P. Magnus *Gladstone* 1954

J. Mallon *Irish Conspiracies* 1910.

N. Mansergh *Ireland in the Age of Reform and Revolution* 1940.
　　　　　" 　　　*The Irish Question* 1965.

F.C. Mather *Public Order in the Age of the Chartists* 1955.
　　　　　　　*Chartist Studies* (Ed. A. Briggs) 1962.

G. Mayer *Friedrich Engels* 1936.

J. McCarthy *Portraits of the Sixties* 1903.
　　　　　" 　　*A History of Our Own Times* 1908.

S. MacCoby *English Radicalism 1858-86* 1938.

D. MacDermot (Ed.) *Stamps of Ireland* (Dublin 1979).

R.B. McDowell *The Irish Administration 1801-1914* 1964.

E. MacLysaght *Irish Families* 1957.

S. MacManus *The Story of the Irish Race* (New York 1969).

P. MacSuibhne *Cardinal Cullen and his Contemporaries* (Naas 1961-77)
5 vols.

M. McDonagh *Irish Graves in England* 1888.

J.S. Mill *England and Ireland* 1868.

J. Mitchell *The Last Conquest of Ireland (perhaps)* (Glasgow 1876)

T.W. Moody (Ed.) *The Fenian Movement* (Cork 1968)

J. Morley *Life of Gladstone* 1903.

E.R. Norman *The Catholic Church and Ireland in the Age of Rebellion
　　　　　　　1859-73* 1965.
　　　　　" 　　*Anti-Catholicism in Victorian England* 1968.

C.C. O'Brien *Parnell and his Party* 1948.
　　　　　" 　　*The Shaping of Modern Ireland* 1960.

L. O'Broin *Fenian Fever* 1971.
" *The Prime Informer* 1971.
" *Revolutionary Underground* 1976.
K. O'Connor *The Irish in Britain* 1972.
J. O'Dea *Story of the Old Faith in Manchester* (Manchester 1910)
B. O'Donnell *The Old Bailey and its Trials* 1950.
F.H. O'Donnell *A History of the Irish Parliamentary Party* 1910.
J. O'Donovan Rossa *Irish Rebels in English prisons* (New York 1882)
" *My Years in English Jails* (Tralee 1967 Edition, New York 1874)
M. O'Donovan Rossa *My Mother and Father were Irish* (New York 1939)
P. O'Farrell *Ireland's English Question* 1971.
T. O'Fiach 'The Clergy and Fenianism' in *Irish Ecclesiastical Record*, 1968 pp. 81-103.
L. O'Flaherty *The Life of Tim Healy* 1927.
P.S. O'Hegarty *A History of Ireland under the Union* 1952.
J. O'Leary *Recollections of Fenians and Fenianism* (Shannon 1969 reprint of 1896 issue)
S. O'Luing *Freemantle Mission* (Tralee 1965)
" 'A Contribution to the Study of Fenianism in Breifne' in *Breifne* (3) 1967 pp. 155-74)
B. O'Reilly *John McHale* 1890.
M.S. Packe *Life of John Stuart Mill* 1954.
T. Packenham *The Year of Liberty* 1969.
E. Pankhurst *My Own Story* 1914.
P. Pearse *Political Writings and Speeches* 1966.
R. Pigott *Recollections of an Irish Nationalist Journalist* 1882.
W.J. Pink *History of Clerkenwell* 1880.
P. Quinlivan *History of High Myddelton North School* 1955.
J.L. Rayner *The Old Bailey and Newgate* 1884.
D. Read *Feargus O'Connor — Irishman and Chartist* 1961.
F. Roney *Irish Rebel and Labour Leader* (Berkeley, California 1931)
P. Rose *The Manchester Martyrs* 1970.
A. Rothstein *A House on Clerkenwell Green* 1966.
T.A. Rothstein *From Chartism to Labourism* 1929.
J. Rutherford *The Secret History of the Fenian Conspiracy* 1877.
D. Ryan (Ed.) *Devoys Postbag* (Dublin 1948 and 1953).
" *The Fenian Chief* (Dublin 1967)
" *The Phoenix Flame* 1937.
M. Ryan *Fenian Memories* (Dublin 1946)
J. Savage *Fenian Heroes and Martyrs* (Boston 1868)
J. Saville *Ernest Jones* 1952.
W. Scott *The Antiquary* (Edinburgh 1816).

R.R. Sharpe *London's Old Bailey* 19 —.

F. Sheehy-Skeffington *Michael Davitt* 1908.

D. Shaw *London in the Sixties* 1908.

W.F. Sinnott 'Charles Bradlaugh and Ireland' in *Cork Historical and Archaeological Society Journal* Vol. LXXVII 1972.

C.G. Smith *The Manchester Fenian Outrage* 1867.

H. Spencer *An Autobiography* 1904.

W.F.B. Stockley *Newman, Education and Ireland* 1937.

R. Straus *Sala* 1942.

E. Strauss *Irish Nationalism and British Democracy 1951*.

A.M. Sullivan *New Ireland* (Glasgow 1882)

T.D. Sullivan *Troubled Times in Irish Politics* (Dublin 1905)

J. Sweeny *At Scotland Yard* 1904.

R. Taine *Notes on England 1861-71* 1872.

C.C. Tansell *America and the Fight for Irish Freedom* (New York 1957)

G. Thompson *The Making of the English Working Class* 1963 revised edition 1978.

W.I. Thompson *The Imagination of an Insurrection* (New York 1967)

D.A. Thornley *Isaac Butt and Home Rule* 1964.

A.P. Thornton *The Habit of Authority* 1966.

M. Trevor *Newman* 1962.

D. Tribe *President Charles Bradlaugh, M.P.* 1971.

C.H. Tsuzuki *H.M. Hyndman and British Socialism* 1961.

J. Tynan *The Irish National Invincibles and their times* (New York 1894)

J. Vincent *The Formation of the British Liberal Party* (Harmondsworth 1966).

G.M. Whalley *Patrick Murphy on Popery in Ireland* 1865.

T. de V. White *The Road of Excess* (Dublin 1946)

J.H. Whyte and P.J. Corish *History of Irish Catholicism* Vol. 5 (Dublin 1967)

M. Williams *Leaves of a Life* (London 1890).

L. Wibberley *The Trouble with the Irish* 1956.

N. Wiseman *The Religion and Social Position of Catholics in England* (Dublin 1864)

C. Wittke *The Irish in America* (Baton Rouge 1956)

*Wolfe Tone* Annual (Dublin 1958)

A. Wood *Nineteenth Century Britain* 1960.

E.L. Woodward *The Age of Reform* (Oxford 1938)

G.D. Zimmermann *Songs of Irish Rebellion* (Dublin 1967)

*Works of Reference*

*Annual Register* 1867, 1868.
*Dictionary of American Biography* (New York 1928)
*Dictionary of National Biography* (22 vols. London 1908-9)
*Encyclopaedia Britannica* 11th edition.
*Finsbury Official Guide* (Ed. M. McDerby) 1958.
J.S. Crone *A Concise Dictionary of Irish Biography* (Dublin 1928)
H. Boylan *A Dictionary of Irish Biography* (Dublin 1978)

# INDEX

# INDEX

Abbott, Albert Henry. 102

Abbott, John. 88

Abbott, Minnie Julia. 90, 142

Adams, Fanny. Murdered by Frederick Baker. 99

Allen, Jeremiah. Police agent. London coroner's court found him guilty of causing Clerkenwell Explosion and murdering Sarah Hodgkinson. 88, 90, 91, 105, 115-6

Allen, William Philip (1848-67). Son of a policeman. Brought up a Protestant. Became a Catholic in 1866. Executed in Manchester 1867. 46-7, 50, 53-61, 72-4, 138

Anderson, Arthur. 23

Anderson, Richard. 95

Anderson, Robert (1841-1918). Born in Dublin. Lawyer. Joined British Secret Service in 1867 as special adviser on fenianism. Assistant Commissioner of Police, Head of CID at Scotland Yard 1888. Writer. Presbyterian lay preacher. 25, 31, opp 135, 135, 162

Applegarth, Robert (1833-1925). British trade union leader. General Secretary of Amalgamated Society of Carpenters and Joiners (1862-71). Member of First International. 155

Archdale, Mervyn Edward (1812-95). Army officer. M.P. for Fermanagh 1835-74. Succeeded as M.P. by brother 1874-85. 135

Archibald, Edward. British Consul in New York. Born in Canada. A descendant of Samuel Archibald who emigrated from Ireland to Nova Scotia in 1761. 112

Armstrong, Frances. Habitual drunkard. Witness at Manchester trials 1867. 59-60

Armstrong, T. Welsh assistant executioner. 73

Baker, Fredrick. 99

Bandon, Earl of (1785-1856). 9

Barlow, Thomas. 61

Barnes, John. 102

Barry, Cathleen. Sister of Ricard O'Sullivan Burke. Lived in Lambeth. 82-3, 113, 120.

Barry, William. 83

Barrett, Edward. 117

Barrett, John. 76

Barrett, Michael (1841-68). Ulsterman. Active IRB member in Glasgow, London and Manchester. Executed in London 26 May 1868. Last man to be publicly executed in England. 85, 87, 106-121, 125, 133-8, 141-2.

Beach, Thomas Billis (1841-94). Colcestrian and doctor. British spy in Fenian Brotherhood in U.S.A. Sent reports to M.P. for Colchester. Wrote autobiography. 85-6, opp 98, 105

Beesley, Edmund Spencer (1831-1915). Radical. Professor of History at University of London. 70

Beesley, Fr. 40

Beck, John. 59

Bell, David (1818-1889). Presbyterian minister. Supported Teant League, National Brotherhood of St. Patrick, IRB. Editor of Irish Liberator (London) and Irish Republic (Chicago). 11, 108

Beales, Edmond (1803-1881). Lawyer. President of the Reform League. President of British National League for the Independence of Poland. 66, 148, 156

Besant, Annie (1847-1933). Theosophist, socialist and fabian. Helped to found Indian Home Rule League and became President of the Indian National Congress. Imprisoned 1917. 69

Birkin, Lieut. 101

Blackmore, J. Member of First International and Reform League. 81

Blackburn, Elizabeth. 62

Blackburne, Lord Chief Justice. Known as the hanging judge. 56-7, 62-3

Blake, John. 109

Blanc, Louis (1811-82). French socialist and historian. 168

Bloomfield, Patrick. Manchester IRB member. 47

Bradlaugh, Charles (1833-91). English radical M.P. Served in British Army in Ireland. Helped draft IRB proclamation of 1867. Member of Reform League. Writer. Republican. opp 68,

68-9, 81, 126, 156, 169, 171

Bradwell, Baron George. 112, 127, 131, 135

Brennan, John. 49, 63

Brett, Baliol. Solicitor General of England. 112

Brett, Charles (1816-67). Manchester police sergeant killed in 1867. 51, 54-56, 60-63, 109.

Brereton, S. Organising Secretary of a non-existent Anglican Clergy Aid Assurance Society. 98-9

Bright, John (1811-89). English radical. Imprisoned for Chartist activities. Writer and M.P. Member of Gladstone's first cabinet. 65-6, 70, 133, 135, 148

Breslin, Michael. Fenian spy in Dublin Castle. 23

Bromley, Sgt. Manchester policeman. 47, 61

Bourke, Thomas Francis (1840-89). Tipperary fenian sentenced to death in 1867. Served in U.S. Civil War.

Buckley, James. Trade union leader. Member of First International and Reform League. 81

Bura, Edward. 108

Burgoyne, Arthur. Glasgow blacksmith. 118

Butt, Isaac (1813-79). M.P. and barrister. Editor and writer. President of Amnesty Association. Protestant founder of Irish Home Rule League. 152

Burke, Ricard O'Sullivan (1838-1922). 7, 9, 10, opp. 10, 25, 44-8, 60, 77-89, 92-3, 107-8, 113, 116, 119-20, 123-31, 139-40.

Cahill, James. 47

Calcraft, William (1800-79). British executioner. 72-3, 136-7

Cambridge, Duke of (1819-1904). Earl of Tipperary, Baron Culloden. Uncle of Queen Victoria. Commander in Chief of British Forces 1856-95. Married Sarah Fairbrother in Clerkenwell 1847. 96

Cantwell, Edward. Catholic priest. 72-3

Carey, Harley. 151

Carey, Martin. Journalist. Sentenced to 5 years penal servitude in 1865 and became insane in gaol. 154

Carlisle, Sgt. Liverpool detective. 23

Carroll, John. 63

Cavell, John. 66

Casey, Joseph Theobald. Kilkenny

cousin of James Stephens. Gaoled 1867-8. Worked in Paris for *New York Herald*. Friend of James Joyce and has been identified as original of Kevin Egan in *Ulyssees*. 77-80, 83-4, 87, 92-3, 115-6, 125-6, 131, 140

Clancy, James (1846-1911). Member of the London IRB. Writer, journalist, lawyer. Joined British Army to get military training. Sentenced to 10 years penal servitude. 108

Clapham, A. Leed's councillor. 148

Clarke, Thomas James (1857-1916). Born in Isle of Wight. Imprisoned 1883-98. Took part in Easter Rising. Executed. 4, 11, 165

Cluseret, Gustave (1823-1900). French soldier and politician. Served in Algeria, Crimea, Italy and in American Civil War. Inspected British army bases for IRB. Member of the First International and Paris Commune. 126, 130

Clutton, William. Tradesman of Leather Lane, Clerkenwell. 90, 142

Cockburn, Alexander. Scottish judge and sociable bachelor. Earl Granville declared that 'the misfortune of Cockburn's son being illegitimate had the compensation of preventing another pauper or idiot son of a law lord being added to the House of Lords'. 112, 119-20, 125, 127, 133, 135, 137

Codd, Rowland (1824-80). Governor Clerkenwell Gaol. 85, 88

Cohen, James. President of the London Association of Cigar Makers. Member of the First International. 148

Condon, Edward O'Meagher (1833-1918). Served in Corcoran's Legion in American Civil War. Helped start Fenian Brotherhood in Toronto (Canada). Author of slogan 'God Save Ireland' when sentenced to death in Manchester 1867. Reprieved because of American citizenship. Gaoled 1867-78 then exiled. Elected Freeman of Dublin 1909. 44-7, 53, 55-8, 60

Connell, John (1850-1929). Had varied career as labourer, sheep farmer, journalist, lawyer, fenian and politician. Secretary of the Workmen's Legal Friendly Society. Wrote 'The Red Flag'. 166

Connoll, J. Manchester policeman. 47, 59

Connolly, James (1868-1916). Born in Edinburgh. Socialist and writer. Ulster organizer for Transport Workers Union. Organized Citizen Army in Dublin and took part in Easter Rising. Captured and executed. 2-3, 161-5, 170

Corydon John Joseph. Informer. 23-5, 31, 46, 108, 127-8

Costello, Augustine. Irish-American army officer. Gaoled 1867-9. 107

Cottingham, James. Lawyer. 53-4, 57, 70

Cremer, William Randal (1804-84). Trade Union leader. Liberal M.P. Member of London Trades Council, British National League for the Independence of Poland, Reform League, Land and Labour League, General Secretary of the First International 1864-6. 81, 126, 156

Cullen, Paul (1803-78). First Irish cardinal. Prominent at First Vatican Council 1870. In 1865 fortynine members of the Cullen family were priests or nuns.

Darragh, Daniel. Teacher in Ballycastle, Co. Antrim. Arrested in Manchester. Died a prisoner in Millbank Gaol. 48, 64.

Davitt, Michael (1846-1906). M.P. Socialist, writer, editor. 3, 23-31, 156-8, 164, 169-70

Day, William. Birmingham house owner. 92

Deasy, Timothy (1841-80). Served in American Civil War and badly wounded at Battle of the Wilderness 1864. Arrived in Ireland 1865. Arrested in Manchester 11 September 1867 and freed by IRB eight days later. Elected to Lawrence City Council 1870 and to Massachusetts House of Representatives 1876. 23, 43-52, 61-2, 70, 93

del Castillo, Canovas. Spanish Premier. 5

Denvir, John (1842-1916). Editor and writer. 19, 20, 33, 37

Derby, Lord (1799-1869). Prime Minister. Held large estates in Ireland. 81

Desmond, Timothy. London-Irish tailor. Took part in tailors strike of 1866. 88, 90-1, 108-121.

Desmond, William. 108, 111-3, 116, 120-1, 137

Devany, John. Police agent. 77, 127, 129

Devoy, John (1842-1928). Leading fenian organiser. Served in French Foreign Legion. Imprisoned 1866-71 then exiled. Writer and journalist. Main source of fenian records. Lived to take salute of Irish troops in Dublin. 4, 5, 24, 26-7, 44, opp 134, 140, 149, 164

Dickens, Charles (1812-70). Novelist. 6

Dimmock, Frederick. London newspaperboy. 88

Disraeli, Benjamin (1804-81). Statesman and novelist. Prime Minister of England 1868 and 1874-80. His novel Lothair has several fenian allusions. 142

Docherty, John. 11

Doheny, Michael (1805-62). Tipperary lawyer and writer. Barrister in London. Colonel of New York 75th Militia Regiment. 166

Donoghue, Morris. 108

Dowling, William. London-Irish Chartist. Transported to Australia 1848. 83

Downing, J. M.P. 148

Duffy, Edward (1840-68). Died in Millbank Gaol. 157

Dunne, Edward. Governor of Illinois 140

Dupont, Eugene (1831-81). French radical. Member of First International. In London 1862-70. 67, 153.

Edinburgh, Duke of (1844-1900). Second son of Queen Victoria. Earl of Ulster, Earl of Kent, Prince of the United Kingdom, Duke of Saxony, Prince of Saxe-Coburg and Gotha. KG., KT., KP., PC., GCB, GCSI, GCMG, GCIE, GCVO, etc. Admiral of the German Navy, General of the Prussian Army. Married daughter of Czar Alexander II of Russia. Shot and wounded at Clontarf (Australia) by Henry O'Farrell (1833-68). 134

Engels, Friedrich (1820-95). Visited Ireland 1855 and 1869. Spoke some Irish. Married Lydia Burns. 6, 11, 67, 126, 153-5, 165, opp 168, 168, 170

English, Nicholas. London-Irish tailor of Dudley Street. President of the Soho Branch of the National Brotherhood of St. Patrick. Held shares in the Irish Liberator. Charged with causing the Clerkenwell Explosion and acquitted. 107-13, 116, 120-1

Evans, Humphrey. 142

Evans, Martha. Died from injuries received in Clerkenwell Explosion. 90, 142

Fallon, Felix. 106, 108, 113, 141

Fariola, Octave. 126

Featherstone, Timothy. 47, 63

Fee, Isabella. 62

Finity, Michael. Employee of Imperial Gas Company. Accused of sedition. 99

Finlen, James (1831-?). Chartist, journalist, lecturer for Reform League. 70, 81-2, 90

FitzGerald, Percy (1834-1925) lawyer, painter, sculptor, writer. 27

Fisher, Henry. An unfortunate witness at trial of Ricard Burke. 131

Flannigan, Mary. Manchester governess. 62

Fordham, Benjamin. London policeman. 77-8

Fox, Peter. Editor of *The Commonwealth*. Active in British National League for the Independence of Poland, First International and Reform League. Died in Vienna in 1869. 81

Flood, John (1841-1909). Dublin journalist. Transported to Australia. Edited *The Wild Goose* on prison ship *Hougoumont*. Founded first branch of Land League in Australia. 19, 26, 108

Gadd, Charles Joseph. Catholic Vicar General of Manchester. 70-74

Garibaldi, Guiseppe (1807-82). Italian revolutionary. 155

Giffard, Hardinge. Lawyer. 112

Gladstone, William Ewart (1809-98). Leader of Liberal Party. Four times Prime Minister of England. 137-8, 146-9, 154-5, 158, 170

Grant, James. Witness at Manchester trials 1867. 62

Gray, Roger. Member of First International, Reform League and League for the Welfare of the Industrious Classes. 81

Greene, J. Baker. Lawyer. 112, 118

Griffiths, Arthur (1871-1922). Politician. Worked in South Africa. Editor of *United Irishman* then *Sinn Fein*. Elected M.P. 1918, jailed 1920-21. Signatory to Anglo-Irish Treaty 1922. 68

Gregory, Lady. 2

Griffiths, John. Manchester barber. 59

Grosvenor, Hugh Lupus (1825-99). First Duke of Westminster. M.P. for Chester. 21

Hales, John. (B.1839). Trade Union leader. Secretary of First International 1871-2. Member of Reform League and Land and Labour League. Expelled from International in 1873. 154

Halpin, William. City Engineer and County Surveyor of Cincinatti, U.S. Commanded Kentucky Regiment in U.S. Civil War. Leader of Dublin District in 1867 Rising. Gaoled 1867-71. 18, 107

Hannen, J. Lawyer. 57

Hardy, Gathorne (1814-1906) Earl of Cranbrook. British politician. Home Secretary. 65, 135, 137

Harris, George. Active in British working class politics. Supported views of Bronterre O'Brien. Member of First International 1869-72. 149

Harrison, Frederick. Vice-President of Reform League. Member of First International. Historian and lawyer. Mother was Irish. 70

Hartwell, Robert. Chartist and printer. Editor of *The Beehive*. On the Executive of the Reform League. Member of First International. Secretary of London Working Men's Union. 81

Hayes, John. Police agent. Suggested Fenians should take Coronation stone from Westminster Abbey. 109

Hayes, Thomas. Wheelwright of Coram Street, London. 109

Haynes, James. Clerkenwell resident. Claimed £5 and got £10. 102

Hennessy, Patrick. First President of the Land and Labour League. Helped in the formation of the Land Nationalization Society, the National Sunday League, National Liberal Union, the League of the Cross, and the Irish Literary Society. 148

Henry, Thomas. Bow Street Magistrate. 92

Higgins, H. Lawyer. 54, 57

Hill, Dr. Doctor at Royal Free Hospital, London. 89

Hodgkinson, Sarah Ann. Killed in Clerkenwell Explosion. 90, 112-5, 125, 142

Hogan, William. Secretary of St. Patrick's Assurance Society, Birmingham. 64

Holland, John (1840-1914). Built first practical submarine. His research funded by Fenian Brotherhood. First British submarines used Holland's design. 5

Hooker, John. Fell off van and got £10. 102

Hopps, John Page. Unitarian Minister in Dukinfield. 39.

Hughes, William. Witness at Manchester trials 1867. 59-60

Hussey, Fr. Catholic priest in Moorfields, London. 135-6.

Ingham, Elizabeth. Manchester witness, 1867. 62

Ingham, Mary. Manchester witness. 62

Jefferson, Dr. Doctor at Royal Free Hospital. 89

Johnson, Andrew (1808-75). President of U.S.A. 1865-69. 6

Johnson, John. Member of Universal Republican League. 148

Johnson, Colonel. 89

Jones, Ernest Charles (1819-69). British radical politician, lawyer, poet and writer. Leading member of Chartist movement. Defended fenian prisoners. Friend of Engels and Marx. 53-5, 57, 70, 127-8

Joyce, James Augustine Aloysius (1882-1941). Novelist and poet. 87, 140

Jung, Hermann (1830-91). Watchmaker. Prominent in First International. 67, 154-5

Justice, Ann. Wife of tailor. 82-3, 87-8, 90-1, 108, 111-2, 115

Justice, Ann. Wife of tailor. 82-3, 87-8, 90-1, 108, 111-2, 115

Karslake, J.S. Attorney General. 57, 112

Kavanagh, Morgan. Linguist and writer. Marx's landlord in Soho. Father of novelist Julia Kavanagh. 109

Keenan, Dr. 108

Kelley, Joseph. 47

Kelly, Thomas J. (1833-1908). Emigrated from Loughrea to America. Served in U.S. Civil War. Wounded and invalided out of army. Took over IRB leadership from James Stephens. Captured in Manchester 1867 but rescued soon afterwards. 7, 13, 19, 23, 26, 43-52, 59, 61-2, 70, 82, 96, 108-9, 113, 126, 141, 156

Kelly, T.M. Manchester dentist. 51

Keliyer, John. 129

Kenealy, Edward Vaughan (1819-80). Lawyer from Cork. Defended London Irish Chartists 1848. Withdrew from Ricard Burke's defence after Clerkenwell Explosion. Leading counsel in Tichborne case. Writer and poet. Published The Englishman. M.P. for Stoke. 82-3, 92

Kennedy, Philip. 108

Kennedy, Magistrate. 50

Kensley, Martha. 115, 123

Keogh, A. Lawyer. 112, 114, 116

Kickham, Charles (1828-82). Poet and writer. Gaoled 1865-9. 165

Kirkland, G. Prison warder. 74

Knowles, John. 59

Knox, P.C. 47, 59

Koppel, M. 119, 123

Kynnersley, A. 35

Kynoch, George. Birmingham arms manufacturer. 131

Labalmondiere, Douglas. Colonel in British Army. Deputy Police Commissioner. 89

Lambert, Miles. 93

Langley, Baxter. Member of Parliament. 148

Larkin, Michael. Emigrated to Manchester 1858. Took part in rescue of Thomas J. Kelly. Executed in public 1867. 47, 53, 56, 58-9, 63 70-74, 138

Larkin, William. Parish priest of Hokitaka, New Zealand. 76

Lavery, James. 47, 49

Leatham, A. 41

Lennon, Michael. 27

Leno, John Bedford. Printer, chartist, trade unionist. Member of Reform League and First International. Published The Workman's Advocate 81

Lessner, Friedrich (1825-1910). German tailor. From 1856 in London. Member of London German Workers' Educational Association and First International. Helped to found Independent Labour Party. 67

Lewis, George Henry (1833-1911). Solicitor. Knighted for services in connection with Parnell Commission. Friend and adviser of Oscar Wilde. 110-1

Lewis, James. Shoemaker. 111

Looney, Francis. London Irish Chartist. Transported 1848. 83

Luby, Thomas Clarke (1822-1901). Son of Protestant Minister. Educated TCD. Took part in 1848 rising. Writer. Gaoled 1865-71 then exiled. 163

Lucraft, Benjamin (1809-97). British trade union leader. Member of First

International. 66, 81, 154-5

Lynch, P. 56, 108

Lynch, John. Died in Woking Gaol, 1866. 157

Maginn, Wiliam (1793-1842). Cork journalist, antiquarian, linguist, duellist, orator, etc. 82

Maguire, Robert (1826-90). Born in Dublin and ordained in Cork. Anglican Rector of St. James, Clerkenwell. Secretary of Protestant Institute. 99-102

Maguire, Robert (1826-90). Born in Dublin and ordained in Cork. Anglican Rector of St. James, Clerkenwell. Secretary of Protestant Institute. 99-102

Maguire, Thomas. Irish marine. Arrested and sentenced to death 1867. Reprieved and set free after press protests. 52-3, 56, 58-65

Mallon, John. Dublin Police Chief. 133

Manning, Henry Edward (1808-92). Cardinal and writer. Educated at Harrow and Oxford. Anglican Archdeacon of Chichester before joining Catholic Church. Archbishop of Westminster. 119

Marston, Henry. Actor. 102

Martin, Mrs M. 115

Massey, Godfrey, 108, 128-9

Mathews, H. Member of Parliament. 148

Marx, Jenny and Laura. *opp 11*

Marx, Karl (1818-83), 6, 11, 65-7, 109, 126, 139, 147-8, 153-6, 167, 169-70

Mayne, Richard (1796-1868). Irish barrister. Commissioner of Police for London for forty years. 85, 89, 96, 98, 124, 137

Mayo, Lord (Richard Bourke)(1822-72). 171

Mazzini, Guisepe (1805-72). Italian revolutionary. 168-9

McCabe, Frank. Priest. 140

McCafferty, John. Soldier. Born in Ohio. Arrested in Ireland and sentenced to death, reprieved. Gaoled 1867-71. 18-20, 24-8, 106, 164.

MacCarthy, Patrick. 40

McCaul, Alexander. Glasgow police officer 110-1, 118, 124

McClure, John. Soldier in U.S. Civil War. Led raid on Knockadoon Coastguard Station 1867. Gaoled 1867-71 then exiled. *opp 134*, 149

McCord, Norman. Historian. 147-8

McCormick, J. Priest. 19

McCorry, Peter, Glasgow journalist. Emigrated to U.S.A. 1868. Editor of various Irish and Catholic papers. 111, 117-9, 137, 141

McDonagh, Christopher. 108

MacDonnell, Joseph Patrick (1847-1906). Secretary of National Brotherhood of St. Patrick. Arrested 1866. Member of First International. Married in Peckham, London. Socialist leader in U.S.

McGee, Thomas D'Arcy (1825-68). Young Irelander. Politician and writer. Minister in Canadian Government. Assassinated in Ottawa. 134

McLean, Edward. 112

McMahon, J. 108

McManus, Charles. 110-1, 116, 118

McNulty, Michael. 110-1, 118, 124

McSweeney, M. 148

Melvin, William 47

Merriman, Josiah. Lawyer, member of First International and Reform League. 145, 148, 154

Mill, John Stuart (1806-73) Economist and philosopher. 68-70, 135, 171

Millen, Frederick F. General in Mexican Army. British agent in Fenian Brotherhood. 13, 86, 105

Mitchell, John (1815-75). Son of Presbyterian minister. Lawyer, editor, writer, Young Irelander, M.P. Gaoled 1848-53, escaped. 11

Moody, T.W. Historian 167

Moore, John. 88

Moore, Louis. 56

Moorehouse, Charles. 47, 63

Morgan, William. Shoemaker. Member of First International and Reform League. 153

Moriarty, Edward. London policeman. 91

Morris, G. 119, 123, 154

Mote, G. 89

Mottershead, Thomas (1825-84). English weaver. Member of First International but expelled in 1873. 155

Mulholland, George. 59, 63

Mullany, Bridget. 123

Mullany, Patrick. Tailor. Joined IRB and London Rifle Volunteers. Arrested 1867. Gave information and was allowed to emigrate to Australia. 84, 105-7, 113-4, 116, 119-20, 123-4, 128, 130, 141

Mulleda, Henry (1840-76). Joined IRB

and 64th Lancashire Volunteers. Arrested in Dublin 1867. Gaoled 1867-71 then exiled. 125-6, 128, 131, *opp 134*, 139-40

Mullen, James. Glasgow shoemaker. 110, 118-9

Murphy, James (1835-91). Soldier. Served in U.S. Civil War and wounded several times. Organized IRB in Scotland. Played Leading part in Clerkenwell Explosion. Married Mary Kelly in Dublin 1865. 44, 46, 48, 85-7, 106, 108-9, 113, 116, 123, 140-1

Murphy, Jeremiah. 108-9

Murphy, William. IRB member. 63

Murphy, William. Anti-Catholic preacher in England. Stirred up riots in several cities. 33-41

Murray, James. 81

Napoleon III (Louis Napoleon Buonaparte 1808-73) Emperor of France 1852-70. 149, 155

Neary, John. Young Irelander. IRB member in Manchester. Died in New York in 1893. 44, 46

Newdegate, C.N. Member of Parliament. Disliked Catholics and Jews. 134

Newton, Thomas. 61

Nolan, John. IRB organiser in Northern England. 47, 108.

Nolan, John (Amnesty). Secretary of Amnesty Association. 140

Nugent, John Francis. Arrested in Drogheda in March 1867 and in Manchester in November 1867. 52, 56

Oakley, J. Catholic priest. 101

O'Bolger, Thomas. 47, 109

O'Brien James Bronterre (1805-64) Chartist Leader in England. Writer. Gaoled 1840-1. 11, 161

O'Brien, Lawrence. Lawyer. 57, 63

O'Brien, Michael (1836-67). Soldier. Served in American Civil War. Executed in public in Manchester 1867. 44-8, 53, 56, 58, 61-2, 73-4, 108, 126, 138

O'Brien, Patrick. 102

O'Connell, Charles Underwood. Soldier in U.S. Civil War. Arrested in Cobh 1865. Gaoled 1865-71 then exiled. Died in New York 1902. *opp 134*, 149

O'Connell, Maurice. Secretary of Soho

Branch of National Brotherhood of St. Patrick. 108

O'Connor, Feargus (1794-1855). Chartist leader. Born in Cork. Lawyer, writer, M.P. Imprisoned 1839-40. Supported alliance between English and Irish working class. 11, 53, 161

O'Connor, James. 150

O'Connor, P. Catholic priest. 114

Odger, George (1820-77). Shoemaker. Trade union leader. Secretary of London Trades Council 1862-72. Member of British National League, Labour Representation League, Reform League. President of First International 1864-7. 70, 81, 126, 153-8

O'Donoghue, Daniel (1831-89). Member of Parliament for Tipperary 1857-75 and for Tralee 1865-85. 56

O'Donnell John (1837-74). Poet and journalist. London correspondent of *Irish People*. Editor of *Universal News*. 108

O'Donovan, Edmund (1844-83). Son of Gaelic scholar John O'Donovan. Linguist, journalist, writer. Served in French Foreign Legion and London IRB. Killed in Sudan. 12, 108.

O'Donovan Rossa, Jeremiah (1831-1915). Editor and writer. Gaoled in England 1865-71. *opp 134*, 139-40, 146, 156-8, 166, 169.

O'Donovan Rossa, Margaret. 10

O'Donovan Rossa, Mary Jane (1846-1916). Writer, lecturer, elocution teacher. 3rd wife of Jeremiah O'Donovan Rossa. Secretary of Fenian Ladies Committee. Thirteen children. 13, 158

O'Flaherty, Liam (1897-    ). Writer. 163

O'Halloran, S.J. 137

O'Halloran, Thomas. 82

O'Keefe, Daniel. 108

O'Keefe, John. 111-2, 116

O'Kelly, Sean T (1882-1966). 2nd President of Ireland. Interned in Wales 1916-8. M.P. 1918. Speaker at First Dail 1919. 4

O'Leary, Ellen (1831-89). 13

O'Leary, John (1930-1907). Educated at TCD, UCC and UCG. Editor of *Irish People*. Gaoled 1865-74, exiled 1874-85. Writer. Had considerable influence on W.B. Yeats. 2, 140, 166-7

O'Leary, Patrick (Pagan). Served in

U.S.-Mexican War of 1846. Recruited British soldiers for IRB. Gaoled 1865-71 then exiled. Writer. 164

O'Mahony, John (1816-77) Linguist and writer. Young Irelander. Founded Fenian Brotherhood in America. 2-4, 85, 126, 141, 166-7

O'Neill, James. Glasgow Irishman arrested with Michael Barrett 1868. 106-7, 110-1, 123

O'Reilly, John Boyle (1844-90). Soldier, poet, journalist, writer. Gaoled 1865-9, escaped from Australia. 145

O'Rourke, Michael. IRB Paymaster in England. 46

Orsini, Cesare. London Italian. Member of First International 1866-7. Brother was executed for attempt to assassinate Napoleon III. 126

Osborne, John. Trade union leader active in many radical organizations. 148

O'Shaughnessy, Mrs. 107

O'Sullivan, Jeremiah. 84, 87-90

Owen, Lloyd. Doctor at Royal Free Hospital, London. 89

Paget, Robert. Clerkenwell clerk. 102

Palin, William Henry. Army officer. 71

Parnell, Charles Stewart (1846-91). Member of Parliament. Chairman of Home Rule Parliamentary Party 1880-90. Gaoled 1881-2. 140, 169

Parry, Sgt. Lawyer. 148

Patterson, Thomas. Manchester puddler. 58

Patton, G. 108

Peak, John. Glasgow shoemaker. 118

Pearse, Padraig (1879-1916). Educationalist, writer, revolutionary, poet, lawyer, Gaelic Leaguer. Commanded 1916 Rising. Executed in Kilmainham Gaol. 2, 140, 163, 165, 169, 172

Perkins, Elizabeth. Sister of Thomas Maguire of Royal Marines. 62

Pickup, George. Manchester bricklayer. 58

Pilsworth, Edward St. Clair. Served with Garibaldi in Italy. Electrometallurgist. Adopted St. Clair as surname. Gaoled 1867-71 then exiled. 11

Poland, Lawyer. 112

Prince of Wales (later King Edward VII) (1841-1910). Eldest son of Queen Victoria. 24

Queensberry, Dowager Marchioness. Born Caroline Margaret Clayton, daughter of General Sir William Clayton and Alice O'Donel. Sent £100 to Manchester fenian prisoners. Paid school fees for children of James Larkin. 70

Quick, T. Catholic priest. 72

Quin, T. 108

Ranger, George. 88

Reddin, Daniel. 48, 63

Rice, Peter. 47, 49, 60-1

Richardson, George. 112

Ridgeway, Edward. 59-60

Roberts, William J. 84

Roberts, W.P. 53-7

Roney, Frank. 166

Rosenberg, Charles. 83

Rowan, Charles. 98

Ryan, Daniel. Dublin Police chief. 85-6

Ryan, Desmond (1893-1964). Journalist and writer. Born in London. Fought in GPO in 1916. 164

Ryan, John. 19-20, 47, 109

Ryan, Mark (1844-1940). Doctor. Joined IRB and Lancashire Volunteers. Had surgery in Clerkenwell. 12

Ryan, Peter. 47

Ryde, J. Police superintendant. 23

Salisbury, Lord (1930-1903). 57

Seward, William. American Secretary of State. 6

Seymour, William Digby (1824-95). Barrister. 57, 61, 63, 70

Shaw, Eyre Massey. Educated at TCD. Captain in North Cork Rifles. Chief Constable of Belfast, then first Chief Officer of London Fire Brigade. 89

Shaw, George. Manchester policeman. 47, 54, 58, 63

Shaw, Robert. Member of First International. 81

Skelly, Thomas. Manchester IRB member sentenced to 5 years penal servitude in 1867. 63

Slack, Henry Wilson Manchester cab proprietor. 61

Sleigh, Warner. Lawyer. 113-4

Smith, Rev. William. 137

Smythe, Patrick James (1826-85). Journalist, lawyer, orator. Member of Parliament. 150, 152

Solly, Rev. Henry. Organizer of Working Mens Club and Institute Union. 68

Sperry, Thomas. Midland Railway employee. 61
Squire, George. 102
Stephens, James (1824-1901). Founder of Irish Republican Brotherhood. 2, 4, 6-7, 13, 18-9, 44-5, 77, 96, 126, 126, 129, 140, 166.
Stoneham, John. 47
Straight, Douglas. Lawyer. 112
Strauss, E. Historian. 170
Stuart, W.E. 102
Sullivan, Alexander Martin (1830-84). Editor, journalist, writer. Member of Parliament. Gaoled 1867-8. 150.
Sylvester, Captain. 71
Sutton, Ambrose. 88

Taylor, Jack. 108
Taylor, John. 47, 61
Teare, G. 41
Thompson, James (1834-82). Poet. Served in British Army in Ireland. Secretary to Polish Aid Committee 1863. Lived with Bradlaugh family. 77-8, 88, 123
Thompson, Martha. 142
Thoresby, T.E. Clerkenwell vicar. 100
Tone, Theobald Wolfe (1763-98). United Irishman. Took part in French expeditions to Ireland 1796 and 1798. 4
Tracy, J. Catholic priest. 51
Trueman, A. 61

Vaughan, James. Tailor of Carnaby Street. Informer at trial of Michael Barrett. 107, 109-10, 113, 116

Victoria, Queen (1819-1901). 6, 99, 133-5, 148
Vilquain, Victor. Belgian soldier of fortune. 126

Walpole, Spencer. 98
Walsh, John. 118
Weston, John. English radical. Member of First International and Land and Labour League. 66, 68, 154
Whalley, G.H. Member of Parliament. Spent his life attacking Roman Catholics in general and Jesuits in particular. 35, 39
Wheeler, J. 122
Williams, Montague. Lawyer. 112-3, 115, 117
Williams, William. Deputy Mayor of Chester. 23, 26
Williamson, Frederick. 106
Wilson, Harold. British Labour Prime Minister 1964-70, 1974-76. 138
Wilson, John. Birmingham gunsmith. 30-1, 62
Wodehouse, John (Baron Wodehouse, Earl of Kimberley) 1826-1902. Lord Lieutenant of Ireland 1864-6. Supported Gladstone on Home Rule Bills. 13, 151.
Woodford, Joyce Ann. 88

Yarwood, A. Manchester policeman. 47, 54, 58
Yates, Frederick. Clerkenwell schoolmaster. 102
Yeats, William Butler (1865-1939). Dramatist, poet, politican. 171